HEBREWS TRUER & GREATER

Visit us online at www.inversiononline.org

Hebrews: Truer & Greater (An iNVERSION Community Resource Book) | First Edition

Copyright © 2014 by iN HOUSE Publishing, 4455 Del Valle Pkwy, Pleasanton CA 94566.
All rights reserved

Cover Design: Rachel Leona Wood & Heath Hardesty
Design & Layout: Rachel Leona Wood

Scripture quotations are from The Holy Bible, English Standard Version (ESV) copyright © 2001 by Crossway Bibles, a publishing ministry of Good News Publishers.
All rights reserved.

ISBN: 978-1-4675-9943-6

Printed in the United States of America

21 20 19 18 17 16 15
8 7 6 5 4 3 2
2 0 1 0

HEBREWS
TRUER & GREATER

An iNVERSION Community Resource Book

Edited by Heath Hardesty & Dane Olney

Table of Contents

Components of this Collaboration	7
Prologue	9
Introduction	11
Historical Context	16
Outline	19
Volume One	**23**
Part 1: Above All Others	25
Part 2: The Greater Messenger	29
Part 3: Gospel Gazing	33
Part 4: The Image of God	37
Part 5: Blood Brothers	41
Volume Two	**45**
Part 6: The Truer & Greater Apostle	47
Part 7: The Truer & Greater Israel	51
Part 8: The Truer & Greater Sabbath	55
Part 9: The Primacy of The Word	59
Part 10: The Truer & Greater High Priest	63
Part 11: Hard Words to an Immature Church	67
Part 12: The Danger of Nominalism	71
Part 13: The Perfect Promise	75
Volume Three	**79**
Part 14: The Priest of Mystery	81
Part 15: The Truer & Greater Tabernacle	85
Part 16: The Truer & Greater Covenant	89
Part 17: The Truer & Greater Holy Place	93
Part 18: Bloodwork	97
Part 19: Once & For All	101
Part 20: The Invincible Confidence of Intimacy	105
Part 21: Endurance & Affliction	109

Table of Contents Cont.

Volume Four	**113**
Part 22: The Deep Reality of Faith	**115**
Part 23: The Truer & Greater Abel	**119**
Part 24: The Truer & Greater Enoch	**123**
Part 25: The Truer & Greater Noah	**127**
Part 26: The Truer & Greater Abraham & Sarah	**131**
Part 27: The Truer & Greater Exile	135
Part 28: The Truer & Greater Abraham & Isaac	139
Part 29: The Truer & Greater Jacob	143
Part 30: The Truer & Greater Joseph	147
Part 31: The Truer & Greater Moses	151
Part 32: The Sea & The Stone	**155**
Part 33: The Truer & Greater Rahab	159
Part 34: The Truer & Greater Judge & King	163
Part 35: The World Was Not Worthy	167
Volume Five	**171**
Part 36: Endurance & Discipline	173
Part 37: The Anti-Esau	177
Part 38: That Which Cannot Be Shaken	181
Part 39: The Idol Factory	185
Part 40: Submission & Leaders	**189**
Part 41: The Good Word	193
"Truer & Greater"	197
Glossary	199
Resources	207

COMPONENTS OF THIS COLLABORATION

The components of this study guide are a result of the collaborative effort of Heath Hardesty, Dane Olney, Chris Kazakevich, Jake Kazakevich, Kyle Tribbey, Jared Johnson, Justin Worley, and Rachel Leona Wood. It was edited by Heath Hardesty and Dane Olney. It was a team effort meant to reflect the *every member mission* mentality that characterizes the iNVERSION church community. Thank you to everyone involved.

Within this study guide you will find:

A note on its use and comGroups: An explanation and overview of the intended purpose of this book and the essential nature of comGroups to the mission and life of the iNVERSION community.

A pastoral introduction: A brief word on the new sermon series by pastor Heath Hardesty.

Historical context & background: A brief but fact-filled overview of the authorship, date of writing, audience and setting of the book of Hebrews. Context is crucial, and we hope this short background information will help you in your study.

Outline of Hebrews: Again, context is crucial. Therefore we have written a comprehensive outline of Hebrews to help you understand the scope and flow of the letter. Additionally, we have broken the outline up by volume and added the title of each sermon to the relevant portion of the letter.

Q's & Cues: These questions and prompts are catalysts, not constraints. They are meant to be springboards to help lead discussion in your comGroups. Know that they are not meant to be limitations or a check-list of questions to rush through. They are to be used in a way that facilitates vibrant, searching conversation rather than kills it.

Prayer primers: We are a people who believe in prayer. It is the language of dependence and it is a way to express our trust in God. And He listens to us because of Jesus. These primers are to help kick-start us to be praying together as a community. Sometimes all we need is a little spark to help us start. These will help us pray together, united, in sync, even as we are going about our lives throughout the week.

Hebrews Song: God's people have been singing since the garden (Genesis 2:23). Why? Frankly, He is too good not to sing about! His salvation is so mighty and undeserved that He commands us to sing *new* songs to Him; it is not enough to rely on familiar melodies (Psalm 98:1). Furthermore, worship music is instruction through song; *singing* the truths of God helps drive them into our hearts in a potent and unique way. For these reasons, gifted members of our team write a new song for each series that tie into the text.

Lexicon: These little word-nerd moments are to help us define terms we may have never heard before, or even words we hear all the time but just could not define. Words are important. They help us understand and communicate reality.

Glossary: Here you will find all the Lexicon bits gathered in one helpful place.

Resources: Take a look at who and what we have been studying. We hope you take the time to look into these and other resources as well.

PROLOGUE:
A Note on comGroups and the use of this book

The Mission of iNVERSION & the Importance of comGroups
The mission of iNVERSION is to *make Gospel-centered disciples for the glory of God*. We desire to advance the kingdom of God in our neighborhoods and communities, to see the broken restored and the dead come alive, to develop in God's people an insatiable hunger for His word, to plant churches that plant churches that plant churches and to hold high the name of our glorious and gracious savior, Jesus Christ. This mission is not carried forward solely by the pulpit but by the people. iNVERSION is *an every member mission* because the church *is* God's mission. The church is the body of Christ on earth, proclaiming the Gospel in word and manifesting the Gospel in love as Jesus did.

This is why comGroups are so crucial. Sundays are the church gathered while comGroups are *the church scattered throughout the city to make disciples of Jesus.* We long to see comGroups spread so densely throughout our cities that there would be Gospel-vitality in every neighborhood. In comGroups the people of God meet together to encourage and equip one another to better know, trust, and proclaim the Gospel of Jesus. This is done as we faithfully and eagerly engage the God-breathed Scriptures that alone are able to pierce to the division of soul and spirit bringing about conviction, affection, and transformation.

Why this book?
This book was designed to serve the comGroups. comGroups are not just *missional* (essential to discipleship and meant to multiply) and *locational* (neighborhood-minded and intergenerational), they are *parallel*. This means they are *Gospel-centered* and *message-based*. Gospel-centered means that comGroups don't meet to fulfill a religious duty. They meet because of the Gospel for the sake of the Gospel to grow in awareness of the Gospel that is our fellowship with God and one another. Message-based means that they do not meet based on gender, convenience, interest in a popular author or subject, etc. Rather, the comGroups gather to study the word and live life by the word.

Specifically, comGroups *study the passage taught at iNVERSION the previous Sunday.* This allows us to go deeper as a whole community into the word, growing together in faith as we confess and repent of the sins that we were convicted of on Sunday. Further, this strategy enables the community to keep our teachers accountable and travel with them through the "whole counsel of God" (Acts 20:27).

Planting and leading a comGroup is a high and difficult calling. We know that our planters have careers, busy lives and families. One night a week to study the Bible is difficult enough without the additional meals, counseling sessions and activities that come along with living life together under the word. Add to that the unavoidable reality of people leaving, criticism, changing schedules and "difficult" people (comGroups are the church in miniature, after all) and we can understand the temptation to simply throw on a video, ask some scripted questions and call it a night. We know the average comGroup leader is not a Bible scholar who speaks in proverbs. That is why this book exists.

In your hands is the labor of leaders you know and (hopefully) trust, ten months of Gospel-centered content so you comGroup planters and members can be prepared each week. This book will provide you with the historical context and a detailed outline of the letter to the Hebrews. We have broken Hebrews into five volumes and each has its own summary to help you understand every passage within the flow of the whole volume and letter. Each week will have a synopsis of the passage that points you to Jesus, questions and cues ("Q's & Cues") to facilitate in-depth conversation, a prayer primer that ties into the passage and several pages for notes with definitions of key terms and relevant quotes from church leaders. In the back of the book you will find a list of resources that helped us with this task and are available for you to study deeper.

This book was written in the conviction that the members of *The Church* are *saints*--those called out of darkness into light, and are set apart for a purpose —and that it is *you* who are doing the work of the ministry to build up the body of Christ (Ephesians 4:12). Our job is simply to equip you. That said: we hope you feel equipped! More than that, we pray that you are as excited as we are to grow in the knowledge of our great savior Jesus Christ by embarking with your comGroup on this journey through the treasure-filled wilderness of Hebrews.

INTRODUCTION TO HEBREWS

The Old Testament is riddled with Gospel gems, precious stones of truth that shimmer alive when the light of the New Testament falls back upon them. The Book of Hebrews is a high-wattage spotlight that makes those once-shadowed treasures of the Old Testament spark and flash in rare, jaw–dropping display. And for all its illuminating of ancient treasures of truth, Hebrews is itself a treasure to behold: a gift of scripture, like a divinely inspired Rosetta Stone, given to God's people for encouragement and orientation in every generation. It is a book of Gospel-marveling to embolden and nourish a people not yet home.

Hebrews is a mystery of a book that calls us to certainty. Its eloquent author remains unknown and elusive (bringing out the Sherlockian theologian in us), but its theme is crystal clear: *the superiority of Jesus Christ.* This Jesus of Nazareth, this famous figure that split our calendars in half, this blue-collar prophet from Podunk-ville, is The Messiah, the one who is *truer* and *greater* than any prophet, priest or powerful king from Israel's long and varied history. He is not an afterthought or accidental note to the symphony of the Jewish tradition—He was the aim all along!

Hebrews is a book often un-attempted and mostly left alone (except for repetition of pithy quotations and the popular tour through its gallery of heroes in chapter eleven commonly known as the *Hall of Faith).* It is rare that Hebrews is preached through and studied in its entirety by a church community. This is due in part to it being considered "too complicated" and in part because it is thought "too archaic" for those of us who live in the digital age. Don't be bullied by such a bad diagnosis.

Hebrews is a weighty and deep book—we won't pretend it is not. It is thick with the wonder of the unfolding mystery of salvation. Some scholars claim that among New Testament books Hebrews is second in difficulty only to the Book of Revelation. True, it takes a good deal of intentionality to understand the implications, warnings and marvels contained in Hebrews, but it is well worth it. Its depth does not mean it is inaccessible; on the contrary, its deep pool of timeless truths makes it timely and welcoming to both the skeptic and the age-old saint. Whether we recognize it or not, the human heart hungers after depth even while flailing about in the shallows of man-made religions. Depth is a reason to dive in, not bow out.

As for being archaic, too antiquated and difficult to connect with in all its talk about temples, sacrificial systems, and rituals, again, we cry "malpractice!" This couldn't be more irrational. It is precisely because of its innumerable references to the Old Testament and its explaining of Israel's sacrificial system that we need to know what this book has within it! And let's be honest, we are a people well acquainted with temples, sacrifices and rituals—though our temples look more like clothing stores, gyms, schools, and the sports parks where we lay down our money, sweat, tears, and time. Far from being irrelevant, all the talk of sacrifices and temple dealings can help us understand our own elusive hearts as well as to navigate even the most mundane challenges of our day-to-day life in a post-Christian culture.

So, why Hebrews and why now? Because we love Jesus and we know we need to mature in the faith and become more like Him—just like the original audience to whom Hebrews was written. This brilliant book was written into a cultural milieu that was growing ever more intolerant and hostile to the truths of the Gospel—just like the western world of 2014. Hebrews is a sermon to a hurting church that needs to reset their gaze upon Jesus Christ. It is a letter, yes, but it is also an elegant and artistic sermon that teaches us how to interpret the Old Testament as well as how to preach. In other words, it teaches us about *hermeneutics* (the art of interpretation) and *homiletics* (the art of preaching). The Old Testament points to Jesus, as should all preaching. Hebrews is a book that teaches us how to read the rest of the Bible and how the grand storyline of salvation uncoils. It teaches us how to assess our hearts, how to hope amidst a culture that is increasingly antagonistic against the claims of Christ, and what to watch out for while we hold fast to love. Such teaching is invaluable life support, nourishment and armament for a church on mission and under fire.

Also, on a more personal level, as this church body is in the wonderful throes of growing pains—opening up a new service, opening up a missional outpost, and welcoming more people into the life of discipleship—this is an opportunity for us all to re-sync and recalibrate on *"Why are we here?"*, *"What is all this for?"* and *"How are we to go about our mission to make Gospel-centered disciples for the glory of God?"* The answer to these questions are found in Jesus—unashamedly and always Jesus. Hebrews puts this superiority of Christ on brilliant display as it takes us on a tour of the past and it trembles in awe as it ties all of the varied threads of salvation history to the person and work of Jesus.

There is nothing more practical, more intellectually satisfying, more existentially moving, than locking our gaze on Jesus. He has brought us to life; He has and is making us His beloved bride. We exist to glorify Him and point others to Him that he might reveal the glory of the Father by the power of His Spirit. Not only does the illumination of Hebrews ignite the Gospel gems of the Old Testament to gleaming life, but it also casts its radiance forward, shining its divine wattage on the hope of our promised future in the presence of The Hero-King. How amazing are the things that have come before! How astounding are the things still yet to come! All of history and all our hope come colliding together in the person and work of Jesus.

My own personal engagement with Hebrews has forever altered my view of the Bible: it has staggered my heart at the grandeur of God's plan come to fruition in Jesus Christ. Hebrews will call us out, call us up, challenge us, and cut the deadwood from our hearts. I believe it is the perfect time for this church community to sink our teeth into the nourishing meat of Hebrews. It is with great joy that we embark on this sermon series with you.

-Pastor Heath Hardesty

HISTORICAL CONTEXT

Author:
There be dragons here—in other words, this is a blank spot on the map of Hebrews, the place of unknown and guesswork. There has been much well-reasoned debate and ridiculous speculation over the authorship of Hebrews. The letter itself does not identify its author, and hundreds of years of tradition has made various claims. In early church history, the authorship was largely ascribed to the Apostle Paul, though there are significant stylistic differences between Hebrews and the Pauline epistles. Other authors put forward in various times and places are Barnabas, Luke (the author of The Gospel of Luke and the book of Acts), Philip, Priscilla, Silvanus, Apollos, and Clement.

What we do know about the author is that they were extremely well versed with the Old Testament Scriptures, knew Timothy (Paul's protégé and recipient of 1 & 2 Timothy) (13:23), personally knew those he was writing to (13:19), was a brilliant sermon writer extremely well-educated in rhetoric, gifted in eloquence, and thought of Jesus in the highest, most exalting of terms.

There is a load of opinions among scholars; however, most are in agreement that the official authorship should remain anonymous. Interesting, is it not, that one of the most eloquent and intellectually rigorous books of the Bible cannot be attributed to anyone? Just a thought, but maybe this eye-catching anonymity is God's way of making sure we focus all of our adoration on Christ rather than lifting up the human writer that was inspired by the Spirit.

Date:
How in the world do we date this book if the author remains unknown? Looking at internal evidence and holding that up against what we know of the historical context of Israel and the Roman Empire, one should take into account the following:

1) The original audience had been Christians a while. (Hebrews 5:11-6:3)

2) The original audience had experienced persecution (Hebrews 10:32-34) but had not yet faced the severe trials of martyrdom (12:4) that would come in the brutal persecution under Nero. This makes sense when considering the troubles Jewish Christians faced under Emperor Claudius when they were expelled from Rome, which eventually came to a bloody climax under the twisted tyranny of Nero decades later.

3) The author of Hebrews also speaks as if the Jewish sacrificial system was still being observed during the time of writing (7:27-28; 8:3-5; 9:7-8, 25; 10:1-3; 13:10-11), so it appears that it was written before the destruction of the Jerusalem temple in A.D. 70. The destruction of the temple put an end to the practice of sacrifices.

With all of these pieces in play, it seems best to date the writing of Hebrews to the mid-60s A.D, just before Nero's persecutions raged. For some extra reference, the Apostle Paul was beheaded by Nero in Rome in the mid to late 60's (sometime before Nero committed suicide in June of 68 A.D). Paul's martyrdom followed Rome's great fire of 64 A.D. that Nero ignited to gain the real estate for his building projects and then blamed the Christians for starting. Classy. And this is why we name our dogs Nero and our kids Paul.

Audience and Setting:
The original recipients of this letter are believed to have been Jewish Christians and/or Gentiles who had converted to Judaism and then converted to Christianity. The reason for thinking this is the book's numerous references and allusions to the Old Testament and to Jewish practices. Within the letter are thirty-five quotations, thirty-four allusions, and nineteen summaries of Old Testament material! That is ton. Clearly, the recipients of the letter were well acquainted with the Old Testament.

Where did they live? To what address did this letter arrive? Another good question with a number of possible answers. One likely answer is that it is addressed to a house church or cluster of churches in or near Rome. Other possible locations are a church community near Jerusalem itself, a church/cluster of churches in Antioch of Syria, while others believe it was written to a group of Christians who were once Essenes—The Dead Sea Sect in Qumran—and who might be falling back into their former pre-Jesus ways or blending them in a dangerous syncretism (a religious mashup).

The 60's were a turbulent time. We're not talking Summer of Love, Haight-Ashbury, hippies, LSD, or Vietnam protests—we're talking 60 A.D. We're talking burning Christians, insane emperors, raging Rome-destroying infernos, apostles losing their heads (literally), and churches meeting in catacombs. This was a time of increasing persecution for the church. The author tells his recipients to "Remember those who are in prison, as though in prison with them, and those who are mistreated" (13:3). Timothy had also just been released from prison (13:23), so we know Christians were being jailed. He also commends them for their endurance through persecution (10:32-34).

Members of the community to whom this letter was written were struggling with commitment to the faith and experiencing a lethargy that seemed to be leading to abandoning the faith and reverting to the Jewish tradition. They were under persecution and facing cultural pressures on all sides. What did they need? They needed to look at the centrality of Christ—and so the anonymous author of Hebrews points the spotlight to Jesus and blasts the readers with a dazzling high-Christology. Jesus Christ is better than anything they have ever had in the past and nothing will eclipse him in the future. He is better (6:9; 19; 22; 8:6; 9:23; 10:34; 11:16, 35, 40; 12:24). He is truer. He is greater than all that has come before. He is the fulfillment of the law and the substance to the shadows of the Old Testament sacrificial system. Though their salvation is guaranteed, the author of Hebrews exhorts the church to persevere and to remain faithful (2:1; 4:14; 6:1-3; 10:23). Only by gazing at Christ and trusting him, the truly faithful one, might we too be faithful and persevere.

OUTLINE OF HEBREWS

The Once & Forever King
- **1:1-2:18 – Jesus is Superior to Angels**
  - **1:1-14 – The Truer & Greater Son**
    - 1:1-4 – The Son's Person and Work *(Above all Others)*
    - 1:5-14 – Evidence of his Sonship *(The Truer & Greater Messenger)*
    - 2:1-4 – Warning Against Neglecting Salvation *(Gospel Gazing)*
  - **2:5-18 – The Founder of Salvation**
    - 2:5-9 – The Son of Man *(The Image of God)*
    - 2:10-18 – The Brother of Man *(Blood Brothers)*

The Exodus
- **3:1-10:18 – Jesus is Superior to the Mosaic Law**
  - 3:1-6 – *(The Truer & Greater Moses)*
  - **3:7-4:13 – Warning Against Failing to Enter God's Rest**
    - 3:7-19 – The Exodus Generation's Failure to Enter *(The Truer & Greater Israel)*
    - 4:1-11 – Our Failure to Enter? *(The Truer & Greater Sabbath)*
    - 4:12-13 – Our Failure: Naked & Exposed *(The Primacy of the Word)*
  - **4:14-10:18 – The High Priesthood of Jesus**
    - 4:14-5:10 – The Answer *(The Truer & Greater High Priest)*
  - **5:11-6:12 – A Digression to Warn Against Falling Away from the Faith**
    - 5:11-14 – A Rebuke *(Hard Words to an Immature Church)*
    - 6:1-12 – A Warning *(The Danger of Nominalism)*
    - 6:13-20 – An Anchor for the Soul *(The Perfect Promise)*

The Wilderness
- 7:1-28 – The Digression Ends: The Eternal Order of Jesus' Priesthood *(The Priest of Mystery)*
- **8:1-13 – High Priest of a Better Covenant**
  - 8:1-5 – A Heavenly Tabernacle *(The Truer & Greater Tabernacle)*
  - 8:6-13 – A Better Covenant with Better Promises *(The Truer & Greater Covenant)*
  - 9:1-10 – The Glory of the Old *(The Truer & Greater Holy Place)*
  - 9:11-28 – The Surpassing Glory of the New *(Bloodwork)*
  - 10:1-18 – Jesus' Perfect Sacrifice *(Once & For All)*
- **10:19-12:29 – The "Therefore": Endure in Faith**
  - **10:19-39 – Hope, Warning & Encouragement**
    - 10:19-31 – Let Us Draw Near *(The Invincible Confidence of Intimacy)*
    - 10:32-39 – We Don't Shrink Back *(Endurance & Affliction)*

The Hero of Faith
- **11:1-40 – By Faith Alone (The Ancients)**
  - **11:1-7 – Act One: Faith in The Unseen**
    - 11:1-4 – What is Faith? *(The Deep Reality of Faith)*
    - 11:4 – *(The Truer & Greater Abel)*
    - 11:5-6 – *(The Truer & Greater Enoch)*
    - 11:7 – *(The Truer & Greater Noah)*
  - **11:8-22 – Act Two: Faith in an Unseen Inheritance (The Patriarchs)**
    - 11:8-12 – *(The Truer & Greater Abraham & Sarah)*
    - 11:13-16 – The Unseen Inheritance: A Heavenly City *(The Truer & Greater Exile)*
    - 11:17-20 – *(The Truer & Greater Abraham & Isaac)*
    - 11:21 – *(The Truer & Greater Jacob)*
    - 11:22 – *(The Truer & Greater Joseph)*
  - **11:23 – Act Three: Faith Under Fire (The Exodus Generation)**
    - 11:23-28 – *(The Truer & Greater Moses)*
    - 11:29-30 – Impossible Odds *(The Sea & The Stone)*
    - 11:31 – *(The Truer & Greater Rahab)*
  - **11:32-40 – Act Four: Conclusion (The Rest of Them)**
    - 11:32-34 – Too Many to Mention *(The Truer & Greater Judge & King)*
    - 11:33-40 – Something Better *(The World Was Not Worthy)*

Walking to Our Now & Future Home
- **12:1-29 – Enduring in the "Already but Not Yet" Kingdom of God**
  - 12:1-11 – The Enduring Son *(Endurance & Discipline)*
  - 12:12-17 – Crucial Christ-like Character *(The Anti-Esau)*
  - 12:19-29 – Kingdom Come *(That Which Cannot Be Shaken)*
- **13:1-25 – Now What?**
  - 13:1-6 – Offer Acceptable Worship *(The Idol Factory)*
  - 13:7-19 – A Final Call to Remembrance *(Submission & Leaders)*
  - 13:20-25 – A Blessing, An Appeal & Greetings *(The Good Word)*

VOLUME ONE

"The Once and Forever King"

The book of Hebrews begins with a triumphant announcement that Jesus is superior to angels. This loaded theme of the first two chapters carries enormous consequences for the author's audience: Jewish Christians. For these readers, steeped in the Old Testament, knew that it was God's holy angels who delivered their beloved Law to Moses on Mt. Sinai. It was angels who were the messengers of God, which meant that every word of the Scriptures they had been raised with was the very Word of God, completely free from error and entirely authoritative over every facet of their lives. Yet now they were being told that One came who was superior to angels in every way. This One was not just a messenger from God, but was God's own Son, fully divine. As the Son of Man, this One claimed to be the final Prophet who carried the final Word, more than that, who Himself was God's Word wrapped in flesh. This One claimed to be the final Priest who would make final purification for their sins in the sacrifice of His own sacred flesh. This One claimed to be the final King who accomplished their salvation and sat down with finality at the right hand of God, the place of final authority. This One claimed that every beloved word of their Scriptures was a shadow that found its substance in Him, the truer and greater. Therefore Volume 1 includes a stern warning: they must pay even closer attention to this Gospel, the word of their Lord Jesus Christ, the Once & Forever King, lest they neglect Him and face Him as Judge. And therefore so must we. Let's glory in Him together.

"The Once and Forever King"

1:1-2:18 – Jesus is Superior to Angels
    1:1-14 – The Truer & Greater Son
        1:1-4 – The Son's Person and Work *(Above all Others)*
        1:5-14 – Evidence of his Sonship *(The Truer & Greater Messenger)*
    2:1-4 – Warning Against Neglecting Salvation *(Gospel Gazing)*
    2:5-18 – The Founder of Salvation
        2:5-9 – The Son of Man *(The Image of God)*
        2:10-18 – The Brother of Man *(Blood Brothers)*

PART 1 | 1:1-4
Above all Others

> Almost every major theme of Hebrews is wrapped tightly into this lightning bolt of an introduction: the contrasting epochs of revelation culminating in the coming of Jesus Christ, the Last Word, the eternal Son of God and the purifier of sins. In these titles and works Jesus is superior even to angels, as much as an author is superior to a character in his own book. This glorious appetizer before the feast of Hebrews boldly declares that Jesus Christ is the truer and greater everything.

Q's & Cues

1 The author states that Jesus both 'created' the world and 'upholds' the universe. Why do you think the author wanted to distinguish the two and why might this be important?

2 If Jesus is the "radiance" of God's glory, what does glory mean? How do the Scriptures show this aspect of Jesus' identity?

3 v3 says that Jesus is the exact imprint of the nature of God. Discuss this.

4 Biblical authors often repeat themselves in order to emphasize a point. This author states that Jesus is the "Heir" and that He "Inherited" (vs. 2 & 4); why do you think the author emphasizes this aspect of Jesus' identity and why is it important?

5 What are examples of the ways God spoke through the prophets?

Prayer Primer

Father
Your Word became flesh and dwelt among us. You have spoken to us through Your Son. May I always long to see Him, may I always long to draw near to Him. Help me to see past the distractions of this world to gaze continually upon Jesus.
In His name
Amen

VOLUME ONE

Prophet (1:1)
The instrument or mouthpiece of God. One upon whom the Spirit of God rested, who by proclamation and demonstration communicated God's Word to His people.

> "The weight of the whole creation is laid upon Christ: he supports the whole and all the parts. When, upon the apostasy, the world was breaking to pieces under the wrath and curse of God, the Son of God, undertaking the work of redemption, bound it up again, and established it by his almighty power and goodness."
> *-Matthew Henry*

Purification (1:3)
The act of making one pure and clean before God and men. To cast out whatever is impure or undesirable.

PART 2 | 1:5-14
The Greater Messenger

Last week, verse 4 trumpeted the theme of the first two chapters of Hebrews: that Jesus Christ is superior even to angels, those powerful, fiery, sinless messengers that surround God's throne and do His bidding. Now verses 5-14 give evidence from the Old Testament to Jewish readers that Jesus Christ is the Greater Messenger. The evidence reveals that He is greater than angels in position, nature and authority as the Son of God, fully divine, seated at God's right hand.

Q's & Cues

1 Read 2 Samuel 7:8-17. This passage records God making His covenant with David, where God promises David that his throne will be established forever and the future kings will be viewed as the sons of God (v14). Why do you think the author used this passage in explaining Jesus' identity to his audience?

2 Read Psalm 2:7-9. In none of the passages is God speaking directly to Christ. So, why is the author of Hebrews citing these examples? How does it connect with 2 Samuel 7:12-17?

3 Why is the author making a comparison between Jesus and Angels?

4 In v8, God calls Jesus God. Dig into this idea.

5 How do angels serve us?

Prayer Primer

Father
Help me to see the value and preciousness of Jesus. He is greater than any other. His words are hope and life. He is more than I could ever comprehend. Creator, Redeemer, Savior. May I never settle for cheap joys, but forever cling to the invaluable treasure of Jesus.
In His Name
Amen

Begotten (1:5)
A New Testament word that describes Christ as the only, or unique, Son of God. Distinctiveness - "one of a kind".

> "In the marvel of the Incarnation, Jesus Christ has spoken to us the words that were given Him from the Father. Jesus is God's last Word."
> – *Edmund P. Clowney*

Anointed (1:9)
To set apart a person for a special work or service

PART 3 | 2:1-4
Gospel Gazing

After proving Jesus to be greater than angels in position, nature and authority, chapter 2 opens with a dire warning to those still clinging to the shadows of Old Testament revelation while rejecting their substance in Christ. If the Law, delivered by angels and full of terrible warnings and astounding promises, was merely a pointer to Christ, then how closely must God's people pay attention to the Gospel of salvation in Jesus Christ? It is then into the magnificent depths of this Gospel, that carries warnings more terrible and promises more astounding, that we gaze today.

Q's & Cues

1 What was the message declared by angels? How has it proved to be reliable?

2 What are some ways we neglect our salvation? How can we as a community protect ourselves from this?

3 If there are people today who still transgress and disobey God, how can it be that "every transgression and disobedience has received retribution"?

4 In v2, whom do you think the author is referring to when the topic of retribution of sin is brought up? How does this line up with our justification in Christ?

5 v3 & 4 tell us that this great salvation was first declared by Jesus and that miracles, signs and wonders also bore witness to this great salvation. Looking at the miracles of Christ through this lens, how do they point to our salvation?

Prayer Primer

Father
Give me a hunger for Your word. You have revealed Your character and Your plan of salvation within the pages of scripture. What else could I ever want to give my time to? Create in me a desire to know You that cannot be satisfied until I meet You face to face.
In Jesus name
Amen

"As God, the incarnate Son is supreme in power and grace, in contrast to the impotence and resourcelessness of fallen mankind. As man, the incarnate Son is able to fully to identify himself with mankind, and in particular in man's place to endure the divine punishment of sin on the cross, thus securing for mankind eternal redemption—a theme developed in this chapter and of major importance throughout the epistle."
-*Philip Edgcumbe Hughes*

Retribution (2:2)
The act of receiving what one deserves, usually referring to punishment for doing evil. Biblically, the judgment of a holy God upon sin.

PART 4 | 2:5-9
The Image of God

The author of Hebrews returns to the evidence for Jesus' superiority to angels, God's messengers, focusing on the fact that Jesus is the Son of Man, an Old Testament title rich with Messianic importance. Here we explore how our father Adam, created in the image of God to rule over God's creation and reflect God's glory, shattered that image by worshiping creation to glorify Himself. Jesus comes as a new representative of mankind, taking on flesh as the restored image of God, and being for a while lower than angels yet now ruling over creation. Though not all things are seen under his rule today, one day all those who trust in Him will reign with Him.

Q's & Cues

1 Early in creation both angels and humans sinned against God; however, God chooses to redeem and restore humanity. What does this say about the relationship God has with humanity?

2 What does it mean to be made in the Image of God?

3 In v8, the author states, "Now in putting everything in subjection to him, he left nothing outside his control. At present, we do not yet see everything in subjection to him." How should this statement affect your life and how you view the future?

4 Read Genesis 1:26-31 and Psalms 8:3-6. The author of Hebrews is suggesting that Jesus is the fulfillment of who Adam/Israel should have been. What other comparisons can be made throughout the scriptures (i.e. both Adam and Jesus were tempted in a garden; Adam sinned at a tree while Jesus bore our sins on a tree, etc.)?

5 The author mentions "the world to come" in verse 5. What is this world and how does it affect v6-8?

Prayer Primer

Father
What joy and relief comes from knowing that there is nothing outside of my Savior's control. Through His suffering He has been lifted up. Through His agony He has been crowned with all glory and honor. Thank You for the life and security I have in Jesus.
In His name
Amen

Reverence
A feeling of profound awe and respect.

Glory (2:7)
A quality of God's character that emphasizes His greatness and authority. Weightiness.

> "The end is this: that He, through divine grace, should be found to have tasted death for the good of us all and each of us, and that He should thus have entered into the lowliness of our death-subjected humanity, in order to exalt that lowliness to the high estate which the eighth Psalm declares to be our ultimate destination, and into which He is already entered himself."
> -F.J. Delitzsch

PART 5 | 2:10-18
Blood Brothers

Last week the author of Hebrews again proclaimed that Jesus was superior to angels in His role as the Son of Man. In verses 10-18, the author unpacks why it is so crucial to this role that Jesus was fully human. The Gospel blows our puny minds by proclaiming that the God "for whom and by whom all things exist" became a man so that He could pay for our sins by His death on our behalf as our Great High Priest. Even more, God's people now have a God who has faced the greatest of sufferings and temptations without sin. Wonder, for God is our blood brother.

Q's & Cues

1 You may have heard this passage referenced in old church hymns, but what does it mean that Christ brought "many sons to glory"? How is this different than just being saved from the penalty of sin?

2 What is sanctification?

3 If the death of Christ destroyed the devil, why are we told elsewhere in Scripture to be on guard against him (1 Peter 5:8)?

4 We all know people who do not know Jesus. Looking at their lives how is it that they are subjected to lifelong slavery? Where else in the Bible is the imagery of slavery used?

5 Going beyond Christ's temptation in the wilderness, in what other ways was Christ tempted throughout his life? In such times, how do the temptations Christ endured help you in overcoming similar temptation?

Prayer Primer

Father
It was my sin that sent Jesus to the cross. My addiction, my inability, my deception, my pride. All I deserve from You is wrath. Yet You love me. You cherish me. You are not ashamed of me. What love is this that I should be called a child of God. Thank You.
In Jesus name
Amen

Sanctification (2:11)
Sanctification is both the gracious event where believers are set apart from sin and for holiness and the process by which God's love is perfected in His people, conforming them to the image of Christ.

Propitiation (2:17)
The act of appeasing God by diverting His wrath onto a substitute. In the Old Testament this was prefigured when blood was sprinkled on the mercy seat on the Day of Atonement, transforming the throne of judgment into a throne of grace. In the New Testament, this was accomplished once for all in the sacrifice of Jesus on the cross.

VOLUME TWO

"The Exodus"

> In Volume 1 (Ch. 1-2), the author of Hebrews focuses on Jesus as superior to the messengers of the Old Covenant, angelic beings. Volume 2 begins a lengthy treatment of Jesus as the mediator of a new and better covenant in His person and work, proving that He is greater than the Mosaic law (3:1-10:17). A call for God's people to persevere in faith follows the establishment of Jesus' infinite superiority to Moses (3:1-6). This exhortation is gravely earnest, for the followers of Moses after the Exodus failed to enter God's rest because of their stubborn unbelief (3:7-4:11). The author purposely draws on imagery from that generation to warn in the strongest possible terms about the ever present danger of falling away from the covenant community (6:1-12). Though Christians have a greater Savior who led us through a greater Exodus from a greater slavery, God's people are always prone to lazy immaturity, as were both the Exodus generation and Hebrews' initial audience (5:11-14). The strong language of this chapter leads believers to despair of their shameful sin and wandering hearts before the ever exposing Word of God (4:12-13), and therefore leads in hope to the very heart of the letter: the superior priesthood of Jesus (4:14-10:17). He is the Great High Priest that we need to represent us to God, sympathizing with our weakness, while also representing God to us as the sinless God-man. That is why this deeply convicting volume ends on a high note: all of God's promises find their "yes" in Jesus Christ, our "anchor for the soul" (6:13-20; 2 Cor 1:20).

"The Exodus"

3:1-10:18 – Jesus is Superior to the Mosaic Law
  3:1-6 – *(The Truer & Greater Moses)*
  3:7-4:13 – Warning Against Failing to Enter God's Rest
    3:7-19 – The Exodus Generation's Failure to Enter
        (The Truer & Greater Israel)
    4:1-11 – Our Failure to Enter? *(The Truer & Greater Sabbath)*
    4:12-13 – Our Failure: Naked & Exposed *(The Primacy of the Word)*
  4:14-10:18 – The High Priesthood of Jesus
    4:14-5:10 – The Answer *(The Truer & Greater High Priest)*
  5:11-6:12 – A Digression to Warn Against Falling Away from the Faith
    5:11-14 – A Rebuke *(Hard Words to an Immature Church)*
    6:1-12 – A Warning *(The Danger of Nominalism)*
    6:13-20 – An Anchor for the Soul *(The Perfect Promise)*

PART 6 | 3:1-6
The Truer & Greater Apostle

After establishing that Jesus is greater than angels, the first mediators of the Mosaic Covenant, the author of Hebrews will spend the next seven chapters revealing Jesus as the better mediator of a better covenant with better promises. He begins by stating that the towering mediator, prophet and apostle Moses was only a faithful servant in the house of God pointing to Jesus, the Faithful Son over the house of God. This holds great significance for the church, the house of God.

Q's & Cues

1 What is an apostle and how was Jesus one?

2 Why do you think the author wanted to compare Jesus to Moses?

3 Why do you think the author waits until 2:9 to mention Jesus by name and 3:6 to call Jesus the Christ?

4 What do you think is meant by if we "hold fast our confidence and our boasting in our hope"?

5 How is endurance important in the life of a believer? What are consequences of not enduring until the end? What are the rewards of endurance?

Prayer Primer

Father
I am so foolish. I am riddled with flaws and continually insufficient. Yet I boast in myself endlessly. I hold up my accomplishments and my victories as if they counted for anything. May I only boast in Christ. May His praises be forever on my lips.
In Jesus name
Amen

VOLUME TWO

Apostle (3:1)
A special messenger of Jesus Christ; a person to whom authority is designated for certain tasks.

Song of Moses
Found in Deut. 32:1-43, this poem is believed to have been written just before Moses' death and illustrates a faithful God who pursues his corrupt and fallen people.

PART 7 | 3:7-19
The Truer & Greater Israel

We have already seen that Jesus is greater than Moses and the angels, the mediators of the Old Covenant. More than that, He is greater than the recipients of the Covenant, Israel. Where the wilderness generation of Israel under Moses failed in their role as the son of God and light of the world, Jesus succeeded. The church, the body of Christ, is warned not to harden their hearts as Israel did, but to hold fast to the true Israel, Jesus Christ. This sub-section that runs from 3:7-4:13 will compare the followers of Moses to the followers of Jesus.

Q's & Cues

1 What is the Church's responsibility as a community to keep each other from falling away?

2 Does the Church's responsibility of watching over one another conflict with tolerance?

3 How do we harden our hearts towards God? How can we counteract the hardening of our hearts?

4 As believers, what are some ways we are similar to Israel when they were being led by Moses?

5 What is unbelief and is it different from doubt?

Prayer Primer

Father
Thank You for sending Jesus to save me. Thank You for His great patience and persistence with me. He is faithful even when I wander. He loves me, He pursues me, and He seeks my good at the sacrifice of Himself. Thank You.
In Jesus name
Amen

Wrath (3:11)
The personal manifestation of God's holy, moral character in judgment against sin. For the believer, God's wrath was absorbed fully by Christ on the cross.

> "We live in an age of sound bytes constantly luring us to new and better products or experiences with instant access to services, information, and opportunities. In this fast-paced age we sprint from one life experience to the next; to some, Hebrew's emphasis on 'long-distance' well-paced faith may seem out of step. Yet, obedience to God must be lived in the daily, often mundane experiences of life over a long period of time, often without immediate gratification."
> *-George H. Guthrie*

Exhortation (3:13)
A message of caution or encouragement with the purpose of motivating persons to action.

PART 8 | 4:1-11
The Truer & Greater Sabbath

Last week the author drew on Psalm 95 to demonstrate that the Exodus generation of Israel under Moses failed to enter the Sabbath rest of God in the Promise Land due to unbelief. Though Joshua's generation did enter the Land, Psalm 95 shows that this event points to a greater Joshua and a greater rest. Paradoxically, Christians must strive to cease their striving if they are to enjoy the very rest that God entered into on the 7th Day of creation, because it is Jesus' work, not ours, that earned this Sabbath rest that we taste now by obeying its Lord and awaiting its consummation in eternity.

Q's & Cues

1 In v2, the author states the message did not benefit Israel because they were not united by faith. What does this look like in the Church? What are some consequences of the church not being united?

2 What is the "rest" the author is referring to?

3 If salvation is based on Jesus' sacrifice and not on our good works, why is it important that we strive or persevere?

4 What was the disobedience of the exodus generation?

5 What do you find most challenging about this verse?

Prayer Primer

Father
For years I have tried to satisfy myself, tried to find fulfillment apart from You. I have exhausted myself searching for joy. But You have found me. And at last I can rest. No longer weary from reaching for unattainable joy. Simply free to rest in Christ. Thank You.
In Jesus name
Amen

Sabbath (4:9)
Originating in creation and perfected in redemption, the practice of observing one day in seven as a time of rest for the people and the land.

PART 9 | 4:12-13
The Primacy of the Word

Drawing on Psalm 95, Hebrews 3:7-4:13 is a comparison of the followers of Moses and the followers of Jesus, warning Christians not to fail to enter God's rest through disobedience and unbelief. The author concludes this section with a climactic warning about the Word of God, a sword that drives through men and women who are naked and exposed before a holy God. This terrifying imagery is used to make us pine for a Great High Priest to stand in our place, to be naked and exposed before His Father, and be found guiltless.

Q's & Cues

1 In the context of this passage, what is the word of God?

2 What is the difference between the soul and the spirit?

3 Why are our thoughts and intentions so important to God?

4 As a community, what are some areas in which we have to be on guard against disobedience?

5 The author is writing to the Church, yet they mention that all believers will give an account for their deeds. How does this fit in with the doctrine of Justification?

Prayer Primer

Father
Open my eyes to the power of Your Word. It is not dead, it is not irrelevant, it is not out of touch. It is alive. Where there is sin in my life, let it be cut out by the power of Your Word. Where there is sorrow, let me find comfort in the pages of Scripture. Where there is joy, let it be increased by the promises You have given.
In Jesus name
Amen

Atonement
At-one-ment. The reconciliation of sinners to a holy God through the death and resurrection of Jesus Christ.

PART 10 | 4:14-5:10
The Truer & Greater High Priest

> Last week we learned about the piercing and exposing nature of God's holy word, which was meant to stir up desperation for a compassionate priest to make atonement for our sins. In Hebrews 4:14-10:18, the author unveils the perfect, eternal High Priesthood of Jesus. The Levitical priesthood and their constant sacrifices have given way to a final one. The shadows have given way to the real. In today's passage, the smoldering wick of our terror in approaching God is put out.

Q's & Cues

1. Who was Melchizedek and why is he important? (Gen. 14:18-20 and Psalm 110:4)

2. How does Melchizedek's role as Priest and King foreshadow Jesus? (Gen. 14:18-20)

3. What do you think the author meant by saying Jesus "learned obedience" and was "made perfect"? How do these concepts interact with Jesus' sinlessness?

4. Since Jesus is a member of the Trinity and lives in perfect unity with the Father and Spirit, why was it necessary for him to pray?

5. Knowing that Jesus is our Big Brother and Advocate to the Father, how does this affect your perception of God?

Prayer Primer

Father
I could cry out for all of my life, I could right every wrong, I could offer myself to You every day, none of it would save me. There is only one who can reconcile me back to you. The sacrifice of Jesus is the only thing that could save me. He alone is able, He alone is sufficient to make atonement for my sins.
In Jesus name
Amen

> "There is indeed, no book in Holy Scripture which speaks so clearly of the priesthood of Christ, which so highly exalts the virtue and dignity of that only true sacrifice which He offered by His death, which so abundantly deals with the use of ceremonies as well as their abrogation, and, in a word, so fully explains that Christ is the end of the Law."
> *-John Calvin*

Great High Priest
Continuing from the line of Aaron, Moses' brother, the High Priest functioned as the executive representative of Israel to Yahweh in the Old Testament. He alone could perform sacrifices on behalf of God's people.

Temptation (4:15)
An enticement or invitation to sin that promises greater good in disobedience than obedience.

PART 11 | 5:11-14
Hard Words to an Immature Church

In 5:11-6:20, the author breaks from his section on the High Priesthood of Jesus (4:14-10:19) to warn about the ever-present threat of apostasy (falling-away from the New Covenant community) and encourage regarding the certainty of God's promise in Christ. The author's tone begins in 5:11-14 as harsh rebuke. The problem is sluggish immaturity: the hearers should be teaching others to cut deep into the juicy steak of the Gospel by now, not being bottle fed the basics like infants.

Q's & Cues

1 How do we, as a community, become dull of hearing?

2 How does the author's claim that the church was dull of hearing interact with his previous warning in 2:1-3?

3 What are the "the basic principles of the oracles of God"?

4 What are some ways we can work towards maturing our faith? What does this look like in a communal setting?

5 Where are some areas that our community is becoming dull of hearing and drifting away from the faith?

Prayer Primer

Father
Take me deeper into the Gospel. Let me never become content with where I am. Create in me an ever increasing desire to get more lost in the beauty of the Gospel. The heights and depths of mercy, the width and breadth of love. May I spend my life searching out the richness of my salvation through Jesus.
In His name
Amen

Discernment (5:14)
Understanding that which is obscure or hidden.

PART 12 | 6:1-12
The Danger of Nominalism

> In a digression from a larger argument about the priesthood of Jesus (4:17-10:18), the author rebuked the listeners for their "sluggish" immaturity to get their attention (5:11-14). They are now challenged to press on towards maturity (6:1-3), warned about the peril of falling away (4-8), encouraged about their present salvation (9-10) and called to persist in faith (11-12). One of the most controversial passages in the Bible, this warning has driven many earnest Christians to tears of doubt. Rest assured, if our hope is in Christ, we can be sure of "better things"—salvation in a better Savior.

Q's & Cues

1 How are those who have "fallen away" (v6) different than those who are "drifting away" (2:1)?

2 How are the people who have fallen away different from believers who struggle with overcoming habitual sin?

3 What is the church's responsibility in dealing with people who have fallen away from the faith?

4 How can we have "full assurance of hope"?

5 How does the author's warning match up with our assurance of salvation (A.K.A. once saved, always saved)?

Prayer Primer

Father
Thank You for the security of my salvation. May I never take for granted the sacrifice of Christ. May I never love the sin that sent Jesus to the cross. Grow in me the desire to pursue righteousness, make me more like Jesus. Let me love what You love and hate what You hate.
In Jesus name
Amen

Nominalism
Identification with a cause in name only. In Christianity, adhering to the external forms of godliness while denying its power (2 Timothy 3:15).

Apostasy
Abandonment of Christian belief and a rejection of Christ by someone who has claimed to be a Christian.

Repentance
Turning away from sin, disobedience, or rebellion and turning back to God. Literally to change one's mind.

PART 13 | 6:13-20
The Perfect Promise

After a harsh rebuke for lazy immaturity and a dire warning about the present peril of falling away, the author's digression ends on a resounding note of hope before entering seamlessly back into the discussion of the priesthood of Jesus (4:14-10:17). Last week ended with a call to imitate past examples of faith in God's perfect promises (v.12) and the example given now is Abraham. God's oath-bound promise to Abraham points forward to God's promise of salvation in Jesus Christ, an anchor of hope for the soul to His New Covenant people.

Q's & Cues

1 What are some promises in scripture we are often impatient to receive?

2 What are the promises we are still waiting to be fulfilled?

3 In the New Covenant, how has God sealed his promises?

4 Read Genesis 12:1-3 and 15:5-6. In what ways is the Abrahamic Covenant in the process of being fulfilled?

5 What are some ways we can practice patience in regards to God's promises?

Prayer Primer

Father
When trials and fear and uncertainty shake my life I can stand firm. I will not be swayed; my faith will not be shaken. You have given me full assurance. Christ has gone before me; He is my soul's anchor. I can rest in Him, knowing that Your promises are tied to my unmovable Savior.
In Jesus name
Amen

Forerunner (6:20)
One who goes before to prepare the way for others.

VOLUME
THREE
"The Wilderness"

The heart of Hebrews throbs with love and mystery. Our author returns in chapter 7 to the fundamental argument of the letter: the superior priesthood of Jesus Christ (4:14-10:18). We must remember chapters 3 and 4, where the followers of Jesus are compared to the followers of Moses who died in the literal wilderness of the desert and in the figurative wilderness of unbelief. We are no better than them, for the word of God cuts through our hearts like butter, exposing our failure before Him (4:12-13). The answer given to this terrifying problem is the priesthood of Jesus: He is fully man so He can sympathize with us but fully God so His sacrifice can atone for us. So, having compared the followers of Moses and the followers of Jesus and found no difference, the author will now compare the Old Covenant under Moses and the New Covenant in Jesus and find all the difference we need for peaceful assurance. In the Mosaic Covenant, Levitical priests after the order of Moses' brother, Aaron, offered animal sacrifices daily in a moveable tabernacle. Followers of Moses were commanded to obey God's Law from the heart. In the new and better covenant (8:1-13), Jesus, after the eternal order of Melchizedek (7:1-28), offered once & for all the sacrifice of Himself (10:1-18) in an immovable, heavenly tabernacle (8:1-5). We too are commanded to obey, but Jesus provides what He commands, the Holy Spirit, to give us new hearts of obedience to the Law that He fulfilled for us (9:11-28). We therefore can (and must!) draw near to Him "in full assurance of faith" for joy and life (10:22).

"The Wilderness"

- 7:1-28 – The Digression Ends: The Eternal Order of Jesus' Priesthood *(The Priest of Mystery)*
- **8:1-13 – High Priest of a Better Covenant**
  - 8:1-5 – A Heavenly Tabernacle *(The Truer & Greater Tabernacle)*
  - 8:6-13 – A Better Covenant with Better Promises *(The Truer & Greater Covenant)*
  - 9:1-10 – The Glory of the Old *(The Truer & Greater Holy Place)*
  - 9:11-28 – The Surpassing Glory of the New *(Bloodwork)*
  - 10:1-18 – Jesus' Perfect Sacrifice *(Once & For All)*
- **10:19-12:29 – The "Therefore": Endure in Faith**
  - **10:19-39 – Hope, Warning & Encouragement**
    - 10:19-31 – Let Us Draw Near *(The Invincible Confidence of Intimacy)*
    - 10:32-39 – We Don't Shrink Back *(Endurance & Affliction)*

PART 14 | 7:1-28
The Priest of Mystery

> Hebrews 6, a dire warning coupled with confidence in God's promise, is a digression from the central theme and thrust of the book, the Great High Priesthood of Jesus (4:14-10:18), a theme to which our author now returns in Chapter 7 with the mysterious, priestly figure of Melchizedek to whom Abraham paid a tithe (Genesis 14). God's sinful people need a better priest than the sinful, mortal ones descended from Aaron that the law requires. And now they have one: a sinless, eternal priest after the order of Melchizedek.

Q's & Cues

1 Read Genesis 14:17-24. Who was Melchizedek?

2 The author states that Jesus is able to save to the "uttermost" those who draw near to God. What do you think this statement means and how should it holistically affect our daily lives?

3 Look up the word guarantor. How does this describe Christ?

4 What does the "word of the oath" refer to?

5 Reread Hebrews 2:10 and 5:9. Within this context, how has Jesus been made perfect?

Prayer Primer

Father
How great is Jesus. How wonderful, majestic, and powerful. Every priest, every sacrifice, every offering, could not take away the sin of even one man. But Jesus, everlasting Jesus, once and for all, swallowed up the sin of His people, that we may now be declared righteous before You. Thank You for the complete sufficiency of Jesus.
In His name
Amen

Patriarch
The founder or ruler of a tribe, family, or clan.

> "Those who have Christ as their high priest and mediator with God have in Him a Savior whose saving power is available without end, not liable to the mischances of mortal life. He lives eternally, eternally engaged to bless and protect those who have committed themselves to Him."
> *-F.F. Bruce*

Intercession
The act of petitioning God or praying on behalf of another person or group.

PART 15 | 8:1-5
The Truer & Greater Tabernacle

What's the point? In this crucial chapter, the author mercifully answers: we have a Great High Priest in Jesus, the mediator of a better covenant, seated at the right hand of God in the heavenly tabernacle having achieved full forgiveness of our sins by sacrificing himself on the cross. Yet Jesus is not only the greater high priest of a greater tabernacle, He Himself is our tabernacle, our meeting place with God, as the covenant Lord who "became flesh and dwelt among us" (John 1:14).

Q's & Cues

1. What is the purpose of the high priest and how does Jesus continue to fulfill this purpose?
2. What are the gifts and sacrifices that the Levitical priests had to offer? What is the gift and/or sacrifice that Jesus offered?
3. The author previously stated that Jesus is a "priest forever, after the order of Melchizedek;" however, they now state that if Jesus was on earth, he would not be a priest. Why do you think this is? Is this a contradiction or is there a deeper meaning?
4. Why was it important that Moses follow a particular blueprint or pattern when building the tabernacle rather than God allowing Moses to build it to his own specifications or to use his own creativity in its design? How does this connect to the idea of the tent being a copy and shadow of heavenly things?
5. What are some examples of copies or shadows in the Old Testament that point to Christ?

Prayer Primer

Father
It's all about Jesus. All Your scriptures point to Him, may my life do the same. May I come to see the gifts you have given me, my relationships, my abilities, my words, my actions as a way to point to Him. They are not supreme, but simply shadows of the joys to be found in Jesus. May all I do honor and glorify the only One worthy of honor and glory.
In Jesus name
Amen

Levite
A member of the Hebrew tribe of Levi, who after the Exodus served the priests and kept watch over the tabernacle. Levitical priests are descended directly from Aaron, the great-grandson of Levi and the brother of Moses.

Tabernacle
Until the temple was built, it was the portable, specifically designed dwelling place for the divine presence of Yahweh after the Exodus.

PART 16 | 8:6-13
The Truer & Greater Covenant

Thus far, we have cherished the glory of Jesus fulfilling every element of the Old Covenant under Moses, specifically in His priesthood (4:17-10:18). We can therefore now confidently assert that the Old Covenant has been made new in Jesus Christ. It is a New Covenant, indeed a better covenant with better promises! The author lists these "better promises" from Jeremiah 31. Though God's people failed to reach God's standards of the Old Covenant externally, Jesus exceeded those standards holistically and has sent His Spirit to transform His people internally.

Q's & Cues

1 What is Christ's ministry? What was the old ministry?

2 How does Christ act as a mediator of the new covenant?

3 Why didn't God begin with a faultless covenant?

4 Carefully read through v8-12. Now looking closely at v9, how would you explain what is being said?

5 Knowing yourself and the sin and rebellion in your own life, share with your comGroup your thoughts and feelings on v12?

Prayer Primer

Father
Thank You for the new covenant brought forth by Jesus. No longer determined by what I can do. I am insufficient and I am weak. I could never hold up my end of the deal. But Christ now holds it all upon Himself. Not any good that I have done, but all the good that Christ has done. His righteousness, His works, His perfection holds this covenant together. That You may be my God and I may be Your child.
In Jesus name
Amen

> "The New Covenant is not only better, and founded upon better promises than the old; but, yet more, it supersedes the old. The characteristics of the New Covenant, and the very name which it bears, point to the abrogation of that which has now become the 'old.'"
> -B.F. Westcott

Iniquity (8:12)
Immorality, unrighteousness, lawlessness.

Covenant (8:6)
In society, an agreement between two people or two groups that involves promises on the part of each to the other. Between God and man, an oath in blood administered sovereignly.

PART 17 | 9:1-10
The Truer & Greater Holy Place

> *Obsolete. Old. Ready to vanish.* These were the words used in Chapter 8 to describe the Old Covenant that was made new in Jesus Christ. These were words that could get one killed. Yet our author is not mocking the Old Covenant, for we are immediately and respectfully ushered back into the inner chambers of the tabernacle in Chapter 9. This illustration of the glories of the old tabernacle system begins with the furniture of the Holy Place, a revered site in the Hebrew conscious saturated with Christological shadows.

Q's & Cues

1 Carefully read verses 1 through 10 how does your idea of worship mesh with how the author of Hebrews defines worship? Does it seem odd to you to have regulations for worship?

2 Now, let's hone in on v1-5. Why do you thing the author of Hebrews goes into such detail about the furnishings within the tent?

3 Why does the author of Hebrews say we cannot now speak in detail of these things?

4 How would you define unintentional sins? How does the necessity of sacrifice for such sins put into perspective our attempts to classify and dismiss some sins as trivial or minor?

5 If gifts and sacrifices could not perfect the conscience of the worshiper, what was the purpose of offering up gifts and sacrifices?

Prayer Primer

Father
Thank You for sending Jesus to put an end to my earning. No longer must I burden myself with laws in an effort to obtain and keep Your favor. Christ has taken that burden upon Himself, He has acted in perfect obedience to You. He has freed me up, not to earn Your love, but to fearlessly claim that which has been graciously given to me. May I strive to walk in obedience, not to keep from losing Your love, but because Your love empowers me to do so.
In Jesus name
Amen

Cherubim (9:5)
Winged angelic beings associated with God's praise and worship.

Most Holy Place (9:3)
Also known as the Holy of Holies, this is the most sacred part of the temple in the Old Testament where the literal presence of God lies behind the veil. Containing the Ten Commandments inside the Ark of the Covenant, only the high priest could enter here to make his annual sacrifice on the Day of Atonement.

Mercy Seat (9:5)
The golden lid on the Ark of the Covenant. Represented God's throne and had atoning blood sprinkled on it for the people on the Day of Atonement.

Conscience (9:9)
A person's inner awareness of conforming to the will of God or departing from it, resulting in either a sense of approval or condemnation.

Reformation (9:10)
To realign or renew. An improvement by change or correction.

PART 18 | 9:11-28
Bloodwork

> Christians today can hardly imagine tabernacle worship in the Old Covenant (9:1-10) under its mediator, Moses, with its bloody sacrifices being offered day after day, year after year by sinful priests, a constant reminder both the system's imperfection and our own. In an astounding passage, the author of Hebrews expounds Jesus as the fulfillment of this system. He is a superior priest who offers a superior sacrifice in a superior tabernacle, and is thus a superior mediator of a superior covenant offering us a superior salvation and therefore a superior joy and a cleaner conscience. He is Truer & Greater indeed.

Q's & Cues

1 Read v8 & 9 of the previous week. Now, looking at v12, what is the holy place that Jesus enters into?

2 Who are "those who are called"? Why is the terminology of "called" being used?

3 Why do you think God demands blood for the atonement of sin?

4 Copies can be copies only if there is first an _____? With that in mind, discuss v23 & 24.

5 If Jesus went to the cross 2000 years ago to atone for our sins. Why would the other of Hebrews tell us that he "appeared once at the end of the ages"?

Prayer Primer

Father
Thank You for the redemption of Jesus. Thank You that His death has brought me life. Through His spilled blood I am invited in to take part in His inheritance. My sin has been absorbed into Him, His righteousness has been imparted to me. I can stand before You now as a perfect son. Because of Jesus' sacrifice I am seen by You as a faithful, obedient servant. Thank You for all that Jesus has given me and all that it took away.
In His name
Amen

VOLUME THREE

> "The symbolism of the high priesthood and sacrifice of Jesus in the heavenly sanctuary is therefore designed to convey the truth that the relations of men with God are based finally upon Jesus Christ."
> -*J. Moffatt*

Redemption (9:12)
Deliverance through the payment of a price. Christians are delivered from slavery to Satan, sin and death through the payment of the blood of Jesus Christ.

PART 19 | 10:1-18
Once & For All

> We have reached the heart of the book, where the author places the capstone on the masterpiece, the focal point of the letter, that Jesus Christ is our Great High Priest. After establishing that eternal redemption is in His blood (9:11-28), our author celebrates the finality of Jesus' sacrifice. We must do away with pining for the glories of the past covenant, for all of its magnificence is but a shadow. Having been sanctified (set-apart) to a Holy God who has forgotten all our sins, there is nothing to do but rest and draw near to Him in confidence and joy.

Q's & Cues

1 The author concludes that we, individually and corporately, are perfect through the transcendent sacrifice of Christ. In what ways do we fail to be who we really are?

2 Christ's attitude wasn't focused on sacrifices and gifts (10:5), but obedience (10:7). What is God calling for us to do as a community? What have we tried to get away with?

3 What do you think is meant by "I will put my law on their hearts, and write them on their minds"?

4 The Holy Spirit has a major role in the New Covenant. As a community, how can we acknowledge His role and presence more?

5 Read 10:16-18. What are some ways we still try to present offerings for our sins?

Prayer Primer

Father
Thank You that Jesus death was sufficient to crush all of my sin. Thank You that I do not have to live in fear that I am still condemned. I do not have to question whether my sin is too great to forgive. Jesus death was not inadequate. Never again will my sin bring down Your wrath. It all fell on Christ, once and for all. I have no need to fear, Jesus completely accomplished what He set out to do.
In His name
Amen

Bread of the Presence
Also known as the showbread, the bread of the presence was twelve cakes on a special table in the Holy of Holies within the Temple that was replaced weekly and eaten by the priests.

Penal Substitutionary Atonement
Jesus willingly taking His Father's punishment on the cross in the place of sinners, reconciling them to God while simultaneously satisfying God's justice.

Ark of the Covenant
A golden box containing the stone tablets upon which the Ten Commandments were written, the Ark of the Covenant was placed in the Holy of Holies within the temple until the first destruction of the Jewish Temple in 586 B.C.

PART 20 | 10:19-31
The Invincible Confidence of Intimacy

> Our author has finished the central thrust of the message: Jesus Christ is our Great High Priest, and the New Covenant in His blood is better in every way than the old. We now enter the "therefore" portion of the letter (10:19-39; 12:1-29), where readers are encouraged to press on in hope in light of these glorious truths. We begin with both assurance and a solemn warning: hope in His grace means a greater intimacy with God than in the Old Covenant, presumption toward his grace means a greater judgment from God than in the Old Covenant. Therefore "let us consider how to stir up one another to love and good works." (v.25)

Q's & Cues

1 Why is it important for the Church to meet regularly? What does this look like?

2 How can individualism and independence get in the way of the purpose of the Church?

3 What does it meant to sin deliberately? What does this mean for believers who struggle with habitual sin?

4 The author states how much worse punishment will be deserved by the one who "was sanctified." Is it possible for a believer to suffer punishment after death? What else could the author be referring to?

5 Why is it a fearful thing to fall into the hands of a living God?

Prayer Primer

Father
Make more aware of my need for community. You did not create me to walk through life alone. Your mission does not move forward on the shoulders of one man, but You have chosen to gather together a body of people to carry Your mission forward. Let me spend my time with followers of Jesus. Let me be built up, and encouraged, and rebuked by those who love You, so that I may do the same for others. Let Your Gospel spread through my life, through the lives of those in my community, and through the world.
In Jesus name
Amen

> "Through God the Son's ultimate vulnerability we have received the ultimate security of becoming the children of God. Exposed, pinned to the tree of our curse, God the Father embraced us through the open arms of Christ."
> *-Heath Hardesty*

Adversary
One who opposes or hinders another. A title often given to Satan in the Bible.

PART 21 | 10:32-39
Endurance & Affliction

> Many years of Christian experience are not always a guarantee of greater passion and maturity. For the original Hebrews audience, the exact opposite was true: the early flames of new birth and endurance in the face of persecution are now smoldering embers in their heart's icy furnace. Laziness has birthed immaturity (5:11-14). Following a terrifying warning in v.31, our author will graciously extol the faith of their early ears, insisting that they are not headed for destruction because they now belong to the "Righteous One" who did not "shrink back" before a greater affliction and is therefore now "partners" with them in their suffering and in ours.

Q's & Cues

1 In what ways do we shrink back like those mentioned in v38 and 39?

2 Is it possible to be bold in our faith while also being winsome?

3 In the context of these passages, what is the most important, how you start or how you finish?

4 As a community, what does it mean to finish well?

5 What is our responsibility in seeing that our brothers and sisters finish well?

Prayer Primer

Father
Give me endurance. Let me finish this race. Keep my eyes set on the perfect face of Jesus. Equip and empower me to battle sin. Give me a strong voice to proclaim Your Gospel. Pour me out. I want to enter Your Kingdom weary. Not tired of giving into sin, I want to be tired from killing it. I want to come home, to rest with You, knowing that I have been freed forever from the penalty, power, and presence of sin.
In Jesus name
Amen

Reproach
To suffer ridicule, rebuke, or shame.

VOLUME
FOUR
"The Hero of Faith"

The author of Hebrews has labored throughout almost seven full chapters (3:1-10:18) to establish that Jesus Christ is truer and greater than every element of the Old Covenant under Moses. Though the Holy Temple, the prophets, priests and kings, the sacrifices, practices and events of the people of Israel existed in flesh and blood history, in the story of redemption they were merely shadows waiting to find their substance in Christ. They were all pointing to something, or Someone, truer and greater than themselves. Our book has now reached its thundering climax with impassioned pleas for perseverance in faith of the promised salvation in Jesus Christ (10:19-39; 12:1-29). Sandwiched in this section, however, is one of the most famous chapters in the Bible, Hebrews 11. Already having given the negative example of the wilderness generation (3:7-19), the author now extols the mighty faith of various renowned yet imperfect Israelites in the perfect promises of God. These examples of confident assurance in an unseen inheritance that inspired endurance in the face of unimaginable opposition and suffering now serves to ignite Christian faith and further point us to Jesus in whom all of these profound figures find their fruition.

"The Hero of Faith"

11:1-40 – By Faith Alone (The Ancients)
  11:1-7 – Act One: Faith in The Unseen
    11:1-4 – What is Faith? *(The Deep Reality of Faith)*
    11:4 – *(The Truer & Greater Abel)*
    11:5-6 – *(The Truer & Greater Enoch)*
    11:7 – *(The Truer & Greater Noah)*
  11:8-22 – Act Two: Faith in an Unseen Inheritance (The Patriarchs)
    11:8-12 – *(The Truer & Greater Abraham & Sarah)*
    11:13-16 – The Unseen Inheritance: A Heavenly City *(The Truer & Greater Exile)*
    11:17-20 – *(The Truer & Greater Abraham & Isaac)*
    11:21 – *(The Truer & Greater Jacob)*
    11:22 – *(The Truer & Greater Joseph)*
  11:23 – Act Three: Faith Under Fire (The Exodus Generation)
    11:23-28 – *(The Truer & Greater Moses)*
    11:29-30 – Impossible Odds *(The Sea & The Stone)*
    11:31 – *(The Truer & Greater Rahab)*
  11:32-40 – Act Four: Conclusion (The Rest of Them)
    11:32-34 – Too Many to Mention *(The Truer & Greater Judge & King)*
    11:33-40 – Something Better *(The World Was Not Worthy)*

PART 22 | 11:1-3
The Deep Reality of Faith

In the midst of agonizing pleas to press on in faith towards the promises of God in Christ, the author of Hebrews pens this legendary chapter to illustrate the faith of God's people in redemptive-history. In the opening act (v. 1-7), the author unpacks the nature of biblical faith. If God's Word has created the material universe from nothing and appeared in human flesh in His ultimate self-revelation, Jesus Christ, faith then is confident trust in God's words about the future with a bold assurance that always bleeds into action.

Q's & Cues

1 How is biblical faith different from "blind faith"?

2 How would you explain faith to someone whom the Christian faith is foreign?

3 How is our faith influenced by the future?

4 What role does knowledge play in faith?

5 What are some of the more difficult aspects of faith with which we struggle?

Prayer Primer

Father
Increase my faith. When I act in my own insufficient strength and fall into sin, it's because I have doubted if You are really strong enough. When I search for my value apart from you, it's because I doubt whether I can really trust what You say. When I dig through garbage to find meaning, or satisfaction, or purpose, it's because I doubt that You can actually give me those things. So increase my faith. I don't need a check list of things to do. I need a heart that fully trusts You.
In Jesus name
Amen

Conviction (11:1)
Aided by the work of the Holy Spirit, the process of being condemned by one's own conscience as a sinner because of failure to meet God's righteous standards.

"Faith has this quality—that it can lift us into fellowship with the Unseen, that it can carry us within the veil...Faith thus has a power of realization, by which the invisible becomes visible and the future becomes present. While hope is the confidant anticipation of a future regarded as future, faith appropriates that future as an experience of the present."
-A.S. Peake

Intercession
The act of petitioning God or praying on behalf of another person or group.

PART 23 | 11:4
The Truer & Great Abel

> The first example of faith comes from one of the first figures of the Bible, indeed the first to taste death. Abel's life reveals that salvation has *always* come by faith and not by works, as demonstrated by his sacrifice of an animal (pointing forward to Jesus Christ). Abel's death reveals that a life of faith, even one cut tragically short, can speak beyond the grave. And as we will see in our final volume, the spilled blood of Abel that cries out for revenge points us to the spilled blood of Jesus, the greater Abel, that declares our forgiveness.

Q's & Cues

1 Why was Abel's sacrifice accepted and Cain's wasn't?

2 What did Abel and his sacrifice have in common with Jesus?

3 What role does faith play in our gifts and offerings to God?

4 What are some reasons God might reject our gifts and sacrifices?

5 Where did Abel get the idea for his sacrifice?

Prayer Primer

Father
Jesus was the perfect one who came to dwell among thieves, murders, and liars. He was the faithful, loving brother who was betrayed and crucified by those whom He loved. My wicked heart cried out for Jesus' blood to be spilled. But rather than crying out for justice, His blood cried out for mercy. He cried out for my forgiveness. Thank You.
In His name
Amen

> "After the fall, God must be worshipped by sacrifices, a way of worship which carries in it a confession of sin, and of the desert of sin, and a profession of faith in a Redeemer, who was to be a ransom for the souls of men."
> - *Matthew Henry*

PART 24 | 11:5-6
The Truer & Greater Enoch

> Little is known about the ancient figure of Enoch, the great-grandfather of Noah, the one whose life caused a remarkable rift in the formulaic genealogy of Seth in Genesis 5. Enoch "walked with God" and was taken, never to see death. His miraculous and faithful life points us to a greater, sinless, eternal Enoch, the only one who truly deserved to escape death, who died willingly and yet "was not found" in his tomb, so that one day death might lose its sting for those who trust in Him.

Q's & Cues

1 Is it possible to please God without walking with Him? In what ways do we act this out?

2 How does God reward those who walk with Him?

3 As a community, how are we called to walk with God together?

4 Is it possible to believe God exists, but not walk with Him? How is this rebellion different from not believing in Him?

5 What is the significance of Enoch not "tasting" death?

Prayer Primer

Father
How impossible it is to fathom that You would reward me? After all my betrayal, after my rejection and rebellion, after Your son was crucified for my sins, How could you have any good thing to give me? You are so generous and gracious. You empower me to walk in obedience and draw near to You, and then You reward me for doing so. How good could You be?
In Jesus name
Amen

Exegesis
Critical interpretation of a text using the text itself to discover meaning.
(Greek: To lead out.)

Hermeneutics
The art of interpreting a text, especially the Bible.

Eisegesis
Projecting one's own ideas into a text.
(Greek: To lead into.)

PART 25 | 11:7
The Truer & Greater Noah

> The ancient tale of Noah and his ark is one of the most beloved and well-known stories of all time. It is also a dark and terrifying story of the awesome wrath of God. Noah's faith in God's Word that led him to obey his God in spite of ridicule and scorn is an example to Christians surrounded by a hostile world. More than that, readers of Hebrews hope in a greater Noah who has safely brought his household, the church, through a greater judgment.

Q's & Cues

1 Read the story of Noah found in Genesis 6 - 9.

2 What were some of the "events yet unseen"?

3 Describe the moral conditions of the world at the time of the flood?

4 If God is the one who caused the flood, why would this verse state that Noah condemned the world?

5 Hebrews 11:7 tells us that Noah was an heir of righteousness and Genesis 6:9 even states that he was blameless. If Noah life was thousands of years before Christ's atonement, how could he be blameless or an heir of righteousness?

Prayer Primer

Father
I am living in a land of death. There is wickedness all around me. It would consume and crush my own heart, were it not for Jesus. He is my shelter. He has allowed me to withdraw into Him so that I would not be destroyed. He took the beating for me, He endured the storm, so that after it was finished, I could step onto solid ground. There will be storms and trials in this life, but what peace comes from being able to retreat into the arms of my Savior, and to be reminded that one day He will remove the sin from this world and reign forever in glory.
In Jesus name
Amen

Righteousness
Holy perfection that adheres to God's objective moral standard.

> "The food we eat, the air we breathe, the streets we walk, the cars we drive, the books we read, the buildings we erect, the universities we establish—all these good things in life have been possible because God constantly upholds a safe place for humanity to multiply and have dominion. As we reflect on God's blessing in the days of Noah, we should be utterly amazed at its tremendous value."
> - *Mark Driscoll*

PART 26 | 11:8-12
The Truer & Greater Abraham & Sarah

In this beloved chapter's Second Act (v. 8-22), the author focuses in on the Patriarchs faith in a promised inheritance. We fittingly begin with the ultimate patriarch, Abraham, who left his home in faith of that inheritance and who, being so old he was "as good as dead," still trusted along his wife, Sarah, and therefore received "innumerable" descendents (v.12). Their faith was revealed to be in a greater Patriarch, Jesus Christ, who would leave a greater home, even heaven, who through his death would secure the promised inheritance for Abraham's spiritual descendents.

Q's & Cues

1 What was the inheritance Abraham was to receive? Read Genesis 12:1-4.

2 Who were Isaac and Jacob? How is it that they were also heirs of the promise God made to Abraham?

3 The author of Hebrews tells us that Abraham was looking forward to a city built by God. Based on God's promise to Abraham in Genesis 12:1-4 and Genesis 17:7-8, does this seem to be the case? How so?

4 v11 states that it was by Sarah's faith that she conceived, yet looking again at Genesis 12:1-4, God has already promised Abraham he would be the father of many nations. Was it by Sarah's faith or God's already established promise? Explain.

5 In v12 what does the author mean by, "and him as good as dead"?

Prayer Primer

Father
Does Your love know no bounds? Is there any heart that You can't change? Is there sin to great for You to forgive? You love so relentlessly, so absurdly different from the love I've known in this world. You reach out to the weak, to the broken, to those who are actively rebelling against You. You save them, and You love them, and You call them to do great things. You are insanely magnificent and unfathomably gracious.
In Jesus name
Amen

Day of Atonement
Known as Yom Kippur in Hebrew, this is the most sacred day of the Jewish calendar. This was the day when the Jewish High Priest would make a sacrifice to Yahweh on behalf of the nation of Israel.

PART 27 | 11:13-16
The Truer & Greater Exile

Christians are by nature exiles. We are in the world but not of the world because our citizenship is in heaven. The author of Hebrews breaks suddenly and significantly in the discussion of the faith of the patriarchs to give perspective to the whole chapter. Like us, Abraham and his descendents died in faith as exiles, never having seen the fulfillment of God's promises. For that reason, God is not ashamed to be called their God and prepare for them a heavenly city, just as Jesus, the Greater Exile who left the heavenly city in faith, is not ashamed to call us his brothers (Hebrews 2:11).

Q's & Cues

1 Do you think it was difficult for Abraham and Sarah to die knowing they wouldn't see the fulfillment of God's promise?

2 If the author is referring to people who were born and lived on earth, how is it that they were strangers and exiles?

3 What are some ways we long for Heaven?

4 As a community, is God ever ashamed to be called our God? Is this surprising to you? Why or why not?

5 How is Jesus the ultimate fulfillment of this promise?

Prayer Primer

Father
These great heroes of the faith, these saints of old, greeted the promise You made to them from afar. How blessed we are to have seen that promise fulfilled? Christ has done it all, it is finished. How blessed are we to have Your Spirit dwelling within us? How much closer could You be? Thank You for the great lengths to which Christ went to unite us to Himself and fill us with the Holy Spirit.
In Jesus name
Amen

Homiletics
The art of preaching a sermon.

> "O what a fair one, what an only one, what an excellent, lovely, ravishing one is Jesus!"
> – Samuel Rutherford

> "Because of their confessional stance of faith in the promise of God, and their wholehearted orientation towards this worthy goal, their heavenly homeland, God is not ashamed to be called the God of Abraham, Isaac and Jacob...just as Christ was willing to be identified with his brothers and sisters."
> - *Peter T. O'Brien*

PART 28 | 11:17-20
The Truer & Greater Abraham & Isaac

> The ultimate patriarch of God's people, Abraham, had already given up his past by leaving his home in faith of God's promise (v.8). Now he is asked to give up his future, to sacrifice his son, the child of promise. He obeyed in faith, and God intervened and provided a substitute, "figuratively" raising Isaac from the dead (v.19). Having received that blessing, Isaac faithfully blessed his sons. These faithful patriarchs reveal to us One greater, who gave up his future at 33 years-old for a greater hope, who like Isaac carried his own wood to His own sacrifice, who was raised literally from the dead to bless us, making us sons of His Father who will one day rise as well.

Q's & Cues

1 Read Genesis 22:1-19. What stands out to you?

2 How does Abraham's call to sacrifice Isaac point to Jesus?

3 What is meant by Abraham's faith being tested? What is the purpose of testing our faith?

4 Why do you think God used Isaac to test Abraham?

5 How was Isaac's faith seen in his blessing?

Prayer Primer

Father
Let there be nothing in my life that I withhold from You. You have given me every good thing that I have, You have every right to do with it what You will. Should Your gifts ever become to me greater than the Giver, rip them from me. Should I ever boast in the strength I have been given rather than the Giver of strength, strip me of it. Make me weak and empty, that I would need to rest in Your arms and seek You for fulfillment. Never let me keep anything from You.
In Jesus name
Amen

Shekinah
Literally meaning dwelling, the Hebrew word describes the divine presence or manifestation of God, especially in the temple in Jerusalem.

> "Jesus loves us with a Never Stopping, Never Giving Up, Unbreaking, Always and Forever Love."
> – *Sally Lloyd Jones*

PART 29 | 11:21
The Truer & Greater Jacob

> The Second Act of Hebrews 11 concerns the faith of the Patriarchs in an unseen inheritance that they would never see fully realized in their lifetime. Last week, Isaac's faith was demonstrated in his blessing of his two sons, Jacob and Esau. Now, his son Jacob blesses his grandsons in faith that God will fulfill his promises through them. Jacob, blessing his sons as he dies, points to a greater Jacob who blessed his enemies as he died and through his death brought the blessings of salvation and sonship to all who would trust in Him.

Q's & Cues

1 Read the story of Jacob's death found in Genesis 47:29 - 48:22.

2 With all of Jacob's life to look at, which involved wrestling with and being blessed by an angel, why do you suppose it is in this situation near his death that the author of Hebrews highlights Jacob's faith?

3 Along with the story of the angel mentioned above, what are some other events in the life of Jacob?

4 Look through some commentaries. Is there any significance to Jacob's "bowing in worship over the head of his staff"?

5 With the blessing mentioned in v21 and of Jacob's life to consider, how is Jesus the truer and greater Jacob?

Prayer Primer

Father
Jesus is so gracious. He is the truer and greater Jacob. Rather than letting us starve, He generously satisfies our every need. He so abundantly fills us up. And He doesn't do it to get something from us. Rather, on top of satisfying our hunger, He gives us His birthright, that we might receive the blessings as children of God. Thank You for the unbelievable grace and generosity of Jesus.
In His name
Amen

Temple
Constructed by King Solomon, the Jewish center of worship where sacrifices to Yahweh were made. It was destroyed by the Babylonians in 587 B.C, rebuilt, and destroyed by the Romans in 70 A.D.

> "Jesus is the true and better Jacob, who wrestled and took the blow we deserved so we like Jacob only receive the wounds of grace that wake us up and discipline us."
> – *Tim Keller*

PART 30 | 11:22
The Truer & Greater Joseph

> Joseph, the last of the Patriarchs, had spent almost his whole life in Egypt, but it wasn't his home. Neither did he pine for the days of his youth, where he enjoyed the favor of his father but ended up being sold into slavery by his jealous brothers. Nearing death, Joseph in faith asked for his bones to be buried in his true homeland, Israel, when God would free his people in the Exodus. His faith points us to a greater Joseph, Jesus, who would be buried in Israel but rise again to lead His people in a greater Exodus.

Q's & Cues

1 Read the story of Joseph's death found in Genesis 50:24-25.

2 Joseph could interpret dreams, was sold into slavery, and became second in command to the pharaoh of Egypt. With all of these amazing things to consider, why do you suppose the author uses his burial instructions as a great demonstration of his faith?

3 God has moved Joseph into a position of high authority in Egypt. He has wealth, status, and power the likes of which we can hardly fathom and his family has been welcomed in to share in it. Why then did Joseph tell them they will one day leave Egypt and go to the land God promised? Why would they want to leave?

4 Why do you suppose Joseph gave specific instructions regarding his bones?

5 With the crazy and amazing life of Joseph to consider, how is Jesus the truer and greater Joseph?

Prayer Primer

Father
When I find it difficult to trust You, let me search Your Scriptures. When I am uncertain and filled with doubt, let me turn to Your Word. Time and time again You have proved Yourself faithful. So full are the pages of Scripture with accounts of You fulfilling Your promises. I can see that You were faithful before and trust that You will continue to be faithful. You do not change. If You loved, and cared for, and kept Your promises to Your people in the past, I can trust that You will do the same for me.
In Jesus name
Amen

Supersessionism
The belief that the Church has superseded Israel as God's people and the promises of the New Covenant have superseded the promises of past biblical covenants such as the Abrahamic, Mosaic and Davidic.

Theology
The rational study of the nature of God.

PART 31 | 11:23-28
The Truer & Greater Moses

This chapter now enters its Third Act, the faith of the Exodus generation (v. 23-31). Having established that faith is the confident assurance of an unseen (v.1-7) inheritance (v. 8-22) from God, we will now explore how faith sustains God's people through suffering and opposition from unbelievers. The author begins, of course, with the towering figure of Moses, who in his suffering for Israel foreshadowed the greater Moses and the greater Israel, the Suffering Servant, Jesus Christ.

Q's & Cues

1. What was the king's edict? Read Exodus 2:22.

2. This passage highlights the faith of Moses, yet v23 speaks of the faith of his parents. Why would their faith be included in passage dealing with his faith?

3. In v26 of Hebrews, the author states that Moses "considered the reproach of Christ greater wealth than the treasures of Egypt." If Moses was alive well before the time of Christ, what is happening in this verse?

4. Who was the "Destroyer of the firstborn?" Read Exodus 12:7-13. What thoughts or feelings are evoked as you read this?

5. How was Moses a foreshadowing of Jesus? How is Jesus truer and greater?

Prayer Primer

Father
You have freed me up from chasing the fleeting pleasures of sin. How many false promises have I been made. How infatuated was I with my sin. I followed it foolishly, intrigued by the grand promises it made to satisfy me. But every time, every time, it led me to death, misery, and self-hate. I have been freed from my slavery to that pathetic sin. I was now as a slave to Christ. I can endure mistreatment and suffering, for they lead me to be more like my blessed Savior. I know the glorious reward that awaits me, not fleeting, not temporary, but to see the eternal face of Jesus Christ.
In His name
Amen

Chiasmus
An ancient rhetorical device in which the structure of a passage is determined by mirrored opposite clauses. (If each letter represented a unit of thought: ABCBA)

"All that Moses suffered was in the cause of God's plan of salvation for his people, culminating in the abuse which was heaped on *the Christ* himself, of which the writer is acutely conscious throughout his epistle."
- *Donald Guthrie*

PART 32 | 11:29-30
The Sea & The Stone

For the last nine weeks we have learned from the exemplary faith of redeemed individuals in the Old Testament. All of these real, flesh and blood persons were "types" that foreshadowed Christ. Now the author discusses the faith of the whole covenant community of Israel that enabled them to pass safely through the Red Sea of judgment and enter the Promised Land through absurd methods and against impossible odds. All of these events looked forward to a greater Israel, Jesus, who through the absurd method of His death would save His people from a greater judgment and to a greater inheritance, the New Heavens and New Earth.

Q's & Cues

1 Read Exodus 14:21-30 and all of Joshua 6.

2 Of all the details the author of Hebrews could have given, why do you suppose he includes the seven days in the Jericho account?

3 The Egyptians and the Hebrews were both in very similar circumstances, however their outcomes were very different. What made the difference?

4 Faith is always accompanied by action. What action of faith might God be calling you to? Share with your comGroup.

5 How is Jesus the truer and greater Israelite?

Prayer Primer

Father
The same path that led to Israel's salvation led to Egypt's destruction. The waves that split and halted for the Israelites plummeted down and crushed the Egyptians. Everything is in Your control. You do whatever You please. From Your Word I can see that You truly do work for the good of those that love You. Whether seas part for me or waves crash down on me, I can endure with confidence knowing that You always work for Your glory and the joy of Your people.
In Jesus name
Amen

> "In verse 29 you have the difference between faith and presumption: faith goes through the sea, presumption is drowned in the sea."
> - *Charles Spurgeon*

Type/Antitype
A "type" (Greek term signifying a mark formed by the impression of something else) is a specific event, person or place found in the Old Testament that prefigures a greater "antitype" that supersedes it in the New Testament.

PART 33 | 11:31
The Truer & Greater Rahab

> Hebrews 11's impressive list climaxes with an utterly scandalous example of faith: a female, *Gentile cult-prostitute.* This unlikely outcast's faith was used by God to provide victory to Israel at Jericho, the seal upon Israel's imminent conquest of the Promised Land. With courage in the face of grave peril, Rahab's faith was shown to be in an unlikely redeemer, an outcast Messiah from Nazareth, who would give His righteousness and His inheritance to the immoral and impoverished. For this reason, Rahab was chosen to be a direct ascendant of the Messiah of the pariah (Matthew 1:5).

Q's & Cues

1 Why was Rahab's friendly welcome considered an act of faith?

2 With your comGroup look up Rahab's genealogy found in Matthew chapter one. Who was Rahab's great grandson? Why is this significant?

3 Rahab's past was no barrier to God's grace. Have you ever met someone or struggled with your own past sin being too much for God's grace?

4 The Rahab account is a clear demonstration of the axiom, "where there is no risk, there is no faith." Do you agree with this? What risk might God be calling you to for his glory?

5 It may seem like an odd comparison, how is Jesus the truer and greater Rahab?

Prayer Primer

Father
Thank You for Your desire to save. I could not earn my salvation, I could not convince You to offer it to me. It flows from You, out of Your overwhelming love and grace. And You reach out to the most broken and vile sinners to bless them with unimaginable love. You are good to Your people. You were good to us while we were Your enemies and You continue to be good to us after You have changed our hearts. Thank You for Your great salvation.
In Jesus name
Amen

Pragmatism
Evaluating truth or validity based on practical application. A methodology that is concerned with "whatever works" in order to get the job done regardless of external pressures or allegiances.

Rhetoric
The art of effective speaking and writing through the use of persuasive techniques.

PART 34 | 11:32-34
The Truer & Greater Judge & King

Our author has run out of breath. After beginning with the exemplary faith of Abel and ending with Rahab and the conquest of Jericho, the author concludes with the Fourth Act of the chapter, an epic sweep of the rest of the history of the Old Testament. Weak, foolish and sinful men by simple faith became conquering judges, wise kings and thundering prophets. Yet their exaltation was not to glorify themselves. It was to foreshadow the coming of a homeless peasant, the Final Prophet, who through His faithful death would become the Judge of all men and the King of Kings.

Q's & Cues

1 What do you know of the men listed in v32?

2 In this passage faith seems to be linked to victory. Tell of a time in your life where you stepped out in faith and a victory followed?

3 Tell of a time in your life when you stepped out in faith and a victory did not follow. What might God have been teaching you?

4 When you read of the great accomplishments of these men that are attributed to their faith, what is brought to mind regarding your own faith?

5 How is Jesus truer and greater than these kings and judges of old?

Prayer Primer

Father
Your will is to build up and not to harm. Make me more like Jesus and help me to accept whatever way You choose to do that.
In Jesus name
Amen

Inclusio
An ancient literary device where information is given and repeated at the beginning and end of a passage for emphasis. (If each letter represented a unit of thought: <u>A</u>BCD<u>A</u>)

Typology
A theological term for the study of events, persons, or places in the Old Testament that foreshadow greater realities in the New Testament.

PART 35 | 11:35-40
The World Was Not Worthy

So often we Christians shame ourselves for not being more like the mighty figures of faith celebrated in this famous chapter. Yet we do not often sit in joyous wonder of the fact that by faith we have received "something better" than they did: fellowship with Jesus Christ, the Son of God and Great High Priest who was "destitute, afflicted, mistreated" yet has given us "all the riches of full assurance and understanding." (Col. 2:2) Rejoice, for we are unworthy but He is more than worthy.

Q's & Cues

1 What Old Testament stories can you recall where women had received back their dead by resurrection?

2 These are Old Testament individuals prior to Christ's being on the earth. If he had not yet atoned for sin on the cross, what is the "better life" that is referenced in v35?

3 In reference to these faithful man and woman, "of whom the world was not worthy." What does this tell us about God's regard for the righteous?

4 Look at v39. If it was "promised," how is it that these faithful saints did not receive it?

5 Who is the "us" in v40 referring to?

Prayer Primer

Father
Your will is to build up and not to harm. Make me more like Jesus and help me to accept whatever way You choose to do that.
In Jesus name
Amen

Believer's Assurance
The idea that once an individual receives salvation, he or she can never lose it.

VOLUME FIVE

"Walking to Our Now & Future Home"

The letter has reached its resounding crescendo, a "word of exhortation" (13:22) aimed at helping members of the New Covenant community in Christ persevere to the end and obtain their inheritance. Hebrews was a letter written to be read as a sermon, and by now the regenerate listeners' heart would be burning for the grace of Jesus Christ, while condemned listeners' blood would be boiling at the offense of Jesus Christ. Jesus has been revealed as the truer, greater, stronger and better Covenant Mediator, Prophet, Judge, Priest, King, Tabernacle, Rest and Son than any person or institution under the Old Covenant that these Hebrews had known. A grander salvation and a more terrible judgment have come on Calvary and are still to come in eternity; therefore, we have been exhorted: hold fast to one another and pursue good works (10:24-25), resist sin (3:13) and most of all, hold fast to our hope, Jesus Christ (6:18). With the foundation laid of Christ's sufficiency, our author will close continuing this earnest exhortation: accept discipline as a child of the King (12:5), crush idols (13:1-6), share, suffer, submit (13:13-17) with eyes fixed on Jesus (12:2) as saints of the most high who are receiving their inheritance, a Kingdom which cannot be shaken (12:28; Daniel 7:18).

"Walking to Our Now & Future Home"

12:1-29 – Enduring in the "Already but Not Yet" Kingdom of God
- 12:1-11 – The Enduring Son *(Endurance & Discipline)*
- 12:12-17 – Crucial Christ-like Character *(The Anti-Esau)*
- 12:19-29 – Kingdom Come *(That Which Cannot Be Shaken)*

13:1-25 – Now What?
- 13:1-6 – Offer Acceptable Worship *(The Idol Factory)*
- 13:7-19 – A Final Call to Remembrance *(Submission & Leaders)*
- 13:20-25 – A Blessing, An Appeal & Greetings *(The Good Word)*

PART 36 | 12:1-11
Endurance & Discipline

> Hebrews 12 is a call for the endurance of those who live in the "already but not yet" age of the Kingdom of God. After commending past examples of faith (Ch.11) that pointed us to Jesus Christ, the author fixes our eyes on the exemplary endurance of our Savior (v.1-3). We then have our religious paradigms flipped upside down as we are led to the uncomfortable subject of discipline. Discipline is not karmic justice, but a marker that one is a child of the king, with the inheritance of the firstborn: eternal joy. We are freed to do more than endure in the face of suffering, we can be thankful for it.

Q's & Cues

1 What was the "joy" set before him for which Christ willing to endure the cross?

2 Is growing weary or fainthearted different from the emotional highs and lows we experience in everyday life?

3 What does holiness mean? What does it mean that we may share in God's holiness?

4 What are some ways, individually and corporately, that God disciplines us?

5 What does the author mean in v8 that if they are without discipline they are not sons?

Prayer Primer

Father
Give me endurance to run this race. Sins from my past seem to strangle me and my own imperfection and nature serve to remind me that there will be new sins in my future, When I am caught up in the guilt of past sins, let me look to Jesus who died to break the grip that sin has on me. When I am intimidated by the sins I have not yet committed, let me look to Jesus who endured the cross when all of my sins were future sins. He has freed me up from every snare and entanglement that, by grace, I may push myself to reach the end.
In Jesus name
Amen

Reprove
To give criticism for a fault.

PART 37 | 12:12-17
The Anti-Esau

> The author of Hebrews has exalted Jesus' endurance and called us to thank our Father for His gracious discipline that makes us more like Christ (12:1-11). Now, Old Testament imagery is used to spur us on to endurance. Our Christ-like character is crucial, for the author insists that without it the world will remain blind to the Lord and His grace. We "firstborn" (12:23) who will inherit by faith the ultimate blessing earned by the Firstborn (Col 1:15), Jesus, must not be like the firstborn Esau who in his exhaustion showed contempt for God's blessing by his immorality.

Q's & Cues

1 As a community, how are we to strive for peace with everyone? Is peace always a possible solution?

2 How can someone fail to obtain the grace of God? As a community, what is our responsibility in seeing that everyone obtains God's grace?

3 Why do you think warnings against sexual immorality is mentioned so frequently in Scripture?

4 How is the person who "sells" themselves into sexual immorality similar to Esau (Gen. 25:29-34)?

5 How is Jesus the anti-Esau?

Prayer Primer

Father
Never let me believe that You are finished with me. I have not yet reached the end of the race. There is still work to be done. I am still weak. Should I ignore my weaknesses and continue to run in ignorance I will inevitably break. Let me bring my weaknesses before You that they might be healed.
In Jesus name
Amen

VOLUME FIVE

Asceticism
Willful self-denial of wordly pleasures in the pursuit of a spiritual goal.

PART 38 | 12:18-29
That Which Cannot Be Shaken

Our letter reaches its rhetorical zenith, painting in stunning contrast the Old Covenant community under Moses encountering God on Mt. Sinai and the New Covenant community under Jesus encountering God on Mt. Zion. V. 18-24 focus on the blessings of the New Covenant, marked by confident, reverential joy as opposed to the utter terror of the Old. All of 10:26-12:29 aims to encourage New Covenant members to press on in faith. However, the tone abruptly changes to an ominous, almost frenzied warning (v.25-29) against ignoring this final revelation. The kindness of God (grace) is to lead us to repentance, not presumption. (Romans 2:4)

Q's & Cues

1 Read Deuteronomy 4:24. How is God's jealousy and being a consuming fire a good thing for the church?

2 What is worship? What qualifies worship to be acceptable to God?

3 As a community, what does acceptable worship look like?

4 How can the warnings in Hebrews 12:18-29 keep us from apostasy and help us to persevere?

5 What are some things on this side of heaven that are eternal and "can't be shaken"?

Prayer Primer

Father
What joy and peace comes from knowing that You are bringing me into a perfect kingdom. There will be no need for it to change, no need for reformation, or redemption. You are establishing a kingdom that cannot be shaken. Never again will sin corrupt Your creation, never again will You people weep, never again will there be a rebellion. Forever we will perfectly dwell with You and You with us.
In Jesus name
Amen

> "Our worship is not less supernatural than the experience of Israel in the wilderness. It is infinitely more so. We have emerged from the shadows into the reality."
> *- Edmund P. Clowney*

Mount Zion
Literally meaning fortification, Mt. Zion was eventually used as a name for the city of Jerusalem, the land of Judah, and the people of Israel as a whole. In the New Testament, the word is used to denote God's Heavenly City, or the New Jerusalem.

PART 39 | 13:1-6
The Idol Factory

Chapter 12 ends with a summoning to "offer to God acceptable worship" (v.28). The author will now explain what that means in the form of urgent exhortation to love, to exercise hospitality, to show compassion, to honor marriage, and to love Christ over money. In doing so our heart's idols of self, comfort, autonomy, pleasure, power and security are smashed, for Jesus has first loved us, welcomed us into His heavenly home, suffered with us, made us His bride and given us spiritual power and eternal security. Indeed, what can man do to us that it did not do to Him?

Q's & Cues

1 Within our community, what does "brotherly love" look like?

2 How is hospitality a vital part of the Christian faith?

3 How are we to honor marriage in our current culture?

4 What action is the author calling the church to when he commands them to "remember" their brothers and sisters in prison? How might this translate into our culture and community today?

5 How is God's promise to never forsake us a defense against the "love of money"?

Prayer Primer

Father
My heart is a factory of idolatry and self-glory. I am in desperate need of help that comes from outside me. When one idol is put to death I create a new one its place. But You do not grow weary. Through Your strength I can crush each idol I create. Until the day that You destroy them all and bring Your people home to worship and glorify the one true God.
In Jesus name
Amen

Idolatry
Ascribing ultimate worth in thought, word or deed to anything other than the creator God (Romans 1:25).

> "The human mind is, so to speak, a perpetual forge of idols."
> - *John Calvin*

PART 40 | 13:7-19
Submission & Leaders

> The readers are called one last time to remember. They are to remember their leaders who have died in faith like the great examples of old (Ch. 11), whose words and deeds pointed to Jesus, our ultimate Example and Sacrifice, who is "the same yesterday, today and forever" and whose grace is our strength (V.8). They are called then to suffer, share and submit to their leaders because, paradoxically, in Jesus, only those who are rejected find acceptance, only those who give have all things only those who obey have freedom.

Q's & Cues

1 As a community, how can we serve and remember our leaders?

2 In recent years, what are some "new" and "trendy" teachings that can lead us away from the truth?

3 As a community, how do we reflect God's grace when we provide for our brothers and sisters in need?

4 As a community, what are some ways we grieve our leaders?

5 How can we practically submit to our leaders?

Prayer Primer

Father
Thank You for the countless ways You have enabled me to walk in obedience. You have given me the life and direction of Your Scripture. You have given me intimate access to the Creator of the universe through prayer. You have filled me with Your Spirit that I may never be without You. You have given me godly lovers of Jesus to guide me and instruct me. May I utilize each precious gift I have been given to honor and glorify Jesus.
In His name
Amen

> "They had been accustomed to think of the 'camp' and all that was inside it as sacred, while everything outside it was profane and unclean. Were they to leave its sacred precincts and venture on to unhallowed ground? Yes, because in Jesus the old values had been reversed. What was formerly sacred was now unhallowed, because Jesus had been expelled from it; what was formerly unhallowed was now sacred, because Jesus was there."
> - *F.F. Bruce*

PART 41 | 13:20-25
The Good Word

This glorious letter concludes with a benediction (bestowing of blessing), a final appeal, and customary news and greetings. The benediction trumpets the theme of the letter, the exaltation of Jesus Christ, the truer & greater, by glorifying the God who raised Him from the dead and asking that He would equip us to do His will. Our author ends with the kind of earnest, heart-felt pleading of a preacher who longs that the word of God would be heard and obeyed.

Q's & Cues

1 How does God equip us, individually and corporately, to do His will?

2 In what ways is this benediction encouraging to the Church?

3 How does the author remind us that the Gospel is different from a "Self Help" book?

4 How is the Trinity represented in the author's concluding words?

5 As a comGroup, what are the key points of Hebrews we should walk away with?

Prayer Primer

Father
May my life be one that is pleasing to You. Equip and empower me to proclaim Your Gospel. Strengthen me to kill the sin that clings to me. Let me rest in the promise of salvation and never tire of gazing upon my gracious and merciful Savior Jesus.
In His name
Amen

Benediction
Usually following a worship service, a benediction is a liturgical invocation for blessing from God.

TRUER & GREATER

A song based on Hebrews by Jake Kazakevich & Thomas Baker

The radiance of glory
The imprint of God's nature
The universe upheld by the word of Jesus power
Twas Him made low to save me
He dwelt with sinful creatures
Now every glory and honor rests upon the Saviors brow

Christ is truer
He is greater
Than the grave could ever dream
He is risen
He is savior
All His people are redeemed
Christ is truer
He is greater
Than any prophet, priest, or king
Let His glory be proclaimed here
Let His people always sing

Of Him who bore our sorrow
Our burden as His own
To make sure every wayward child and prodigal comes home
The righteousness of Jesus
Imputed to the slave
Of sin and death, now every breath is drawn to sing His praise

Christ is truer
He is greater
Than the grave could ever dream
He is risen
He is savior
All His people are redeemed
Christ is truer
He is greater
Than any prophet, priest, or king
Let His glory be proclaimed here
Let His people always sing

We stand as new creations
We rest on Jesus word
Let every heart and mind obey the law that they have heard
And let us cling with hope
To the covenant He gives
That He shall be forever ours and we forever His

Christ is
The confession that I hold
The anchor for my soul
Once for all the cure for sin

GLOSSARY OF TERMS

Adversary (10:27)
One who opposes or hinders another. A title often given to Satan in the Bible.

Anointed (1:9)
To set apart a person for a special work or service.

Apostasy
Abandonment of Christian belief and a rejection of Christ by someone who has claimed to be a Christian.

Apostle (3:1)
A special messenger of Jesus Christ; a person to whom authority is designated for certain tasks.

Ark of the Covenant
A golden box containing the stone tablets upon which the Ten Commandments were written, the Ark of the Covenant was placed in the Holy of Holies within the temple until the first destruction of the Jewish Temple in 586 B.C.

Asceticism
Willful self-denial of wordly pleasures in the pursuit of a spiritual goal.

Atonement
At-one-ment. The reconciliation of sinners to a holy God through the death and resurrection of Jesus Christ.

Begotten (1:5)
A New Testament word that describes Christ as the only, or unique, Son of God. Distinctiveness - "one of a kind".

Believer's Assurance
The idea that once an individual receives salvation, he or she can never lose it.

Benediction
Usually following a worship service, a benediction is a liturgical invocation for blessing from God.

Bread of the Presence
Also known as the showbread, the bread of the presence was twelve cakes on a special table in the Holy of Holies within the Temple that was replaced weekly and eaten by the priests.

Cherubim (9:5)
Winged angelic beings associated with God's praise and worship.

Chiasmus
An ancient rhetorical device in which the structure of a passage is determined by mirrored opposite clauses. (If each letter represented a unit of thought: ABCBA)

Conscience (9:9)
A person's inner awareness of conforming to the will of God or departing from it, resulting in either a sense of approval or condemnation.

Conviction (11:1)
Aided by the work of the Holy Spirit, the process of being condemned by one's own conscience as a sinner because of failure to meet God's righteous standards.

Covenant (8:6)
In society, an agreement between two people or two groups that involves promises on the part of each to the other. Between God and man, an oath in blood administered sovereignly.

Day of Atonement
Known as Yom Kippur *in Hebrew, this is the most sacred day of the Jewish calendar. This was the day when the Jewish High Priest would make a sacrifice to Yahweh on behalf of the nation of Israel.*

Discernment (5:14)
Understanding that which is obscure or hidden.

Eisegesis
Projecting one's own ideas into a text. (Greek: To lead into.)

Exegesis
Critical interpretation of a text using the text itself to discover meaning. (Greek: To lead out.)

Exhortation (3:13)
A message of caution or encouragement with the purpose of motivating persons to action.

Forerunner (6:20)
One who goes before to prepare the way for others.

Glory (2:7)
A quality of God's character that emphasizes His greatness and authority. Weightiness.

Great High Priest
Continuing from the line of Aaron, Moses' brother, the High Priest functioned as the executive representative of Israel to Yahweh in the Old Testament. He alone could perform sacrifices on behalf of God's people.

Hermeneutics
The art of interpreting a text, especially the Bible.

Homiletics
The art of preaching a sermon.

Idolatry
Ascribing ultimate worth in thought, word or deed to anything other than the creator God (Romans 1:25).

Inclusio
*An ancient literary device where information is given and repeated at the beginning and end of a passage for emphasis. (If each letter represented a unit of thought: **A**BCD**A**)*

Iniquity (8:12)
Immorality, unrighteousness, lawlessness.

Intercession (7:25)
The act of petitioning God or praying on behalf of another person or group

Levite
A member of the Hebrew tribe of Levi, who after the Exodus served the priests and kept watch over the tabernacle. Levitical priests are descended directly from Aaron, the great-grandson of Levi and the brother of Moses.

Mediator
One who intervenes between two persons or groups as an arbitrator in order to help them come to an agreement.

Mercy Seat (9:5)
The golden lid on the Ark of the Covenant. Represented God's throne and had atoning blood sprinkled on it for the people on the Day of Atonement.

Most Holy Place (9:3)
Also known as the Holy of Holies, this is the most sacred part of the temple in the Old Testament where the literal presence of God lies behind the veil. Containing the Ten Commandments inside the Ark of the Covenant, only the high priest could enter here to make his annual sacrifice on the Day of Atonement

Mount Zion
Literally meaning fortification, *Mt. Zion was eventually used as a name for the city of Jerusalem, the land of Judah, and the people of Israel as a whole. In the New Testament, the word is used to denote God's Heavenly City, or the New Jerusalem.*

Nominalism
Identification with a cause in name only. In Christianity, adhering to the external forms of godliness while denying its power (2 Timothy 3:15).

Patriarch (7:4)
The founder or ruler of a tribe, family, or clan.

Penal Substitutionary Atonement
Jesus willingly taking His Father's punishment on the cross in the place of sinners, reconciling them to God while simultaneously satisfying God's justice.

Pragmatism
Evaluating truth or validity based on practical application. A methodology that is concerned with "whatever works" in order to get the job done regardless of external pressures or allegiances.

Prophet (1:1)
The instrument or mouthpiece of God. One upon whom the Spirit of God rested, who by proclamation and demonstration communicated God's Word to His people.

Propitiation (2:17)
The act of appeasing God by diverting His wrath onto a substitute. In the Old Testament this was prefigured when blood was sprinkled on the mercy seat on the Day of Atonement, transforming the throne of judgment into a throne of grace. In the New Testament, this was accomplished once for all in the sacrifice of Jesus on the cross.

Purification (1:3)
The act of making one pure and clean before God and men. To cast out whatever is impure or undesirable.

Redemption (9:12)
Deliverance through the payment of a price. Christians are delivered from slavery to Satan, sin and death through the payment of the blood of Jesus Christ.

Reformation (9:10)
To realign or renew. An improvement by change or correction.

Repentance (6:1)
Turning away from sin, disobedience, or rebellion and turning back to God. Literally to change one's mind.

Reproach (10:33)
To suffer ridicule, rebuke, or shame.

Reprove (12:5)
To give criticism for a fault.

Retribution (2:2)
The act of receiving what one deserves, usually referring to punishment for doing evil. Biblically, the judgment of a holy God upon sin.

Reverence (5:7)
Profound awe and respect.

Rhetoric
The art of effective speaking and writing through the use of persuasive techniques.

Righteousness
Holy perfection that adheres to God's objective moral standard.

Sabbath (4:9)
Originating in creation and perfected in redemption, the practice of observing one day in seven as a time of rest for the people and the land.

Sanctification (2:11)
Sanctification is both the gracious event where believers are set apart from sin and for holiness and the process by which God's love is perfected in His people, conforming them to the image of Christ.

Shekinah
Literally meaning dwelling, *the Hebrew word describes the divine presence or manifestation of God, especially in the temple in Jerusalem.*

Song of Moses
Found in Deut. 32:1-43, this poem is believed to have been written just before Moses' death and illustrates a faithful God who pursues his corrupt and fallen people.

Supersessionism
The belief that the Church has superseded Israel as God's people and the promises of the New Covenant have superseded the promises of past biblical covenants such as the Abrahamic, Mosaic and Davidic.

Supplication (5:7)
To humbly and diligently ask of God.

Tabernacle
Until the temple was built, it was the portable, specifically designed dwelling place for the divine presence of Yahweh after the Exodus.

Temple
Constructed by King Solomon, the Jewish center of worship where sacrifices to Yahweh were made. It was destroyed by the Babylonians in 587 B.C, rebuilt, and destroyed by the Romans in 70 A.D.

Temptation (4:15)
An enticement or invitation to sin that promises greater good in disobedience than obedience.

Theology
The rational study of the nature of God.

Type/Antitype
A "type" (Greek term signifying a mark formed by the impression of something else) is a specific event, person or place found in the Old Testament that prefigures a greater "antitype" that supersedes it in the New Testament.

Typology
A theological term for the study of events, persons, or places in the Old Testament that foreshadow greater realities in the New Testament.

Wrath (3:11)
The personal manifestation of God's holy, moral character in judgment against sin. For the believer, God's wrath was absorbed fully by Christ on the cross.

Handbook for the Young Athlete

Bob Gaillard, University of
  San Francisco
William Haskell, Ph.D., Stanford University
  Medical Center
Nathan Smith, M.D., School of Medicine,
  University of Washington
Bruce Ogilvie, Ph.D., California State
  University at San Jose

Bull Publishing Co.

GV
704
.H36

Library of Congress Cataloging in Publication Data

Main entry under title:

Handbook for the young athlete.

    1. Athletics--Handbooks, manuals, etc.
2. Athletes--Recruiting. I. Gaillard, Bob,
1940-
GV704.H36   796   78-16444
ISBN 0-915950-18-9 pbk.

Cover Design: Tonya Carpenter
Illustrations: Mary Burkhardt
Composition: The Bookmakers, Inc.
Printing and Binding: George Banta Company, Inc.

© Copyright 1978
Bull Publishing Co.
P.O. Box 208
Palo Alto, California 94302
(415) 322-2855

ISBN 0-915950-18-9

Library of Congress
   Catalog No. 78-16444

Manufactured in the United States of America

Handbook for the Young Athlete

Contents

INTRODUCTION   9

One

YOUR ATHLETIC POTENTIAL   11
William Haskell, Ph.D

THE NEED FOR SELF-EVALUATION   13

UNDERSTANDING YOUR ATHLETIC POTENTIAL   14
    MENTAL ATTITUDE, ATHLETIC SKILL,
    ATHLETIC FITNESS

HOW TO EVALUATE YOUR ATHLETIC FITNESS   26
    THE ATHLETIC FITNESS OF OUTSTANDING
    ATHLETES, A SIMPLE TEST OF YOUR
    ATHLETIC FITNESS

Two

TRAINING TO IMPROVE
YOUR ATHLETIC FITNESS   39
William Haskell, Ph.D.

GENERAL PRINCIPLES OF ATHLETIC TRAINING   42
    OVERLOAD, PROGRESSION, SPECIFICITY,
    INDIVIDUALITY

HOW TO IMPROVE YOUR ATHLETIC FITNESS   45
    BODY COMPOSITION, SPEED, MUSCULAR
    STRENGTH/POWER/ENDURANCE,
    CARDIORESPIRATORY ENDURANCE,
    FLEXIBILITY, SPECIALTY TRAINING

YEAR-ROUND TRAINING PATTERNS   67

ANNUAL TRAINING SCHEDULE   70
    PRE-SEASON, COMPETITIVE SEASON,
    POST-SEASON

Three

FOOD FOR SPORT   75
    Nathan J. Smith, M.D.

NUTRIENTS: THE BASIC BUILDING BLOCKS   77
    WATER, MINERALS, VITAMINS, FATS,
    CARBOHYDRATES, PROTEINS

THE BASIC DIET   89
    THE IMPORTANCE OF A WELL-BALANCED
    DIET, THE FOUR FOOD GROUP PLAN,
    THE BASIC DIET PLAN

NONTRADITIONAL DIETS AND
DIETARY SUPPLEMENTS   94
    VEGETARIAN AND OTHER MEATLESS DIETS,
    NONCONVENTIONAL DIETS THAT
    WILL NOT WORK

GAINING OR LOSING WEIGHT   103
    THE BODY'S USE OF ENERGY, ENERGY
    EXPENDITURE IN VARIOUS SPORTS,
    WEIGHT GAIN/LOSS

THE ENERGY DEMANDS OF THE ATHLETE   113
    TRAINING AND DIET, DIETARY
    CONSIDERATION FOR: ALL-OUT EFFORT
    OF SHORT DURATION, INTERMEDIATE
    LENGTH EVENTS, ENDURANCE CONTESTS

THE ATHLETE'S NEED FOR WATER AND SALT   121
    BODY WATER, THE WATER REQUIREMENTS
    OF THE ATHLETE, THE ATHLETE'S NEED FOR
    SALT, THE CRITICAL ROLE OF WATER IN THE
    PREVENTION OF HEAT DISORDERS

IRON NUTRITION   127
    IRON IN THE DIET, THE PREVENTION OF
    IRON DEFICIENCY

THE PRE-GAME MEAL AND EATING
    DURING COMPETITION 129
    THE PRE-GAME DIET, FOOD INTAKE BEFORE
    COMPETITION, FLUID INTAKE BEFORE
    COMPETITION, TRAVEL

WRESTLING AND OTHER WEIGHT
    CONTROL SPORTS 133
    THE EFFECTS OF INADEQUATE WEIGHT
    PROGRAMS, THE HIGH PERFORMANCE DIET,
    HIGH SALT-CONTAINING FOODS, THE IDEAL
    COMPETING WEIGHT, GROWTH DEMANDS OF
    THE HIGH SCHOOL WRESTLER, DIURETICS
    AND CATHARTICS

Four

TAKING CARE OF INJURIES 143
Nathan J. Smith, M.D.

LEVELS OF RISK 145
    THE MANAGEMENT OF COMMON SPORTS
    INJURIES, WHAT NOT TO DO IF INJURED,
    WHAT TO DO WHEN INJURED, WHY DOES
    ICE WORK?, THE MANAGEMENT OF AN
    INJURY—A CASE IN POINT, PREVENTING
    INJURIES, BE PREPARED FOR EMERGENCIES,
    CALL FOR HELP, SOME IMPORTANT DON'TS

Five

THE YOUNG WOMAN ATHLETE 155
Bruce Ogilvie, Ph.D.

MALE-FEMALE PHYSICAL DIFFERENCES 158
    CARDIORESPIRATORY ENDURANCE,
    STRENGTH, INJURY VULNERABILITY,
    MENSTRUAL CYCLE, SPORTS ACTIVITY

INTERNALIZED STEREOTYPES 164
    BOY-GIRL DIFFERENCES, TOM BOYS

A SELF TEST   165

HISTORICAL ORIGINS OF PREJUDICE   170
    SPORT AND DANCE, UNDERSTANDING
    YOURSELF

Six

RECRUITING AND HOW TO HANDLE IT   173
    Bob Gaillard, Coach

THE RECRUITER'S PERSPECTIVE   176
    EVALUATING PLAYERS, THE SCOUTING
    PROCESS, MASS RECRUITING, SPECIFIC
    RECRUITING, THE THREE-VISIT RULE, THE
    CAMPUS VISIT

THE ATHLETE'S PERSPECTIVE   186
    ANALYZING YOUR ABILITY, HELPFUL
    CRITICISM, ESTABLISHING PRIORITIES,
    NARROWING THE LIST OF SCHOOLS, A
    COLLEGE RATING SYSTEM, SETTING
    RECRUITING DEADLINES, THE CAMPUS
    VISIT, THE LETTER OF INTENT

Introduction

This book was written for you, the young athlete, and for your coach, parent or teacher. The authors have long experience in their fields and have worked with thousands of young athletes. In this book, they answer the questions that those athletes have asked them through the years about nutrition, injuries, athletic potential, training, women athletes and recruiting. They give the very latest information available and tell you how you can apply it to your training and your sport.

What questions do you have?—Can I go on a vegetarian diet and still have enough strength for wrestling? Is it usually better to apply heat or cold to an athletic injury? What sport is best for me? How should I change my training schedule throughout the year? Why don't women play football? How can I choose the right college during recruiting? What are the recruiters looking for?

We have provided a detailed table of contents so that you can quickly find the answers to the questions that interest you most. Or you might want to read straight through and discover facts about yourself as a young athlete that you hadn't thought about before.

one

Your Athletic Potential

William Haskell

THE NEED FOR SELF-EVALUATION

What is your potential as an athlete? How far can you expect to go in your sport? Are you good enough to make first string in college? ... to pursue a professional career in athletics?

An objective self-evaluation of your athletic abilities is extremely important in planning your athletic future. To evaluate your abilities, you need to know how you stack up against those who will be competing on the team next year, or the year after in college. How tall, heavy, strong or quick are you now in comparison to champion athletes and how much can you expect these qualities to develop in the next several years? This chapter will explore these questions.

UNDERSTANDING YOUR ATHLETIC POTENTIAL

Have you ever watched a baseball player with such a natural, easy swing that you thought he must have been born with a bat in his hands? He's the kind of athlete we often call a "natural." He seems to have inherited just the right genes to do well in his sport. He makes things look easy and has an "instinct" for the right move at the right time.

On the other hand, some athletes appear to have to work very hard at their sports. They make up in "hustle" what they may lack in natural grace, size, or power. They train long hours to develop their skills and to attain the highest possible level of physical fitness.

For most outstanding athletes, ability is a combination of "good genes" and hard work. The genetic component sets the limits of athletic potential, but it's up to the athlete to develop that potential to its fullest. How much of his potential each athlete develops depends on his willingness to train, practice and, if necessary, sacrifice other interests.

In this section, we will look at the three aspects of athletic potential, some of which have a large genetic component and some of which are mostly under the control of the athlete. Then in the next section we will help you determine your athletic potential.

MENTAL ATTITUDE

Good mental attitude is vitally important to the success of any athlete. Many outstanding athletes have made up for physical deficiencies by having the right mental attitude, during both practice and competition. A proper mental attitude includes being willing to accept instruction; having a strong desire to win and a willingness to work hard and sacrifice other interests in order to be successful. It also means having the self-control and self-confidence which enables you to perform well during highly competitive and demanding situations.

Coachability Some athletes take instruction well. They are able to accept advice from a coach without taking it as personal criticism. Others do not seem able to listen, may think they know better, or may have difficulty converting instructions into improved performance. As Bob Gaillard emphasizes in the last chapter, recruiters are looking for the athlete who is able to listen and learn from his coach. Athletes at all levels, even professionals, need to be able to take and even seek instruction.

Learn to relax and accept suggestions or instructions on how to improve your skill or level of physical fitness. Analyze what is said and try to see how you can take advantage of your coaching.

Desire Strong desire shows up as hustle, aggressive play, or enthusiasm, not only when things are going well—in fact, more importantly, when things go badly. It is the willingness to spend extra time at practice, to give up other interests, to strive during times of pain or exhaustion. The athlete with desire is quickly recognized by the coach and other players.

Desire alone will not make you successful, but it can make up for limitations in skill, size, speed, or power. The basis of desire is one of the great mysteries of coaching. We cannot teach it to you in this or any other book; you must find it within yourself.

Self-Control The ability to maintain self-control, and particularly not to lose your temper during competition, is a definite plus. Even though some otherwise outstanding athletes have been prone to temper tantrums, using bad language or throwing equipment or even punches at opposing players, no one should want to copy them—such behavior only reduces their effectiveness as athletes.

Some athletes seem naturally to have more self-control than others, but it can be developed, by first recognizing its benefit, and then through practice, especially during competitive or highly emotional situations.

Self-Confidence An athlete who performs well consistently knows he* is good. That is not to say he brags or is cocky, but that he believes in his own abilities. In all sports, but particularly in those where the athlete is on his own or where there is direct competition between two individuals, having the self-assurance that he can win makes the difference between being just a good athlete or a champion. As soon as the athlete begins to have self-doubts, his chances of success quickly fade.

ATHLETIC SKILL

Skill is the ability to perform a specific task efficiently. Skill is different from fitness in that skill is very specific to a particular sport. A good baseball pitcher may appear awkward and uncoordinated when playing another sport, such as basketball, soccer, or tennis. It is not that he couldn't develop skill in these other activities, but in order to do so he would have to practice them as patiently as he has his pitching. Some heredity comes into play here, but development of a skill largely results from practice.

Developing a skill is much like programming a computer. Once you put a program into the computer, it will continue to execute that program until it is reprogrammed. Once you learn a skill, it's as if you programmed a nerve-muscle computer which will perform the skill over and over again just as you have learned it. This is why good teaching or coaching is so important early in learning a sport. If you learn the skill improperly, you will continue to perform it improperly until you relearn (reprogram) it correctly. Once you have learned and practiced a skill for some time, you will retain most of it for many years without practice. For example, once you've learned, you never really forget how to ride a bike or swim.

---

*Because there is no bi-sexual singular pronoun, we've let male nouns and pronouns stand for both sexes. We hope there will soon be appropriate words in our language.

Your Athletic Potential

When you begin to learn a new skill, your ability level increases rapidly at first, then more slowly as you refine the precise movements involved. As you improve the skill, performing it takes less energy, and gradually less concentration, until you may reach the point where you can perform while thinking about something else. A good basketball player is unconscious of his dribbling, and can concentrate on the other nine players on the court.

Developing and maintaining a skill takes hours of practice performing a particular movement. It is important to perform a movement which is as close as possible to or exactly the same as the actual skill involved. For example, although a volleyball serve and a tennis serve are somewhat similar, playing tennis will not develop volleyball skills. The volleyball player must practice the particular movements for volleyball serving—throwing the ball up straight, cocking the hand behind the ear, and finally whipping the hand out to meet the ball and following through.

ATHLETIC FITNESS

"Athletic fitness" is the composite of your physical characteristics, as opposed to your specific skills. The components include body size (weight, height, and composition), muscular strength, power and endurance, speed, cardio-respiratory endurance, flexibility, and agility. How much an athlete has of any one or combination of these components is determined both by what he is born with and what he does with it.

Body Size Most boys and girls reach their maximum height by the time they are sixteen to eighteen years of age, and some even sooner. There are exceptions—some will gain one, two or even three inches in height after high school—but the average athlete reaches nearly full stature before high school graduation. For example, the average height of the All-American college basketball team for 1977-78 was six feet, eight inches and most of these players were seniors. That team's average height before high school graduation was six feet, seven inches. Similarly, at Stanford University the height of the players on the varsity basketball team in 1977-78 averaged six feet, six inches, only one inch taller than they averaged as seniors in high school.

For many sports a heavy body weight is a desirable characteristic; for some, such as football, it can be essential. Though a few grow substantially after graduation from high school, as a general rule, boys reach full growth in terms of effective weight by the time they are seventeen or eighteen, and girls by sixteen or seventeen. "Effective weight" refers to the amount of muscle mass and bone, not fat (which usually increases with age). The exception is usually the athlete who has a large bone structure (wide shoulders, big hands, thick wrists), who can often gain a moderate amount of muscle mass after high school through weight training.

Some athletes find they must increase their body weight after high school in order to be effective at their regular positions on a new team or at a new position. Most of them accomplish this by increasing muscle mass through weight training programs. Tommy Hart, formerly a defensive tackle for the San Francisco 49'ers, needed to gain a considerable amount when he signed on at 205 pounds. Through a systematic program of heavy weight training and good nutrition designed by Coach Paul Wiggen, Tommy gained forty pounds in two years and became a premier player with excellent speed.

Obviously all body weight is not the same! For many athletic events, especially those requiring strength and power, an increase in body weight is useful, but only if it is an increase in effective weight, not fat. Also, sports that require athletes to move their bodies rapidly (sprinting), against gravity (gymnastics), or over long distances (distance running) are best performed by individuals with very little body fat. Thus, most athletes (ocean swimmers and sumo wrestlers are exceptions) benefit from having a limited amount of fat. The best way to describe how much fat one has is to determine the relationship of his

AVERAGE PHYSICAL SIZE AND BODY COMPOSITION OF CHAMPION ATHLETES

Sport	Males Height	Males Weight	%Fat	Females Height	Females Weight	%Fat
Baseball	6-0	195	10-14%	—	—	—
Basketball	6-5½	201	8-10%	5-6½	139	18-24%
Cycling	5-10½	148	8-10%	—	—	—
Football						
Lineman	6-4¾	255	16-18%	—	—	—
Defensive backs & receivers	6-½	183	6-9%	—	—	—
Offensive backs	6-0	208	10-12%	—	—	—
Gymnastics	5-10	153	4-8%	5-2½	110	12-14%
Running						
Sprint	5-11	151	4-8%	5-5	117	8-10%
Distance	5-9½	138	4-8%	5-6¾	126	12-16%
Field—shot/discus	6-2	224	17-21%	5-6	164	24-30%
Skiing	5-10½	158	6-10%	5-4¾	126	14-17%
Soccer	5-9½	167	8-12%	—	—	—
Swimming	6-0	174	6-10%	5-5½	139	17-21%
Tennis	5-11	161	13-15%	5-5¾	125	21-27%
Your Values						

*Values taken from measurements made at Stanford University, the National Athletic and Health Institute and from published literature.

pounds of fat to total body weight and express this value as a percentage. For example, if you weighed 100 pounds and you had 20 pounds of fat, 20% of your weight would be fat, whereas if you weighed 200 pounds and had 20 pounds of fat, only 10% of your weight would be fat. In the table on page 19, we have listed the average physical size and body composition of selected national college and professional champion athletes in a variety of sports. One can be of substantially different body size or composition and still be a very successful athlete, but these values will give you a good idea of the size of champion athletes in each of these sports.

Since the average American male's body weight is about 22% fat and the average female's is about 28%, it is evident that champion athletes in most sports carry relatively little fat.

Estimate Your Body Fat You can obtain a good estimate of how much of your total body weight is fat by measuring the thickness of your skin on the back of your upper arm (actually your skin is very thin and the amount of underlying fat determines the thickness). The following procedure applies to both boys and girls and will allow you to estimate what percent of your weight is fat.

PERCENT FAT ESTIMATION: BOYS AND GIRLS

What You Will Need:
1. A friend to measure your skinfold thickness.
2. A ruler.

Directions:
1. You will not be able to measure your own skinfold. Have a friend measure yours and you can measure theirs.
2. Let the right arm hang down to the side.
3. Locate the skinfold site.
    a. On the back of the upper right arm.
    b. Midway between the shoulder and the elbow.

Your Athletic Potential

4. Firmly grasp a fold of skin between your thumb and first finger. Pull the skin away from the arm.
   a. Make sure the fold does not include any muscle, just skin and fat.
   b. Practice pinching and pulling the skin to be sure there is no muscle included.
5. Using the ruler, measure the thickness of the skinfold to the nearest ¼ inch.
   a. BE SURE TO MEASURE THE DISTANCE BETWEEN YOUR THUMB AND FINGER. Sometimes the top of the skinfold is thicker than the distance between your thumb and finger. To help avoid this problem make sure the top of the skinfold is level with the top of your thumb.
   b. Do not press the ruler against the skinfold. This will flatten it out and make it appear thicker than it really is.
6. Take two separate measures of this skinfold thickness, releasing the skin between each measure.
7. Calculate the average skinfold thickness.

_____   _____   _____
Skinfold #1   Skinfold #2   Average Skinfold

8. Now use the chart on page 22 to estimate your percent body fat.

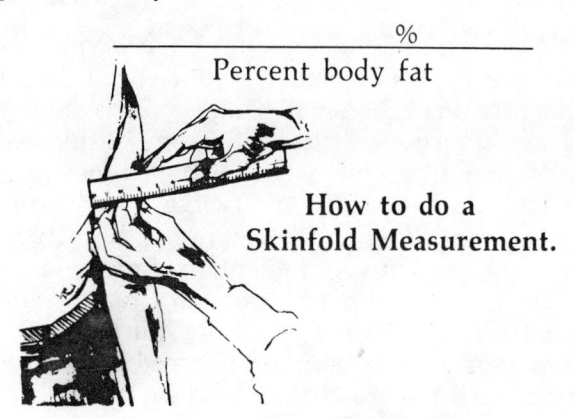

_____%_____
Percent body fat

How to do a Skinfold Measurement.

Handbook for the Young Athlete

Speed Your speed is your ability to move your body or any one of its parts rapidly. How fast you can run or move is determined by several factors, mostly all genetically determined. Your speed is dependent on characteristics of your nervous system (how fast impulses can travel through it), the connection sites of nerves and muscles (how many muscle fibers for each nerve ending), the arrangement of bones and the attachment of bones by ligaments and tendons, and the type of muscle fibers you have. Speed also is dependent on adequate muscle strength and power.

Percent Body Fat—Boys

Skinfold Thickness (inches)		
¼	5%–9%
½	9%–13%
¾	13%–18%
1	18%–22%
1¼	22%–27%

Percent Body Fat—Girls

Skinfold Thickness (inches)		
¼	8%–13%
½	13%–18%
¾	18%–23%
1	23%–28%
1¼	28%–33%

The type of muscle fibers you have is an especially important factor in determining your speed. In a recent study, doctors analyzed small samples of tissue from the muscles in the arms and legs of various athletes. They discovered that there were two distinct types of muscle fibers, which they named "slow twitch" and "fast twitch" fibers. All the athletes in the study had both types, but those who excelled in speed events had more fast twitch fibers. Fast twitch fibers contract very rapidly and with substantial force, but they tire quite quickly. Individuals who have a great deal of natural speed tend to fatigue quickly and are not good in events or sports requiring

Your Athletic Potential

endurance. Slow twitch fibers, on the other hand, do not contract as rapidly, but they have much better staying power. Consequently, well-trained cross country runners can run for hours, but are not capable of short bursts at a high speed.

Figure 1-1 shows the relative percentages of slow and fast twitch fibers in the leg muscles of world class athletes in different sports. The experts agree that our make-up of slow and fast twitch muscle fibers is generally determined by heredity—training has little effect.

Sport	% Fast Twitch	% Slow Twitch
Track, Sprinter	60%	40%
Marathoner	40%	60%
Speed Cyclist	55%	45%
Soccer Player	45%	50%

Figure 1-1: Ratios of leg muscle fiber types of various athletes

Thus, although you *can* improve your time somewhat in a particular event by improving your muscle strength or power and your skill (i.e., improvement of starting techniques will improve a 100-yard dash time), your basic speed will not increase greatly. The top sprinters demonstrate this principle. Houston McTear, who currently holds the 40, 50 and 60-yard sprint records, ran a 9.7 second 100-yard dash in the eighth grade, before any significant training or coaching. He ran an unofficial 9.0 before graduating from high school. David Sime provides another example. In the 1950s he was the world record holder for the 100-yard dash, 100 meters, 220-yard dash, 200 meters, 220-yard low hurdles and the 60, 70, 80, and 100- yard indoor dash. In 1956, he won his final major 100-yard dash competition in 9.5 seconds. Fifteen years later at age thirty-five, after no formal conditioning or training beyond regular tennis and jogging, he ran 100 yards in 9.6 seconds, only one-tenth of a second slower than at age twenty.

Muscle Strength Muscle strength is the ability to apply maximal force. It may be used to move or lift heavy objects (weight lifting), to resist the force applied by an opponent (wrestling), or to maintain body position (gymnastics). Maximum strength is determined by the size of the muscle mass and the chemical characteristics of the muscles being used. When muscle strength is increased with training, there usually is an increase in the size of the muscle fiber in boys but not in girls. This sex difference is due to the different levels of sex-related hormones in boys and girls after about age twelve or thirteen. The *number* of muscle fibers (which is genetically determined) does not change with training of any type.

The strength of specific muscles or muscle groups, such as the upper arms, can be increased quite substantially and rapidly by a program of heavy resistance exercise. Improvement in strength by as much as 30% to 50% can be obtained in three to six months by such a program (see pages 47-56).

Power Power is the combination of both speed and muscular strength or force. It is the ability to apply force rapidly and is a very important characteristic for success in many sports. Power is necessary in order to start quickly, change direction rapidly (a must for a defensive back in football), and for good jumping ability. It is needed to hit a baseball or golf ball a long distance or to serve a tennis ball very hard. Power appears to be quite specific to a specific type of event; a powerful football lineman may not have a powerful tennis serve or be able to hit a long ball on the golf course.

Absolute power is dependent on body size, or to be more specific, on the muscle mass being used for the task. For example, Muhammad Ali has been considered a very powerful fighter. He has obtained this power as a result of both his large size (usually 220 to 230 pounds) and his exceptional speed. This combination of quick movement with a large muscle mass produces the type of power so very effective in such sports as shot-putting, or line play in football.

Muscle Endurance Local muscle endurance is the capacity to perform repeated muscle contractions without limiting fatigue. The ultimate capacity of a muscle for endurance is genetically determined—those individuals who have inherited a large number of slow twitch fibers can contract their muscles repeatedly without fatigue.

But the extent to which a person can realize his ultimate muscle endurance capacity depends on physical training of the specific muscle group used in the particular athletic event. For example, if you want to increase your endurance capacity for swimming the crawl stroke, then you should perform the specific action of the stroke, or one very close to it, in your training.

Cardiorespiratory Endurance (Aerobic Capacity) Cardiorespiratory endurance makes it possible to perform large muscle activities at high intensity for extended periods of time. It is the ability to transport oxygen from your lungs to your working muscles, and for the muscles to use this oxygen effectively in the required athletic activity.

This capacity is dependent on the integrated function of the lungs, heart, blood vessels, and muscles. Good cardiorespiratory endurance is essential for such events as long distance running, swimming, cycling, cross country skiing, rowing, soccer, and basketball. It can be improved substantially by regularly performing activities that require a lot of "wind" for fifteen minutes or longer.

Agility Agility is the ability to change directions rapidly and with control at high speeds. Good agility is essential to the basketball player, the defensive back in football, and the tennis player (especially during a serve and volley game). Agility is partly an inherited trait, but it can be substantially improved by repeated practice of a specific skill or move. Again, for maximum improvement the exact movement needed in competition should be performed in practice.

Flexibility Flexibility is the ability to move joints through their full range with ease. It is dependent upon several factors, including the structure and alignment of bones, the degree of stretch of ligaments and tendons, and the amount of muscle and fat tissue which may restrict movement. Flexibility may be greatly improved by exercises or sports requiring substantial stretching. It is very specific to a given joint or area of the body: warming up or stretching one area has no effect on other joints or tissues.

HOW TO EVALUATE YOUR ATHLETIC FITNESS

One way to evaluate your athletic potential is to compare yourself with other athletes. How you stand now, compared to other team members, other players in your league, or conference or state, indicates reasonably well how you might achieve in the future. If you are not first string now, or scheduled to be first string during your last season in high school, it is not likely (although there are exceptions) that you will become first string in college or be considered pro material. This does not mean that you are as good now as you will become. Rather, it means that coaches or scouts will usually spot natural talent even before it's fully developed.

Generally speaking, top athletes in college or the pros were very good or outstanding in their sports when in high school or college. But, of course, there are exceptions. Ron LeFore, center fielder for the Detroit Tigers, is an example of a natural athlete who did not participate in sports in high school or college but quickly became an outstanding baseball player once he began to compete seriously. While in prison, for armed robbery, he decided to play softball. His ability was immediately recognized (he could run 100 yards in 9.6 seconds without any special coaching), and after playing two years of baseball for the

Your Athletic Potential

Jackson State Prison, he was signed by the Detroit Tigers. He played minor league ball for 1½ years and then moved up to first string for the Tigers. After only two years of major league baseball and 5½ years after his first baseball games in prison, he made the American League All-Star Team.

However, very few players ever reach the NFL or NBA without first being a good, if not outstanding, college player. All of the regular players on the rosters of the NFL football teams in 1977-78, played previously on a college team; and in the NBA only one player, Moses Malone of the Houston Rockets, had not played college basketball.

The Fitness of Outstanding Athletes

How does your level of fitness for athletic performance compare to that of outstanding athletes? In this section, we will show you how you can precisely compare your athletic fitness to that of athletes successful in different sports.

During the past ten years the athletic fitness of top collegiate and professional athletes has been measured by many different fitness experts. We took this data and rated the athletes' capacity on the various components of fitness using the following scale:

1 = above average
2 = good
3 = very good
4 = excellent

The "Athletic Fitness Rating Chart" on page 28 contains these ratings for champion athletes. Where appropriate these ratings apply to both men and women.

As you can see, outstanding athletes are not always outstanding in every component of fitness. For example, a world class distance runner will usually score 1s, or at best 2s, in all categories except muscular and cardiorespiratory endurance. Conversely, a football lineman usually scores low in cardiorespiratory endurance, but very high in muscular strength and power.

ATHLETIC FITNESS RATING CHART

Fitness Components*

Sport	Muscular Strength	Muscular Power	Speed	Agility	Flexibility	Muscular Endurance	Cardio-respiratory Endurance
Baseball	2	3	3	2	2	1	1
Basketball	2	3	2	3	2	2	3
Football—linemen	4	3	2	2	2	2	1
backs & receivers	2	3	3	3	3	2	2
Soccer	2	2	2	3	2	3	3
Tennis	1	2	2	3	2	2	2
Alpine Skiing	2	2	2	2	1	4	4
Cross Country Skiing	1	1	1	1	1	4	4
Gymnastics	4	4	2	4	4	3	2
Cycling—sprints	3	3	4	2	1	2	2
distance	2	1	1	1	1	4	4
Swimming—sprints	3	3	3	2	3	1	1
distance	2	1	1	1	3	4	4
Track & Field—sprints	3	3	4	2	3	1	2
distance running	1	1	1	1	1	4	4
throwing events	4	4	2	2	2	2	1
jumping events	2	4	3	2	3	2	2
YOUR SCORE							

*1—Above Average; 2—Good; 3—Very Good; 4—Excellent.

Your Athletic Potential

This chart can be used as a general guide to the levels of athletic fitness needed for top success in each sport. For example, to be able to compete with an outstanding gymnast, you will need "excellent" flexibility, agility, and muscular power—but only "good" speed.

In using this chart, however, keep in mind that the values listed are averages from many scores. In some sports, those which depend primarily on athletic fitness and not on skill, such as long distance running, most of the tested athletes obtained similar scores; all long distance runners scored very high in cardiorespiratory endurance. It is easy to see which abilities are most needed in such sports. However, in those sports which require a high degree of skill, the scores varied widely. For example, professional tennis players vary greatly in speed, strength and agility. It is not possible to identify a potentially great tennis player solely by his or her physical attributes. Success is determined more by the degree of skill developed, and by mental factors, such as concentration.

It is also important to remember that there are exceptions. Some, albeit a very few, top collegiate and professional athletes do not possess abilities at levels indicated on the chart. Also, a higher level of one ability might help compensate for a lower level of another. For example, a very fast basketball player (with a speed rating of 3 or 4) might be very successful even though he had only average muscle power and jumping agility. Nevertheless, this chart is a good general indicator of the fitness levels you will need in your sport to win against outstanding athletes.

A question which may have arisen in your mind as you studied the chart is: How do I stand in comparison to top collegiate and professional athletes?

A SIMPLE TEST OF YOUR ATHLETIC FITNESS

In order to answer that question, we have devised a simple test consisting of seven exercises similar to the ones that the collegiate and professional athletes performed. By taking this test you can rate yourself in comparison to these outstanding athletes.

How to Take the Test You will need another person to help you with some of the exercises, so it's best to take the test with one or more friends. First, look over the test instructions and scoring. All that you need for equipment is a stopwatch, a twelve-inch ruler, a chinning bar and a piece of chalk. We suggest you take the test at your local high school track, and that you wear gym shorts and running shoes. If possible, it's best to take the parts of the test in the order listed.

When you have completed each part of the test, enter your score on the "Athletic Fitness Score Card" (page 37 for girls; page 36 for boys). Using the chart, find your athletic rating (0-4). For example, if you are a boy and ran 1¾ miles in twelve minutes, you would receive a rating of 2 for cardiorespiratory endurance. This means that you are considered good in that category. Enter your ratings in the appropriate boxes on the Score Card.

1. *Pull-Ups—Test of Arm Strength* A test of your upper body strength is the maximum number of pull-ups you can perform. Locate a bar you can hang from without your feet touching the ground. Grasp the bar with the palms away from your face (overhand grip). From the hanging position raise your body using your arms until your chin is just over the bar and then lower your body to the starting position. Repeat as many times as possible. Do not swing your body forwards or backwards and do not raise your knees or kick your legs. Record your maximum number of properly executed pull-ups in the "Your Score" box of the Athletic Fitness Score Card. Then determine your rating and enter it in the "Rating" box.

2. *Standing Long Jump—Test of Leg Power* Leg power can be measured by how far or high you can jump from a standing position. Mark a starting line on the floor with chalk,

Your Athletic Potential

and six feet (seventy-two inches) from that line in the direction you are going to jump, mark a second line. Additional lines should be marked at seven, eight, and nine feet. To perform the test, get in a semi-crouched position with your feet about shoulder width apart and your toes at the starting line. From this position (without any steps or movement of the feet) jump forward as far as possible. Have your friend use the chalk to mark on the floor where the back of your shoe that hit nearest the starting line landed. Measure the distance from the starting line to where you landed. Repeat as many times as you want. Record your longest jump in inches in the "Your Score" box of the Athletic Fitness Score Card. Enter your rating in the "Rating" box.

3. *50-Yard Dash—Test of Speed*   Many professional teams test the speed of their athletes using the 40 or 50-yard dash. For best results try to perform this test on a running track, and if possible have your coach time you. Your coach should stand fifty yards away and give you the instruction, "On your mark, get set, go." On "go" he should start the stop watch while you sprint as fast as possible the fifty yards. He should stop the watch as your body crosses the line at fifty yards. You may want to practice this event several times on different days before actually taking the test. Test yourself several times and record your best time in the "Your Score" box of the Athletic Fitness Score Card. Enter your rating in the "Rating" box.

4. *Six-Count Agility Exercise—Test of Agility*   A good test of your agility is how many times you can complete this sixcount agility exercise in twenty seconds. You will want to practice the exercise a few times before taking the test, to get your best score. The exercise is performed as follows:

Starting position = standing, feet shoulder width apart, arms at sides.

Handbook for the Young Athlete

Position 1	= full squat with palms of hands on floor between feet
Position 2	= extend legs to rear so you are in the up position for a push-up (front leaning rest position)
Position 3	= swing legs to the side and forward so that your feet are pointing in the direction opposite from position 2; your back now will be toward the floor
Position 4	= turn body over so you are in front leaning rest position (same as position #2)
Position 5	= bring legs up to full squat position (same as position #1)
Position 6	= stand up, so you are once again in standing position

Have a friend time you for exactly twenty seconds. Perform the exercise as rapidly as possible and count the number of times you can complete the full six-count exercise plus the number of positions you reach in the last exercise at twenty seconds. For example, if you complete five full exercises and are in position 4 of your sixth exercise when twenty seconds are up, your score would be 5-4. Record your score in the "Your Score" box of the Athletic Fitness Score Card. Enter your rating in the "Rating" box.

Six-Count Agility Exercise

Position 1    **Position 2**

Your Athletic Potential

Position 3

Position 4   Position 5   Position 6

5. *Forward Flexion—Test of Flexibility* How flexible are you? This test is a measure of your lower back and hip flexibility. Take a twelve-inch ruler and have your friend hold it firmly on the floor or grass. Sit down with your legs straight out in front of you, feet together, and place the bottom of your heels at the three-inch line. The short end of the ruler should be pointed directly at you. While keeping the backs of your legs in contact with the floor, slowly reach forward with both hands together and see how far you can reach down the ruler: the higher the value the better the score. Your score is how many inches you can reach with your fingertips *without* bouncing or jerking your body or arms. Put the highest reading in inches that

you obtained in three tries in the "Your Score" box of the Athletic Fitness Score Card. Enter your rating in the "Rating" box.

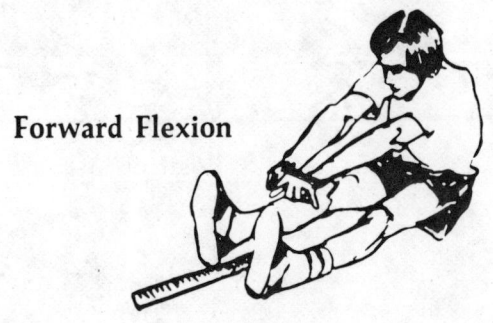

Forward Flexion

6. Sit-ups for One Minute—Test of Muscular Endurance The good old sit-up is an excellent index of the muscular endurance capacity of your stomach muscles: that is, their ability to contract repeatedly without limiting fatigue. Lie on the grass or floor with your knees bent so that the bottoms of your feet are flat on the floor (have your friend hold them firmly). Clasp your hands behind your head. As you do sit-ups, time yourself, or have someone time you, for one minute. Keep your knees bent and feet on the floor, and sit up so that your back is perpendicular to the floor (don't worry about touching elbows to knees). Once you have sat up all the way, return to the starting position so that your hands touch the floor. Repeat as many times as you can in one minute. Record the number of sit-ups you completed in the "Your Score" box of the Athletic Fitness Score Card. Enter your rating in the "Rating" box.

7. Twelve-Minute Run—Test of Cardiorespiratory Endurance Here is a test of your capacity to perform vigorous exercise for an extended period of time. The objective is to see how far you can run in twelve minutes. You should plan to run around a regulation track that is 440 yards, or ¼ mile, per lap. After you have warmed up with some stretching and slow jogging, get ready to time yourself or,

Your Athletic Potential

preferably, have your friend or coach time you. When ready, begin running around the track at a pace that you think you can continue for twelve minutes. A proper pace is very important for your best time. Count the number of miles you complete (four laps to the mile) and record this value on your score card. Delay taking this test if you have any medical problems, including a cold or generalized infection. Record the number of laps you complete in the "Your Score" box of the Athletic Fitness Score Card. Enter your rating in the "Rating" box.

Rate Yourself When you have completed all the exercises and filled in all your scores and ratings, look back at the "Athletic Fitness Rating Chart" on page 28. Fill in your ratings at the bottom of this chart, and then see how you compare. For example, if you are a boy and can run ¾ miles in twelve minutes, you would have received a score of 2 for cardiorespiratory endurance. This would be the level recommended for tennis players, football backs and receivers, but would be lower than that desirable for sports such as soccer, distance running, cycling or swimming.

To be a serious athlete, you should have scored at least 1 on each test if you are fifteen years of age or older. But remember, the standards given here are very high, so don't be discouraged if you don't meet all of them. It would be the rare high school student who would be able to attain a rating of 3 or 4 on all the fitness components listed in the "Athletic Fitness Rating Chart." You have several years of training and growth yet before you will be competing with college or professional players.

In order to determine whether you will ever meet these standards, think of how much you have improved in the last year or two. In your mind, extend that rate of improvement into the future. What levels of ability can you reasonably expect to achieve by the time you get to college or turn pro?

Now that you know what you need to work on, go on to the next chapter where we have outlined several programs to improve your athletic fitness.

ATHLETIC FITNESS SCORE CARD—Boys and Men

Test	0 = Below Athlete Level	1 = Above Average	2 = Good	3 = Very Good	4 = Excellent
1. *Strength*—Pull-ups (no.)	fewer than 7	7 to 9	10 to 12	13 to 14	15 or more
2. *Power*—Stand. long jump (ins.)	fewer than 85	85 to 88	89 to 91	92 to 94	95 or more
3. *Speed*—50-yd. dash (secs.)	slower than 6.7	6.7 to 6.4	6.3 to 6.0	5.9 to 5.6	5.5 or less
4. *Agility*—6-ct. agility (cts.)	fewer than 5-5	5-5 to 6-3	6-4 to 7-2	7-3 to 8-1	8-2 or more
5. *Flexibility*—Forward flexion (ins.)	not reach ruler	1 to 2	3 to 5	6 to 8	9 or more
6. *Muscular Endurance*—Sit-ups (no.)	fewer than 38	38 to 45	46 to 52	53 to 59	60 or more
7. *Cardiorespiratory Endurance*—12-min. run (miles)	fewer than 1½	1½	1¾	2	2¼ or more

YOUR SCORE

	Strength	Power	Speed	Agility	Flexibility	Muscular Endurance	Cardiorespiratory Endurance
Your Score							
Rating (0–4)							

Your Athletic Potential

ATHLETIC FITNESS SCORE CARD—Girls and Women

Test	0 = Below Athlete Level	1 = Above Average	2 = Good	3 = Very Good	4 = Excellent
1. *Strength*— Pull-ups (no.)	fewer than 2	2 to 3	4 to 5	6 to 7	8 or more
2. *Power*—Stand. long jump (ins.)	fewer than 63	63 to 65	66 to 68	69 to 71	72 or more
3. *Speed*— 50-yd. dash (secs.)	slower than 8.2	8.2 to 7.9	7.8 to 7.1	6.9 to 6.0	5.9 or less
4. *Agility*— 6-ct. agility (cts.)	fewer than 3-5	3-5 to 4-3	4-4 to 5-2	5-3 to 6-2	6-3 or more
5. *Flexibility*—Forward flexion (ins.)	fewer than 3	3 to 5	6 to 8	9 to 11	12 or more
6. *Muscular Endurance*— Sit-ups (no.)	fewer than 26	26 to 31	32 to 38	39 to 45	46 or more
7. *Cardiorespiratory Endurance*—12-min. run (miles)	fewer than 1¼	1¼	1½	1¾	2 or more

YOUR SCORE

	Strength	Power	Speed	Agility	Flexibility	Muscular Endurance	Cardiorespiratory Endurance
Your Score							
Rating (0–4)							

two

Training to Improve Your Athletic Fitness

William Haskell

In this chapter, we will concentrate on how to improve and maintain physical fitness. Because mental attitude and sport skill are also important to athletic success, you should realize that outstanding fitness—strength, speed, or endurance—will not ensure outstanding performance. However, if physical fitness is neglected, you will have little or no chance of being a successful athlete.

Previously, we learned that heredity has set potential "limits" of physical fitness for you and everyone else. Unfortunately, some people are born with only average speed or agility and no amount of training will change that fact. But don't use this as an excuse for poor performance or as a rationalization for dropping out of athletics. One cannot truly evaluate fitness potential until he or she is fully grown and has trained vigorously (more than just sport play) for one to two years. Any conclusion you might make about your own fitness potential before fulfilling these requirements would only be a guess.

A few young athletes mature early. With their size and strength advantage, they may dominate their competition for one or two years even without physical training. However, even the bigger young athlete should avoid becoming complacent about his need for regular workouts. By the time the athlete who matures early reaches college, many of his teammates and competitors will have caught up with him in growth, and who is more successful will depend on skill and fitness development.

Remember also that competition in college is much tougher than in high school, so no matter how well you are doing now, continual physical training will help you prepare for college.

GENERAL PRINCIPLES OF ATHLETIC TRAINING

The first step in developing a sound physical training program for yourself is to understand the general principles that such a program should be built upon.

Overload

Physical condition can be improved to the limit of your genetic potential according to the amount you train. It will deteriorate if you are inactive and it will improve if you are more active than usual (see Figure 2-3). Increasing activity, called "overload" is the essence of physical training. The overload can come in the form of increased work, such as running farther distances or lifting heavier weights, or it can come from an increased work rate, such as running or swimming faster.

It is important to note that improvement in physical condition is not proportional to the increase in overload. For example, running three half-hour sessions each week may improve endurance capacity 10%. Running twice as much, or six half-hour sessions each week, will probably not result in a 20% increase—more likely 12 to 15% instead.

PROGRESSION

The body will adapt to an overload by improving its physiological function. This adaptation will occur in about one to four weeks, depending on the size (intensity and duration of exercise) of the overload, the frequency of exercise, and the initial condition of the athlete. Once the change is complete, there will be no new improvements in physiological function unless an even greater overload is imposed. This increase, necessary for continued advancement in physical fitness, is known as the *principle of progression.*

It is normal for a deconditioned athlete to progress rapidly through the initial levels of overload exercise, and then more slowly at levels near peak condition. Champion athletes virtually spend years training to shave a few seconds off a mile run time or to add a half an inch to their personal best in the high jump.

SPECIFICITY

Every type of training should be planned to produce a very specific physiological response. For example, a particular program of isometric strength training (exerting force against an immovable object) will significantly increase isometric strength in the particular arm or leg used, and at that particular joint angle. But the same trained muscle tested dynamically (lifting a weight through the range of motion), will show no evidence of significant strength improvement.

Fitness evaluations of female varsity swimmers at the University of California, Davis, provide a striking example of the specificity of training. When endurance was measured during arm work, the swimmers had a 25%

greater maximal oxygen uptake than female varsity runners. However, when leg endurance was measured (on a treadmill), maximal oxygen uptake was no different than that of non-athletic college females. These kinds of results have been confirmed in a variety of scientific studies and are the cornerstone of our next principle of training, the *principle of specificity.*

The practical implications of this principle are of major importance to you as an athlete. Unless training routines closely resemble the actions of your particular sport and, more specifically, the actions of the position you play in that sport, you will not receive the optimal training benefits. In a later section we will consider "specialty training"—drills which attempt to narrow the gap between general training exercises and the particular physical requirements of the athlete's sport, in order to develop a more efficient training program.

INDIVIDUALITY

The last general principle of athletic training is the *principle of individuality.* Not all athletes will improve their physical condition at the same rate or to the same level. Some of the factors that affect the rate of response are age, sex, body size, rest and sleep habits, initial level of condition, nutritional habits, injury and disease, and motivation. Individual training programs should be adjusted accordingly; in particular, progression should be slowed when necessary. For example, the strength training programs outlined in this chapter call for successive increases in weight or in repetitions every week. If at any point you find you have not "comfortably" finished the previous week's requirements, do not progress. Spend an extra week at the same training level.

All training programs described in this chapter have been constructed to serve the expected responses of the average young athlete. Try your best to stay with the programs but don't be ashamed to remain a second week at a particular level. Remember, slow progression does

Training to Improve Your Athletic Fitness

not mean you can't ultimately reach championship performance.

HOW TO IMPROVE YOUR ATHLETIC FITNESS

As discussed previously, there are several components of physical fitness: body size and composition, speed, muscle strength-power-endurance, flexibility, agility, and cardiorespiratory endurance. Athletes in the more physically specialized sports, such as track, field, or swimming, need only focus on one or two of these, but athletes involved in sports requiring a greater variety of abilities, such as basketball, soccer, or gymnastics, need to be concerned with all aspects of physical fitness. Unfortunately, training in one area (such as speed) does not cross over to another area (such as flexibility). Separate attention must be given to each.

The following sections will discuss some of the basic physiological facts behind physical fitness, and outline training programs designed for the development of the different components of fitness. These specific training programs will then be integrated into a single two-month pre-season training schedule.

Although the schedule and programs which follow represent the best general training procedures known to sport science, they will not suit every athlete exactly. Different athletes respond to training differently. Plan to modify the programs slightly according to the results of your physical evaluation tests and according to your own opinion of your needs.

TRAINING TO IMPROVE BODY COMPOSITION

As discussed in the last chapter, body size and composition are mainly determined by heredity. Most athletes attain their full height and weight by the end of high school or within one or two years thereafter. Body composition, however, can be substantially altered with training and diet, depending on the individual athlete.

Compare your body fat with that of champion athletes by using the chart on page 19. Do you need to lose fat weight? If so, you must alter both your eating and exercise habits in an attempt to burn up more calories than you eat. See Chapter Three for a complete discussion of the nutritional factors in weight loss. Losing fat weight is a reasonably slow process, so be patient. And remember, some athletes need more body fat than others to feel strong, so it's best not to lose a lot of weight all at once. Instead, do it in one-month intervals. Reduce for a month, then maintain that weight for two weeks. Be sure you feel good before losing the next four to eight pounds.

Starvation diets are ill-advised for anyone, but they are especially bad for the athletes. During the first twenty-four hours of a fast, significant amounts of muscle tissue are metabolized for energy. Loss of muscle tissue means less strength and poor performance. It is highly important to maintain proper nutritional habits when you are on a fat weight-reduction program.

The best exercises for fat reduction are those which are moderate, continuous, and use mainly the large muscles of the leg, such as running and cycling.

If you need to gain weight, be sure to do it by adding muscle tissue, not useless fat. Unfortunately, this is another area where genetics can deal us a bad hand—not all athletes can add the same amount of muscle bulk. Being able to increase muscle depends on the number of muscle fibers you are born with, and the amount of circulating testosterone, the male sex hormone. Females have fewer muscle fibers and very little circulating testosterone, and therefore are not able to gain much muscle bulk. Males can expect to add some pounds with muscle training (usually five to twenty). See Chapter Three, pages 108 to 111 for specific information about nutrition and weight gain.

TRAINING FOR SPEED

The speed at which the individual muscle fibers contract is probably the most important factor in determining the speed of an athlete and, as we learned in the last chapter, this is mainly genetically determined. Those who inherit a greater proportion of fast-twitch fibers will tend to have good natural speed.

But no matter what your genetic potential, specific speed training is necessary to realize this potential. For a sprinter, this means practicing your event over and over; for other athletes, it means repeating short movement patterns that would be used in competitive situations. This will all be spelled out in greater detail later in this section, when we present the "specialty training" drills which should be used to optimize speed.

There are other training methods to be considered when you are attempting to improve speed. Running, cycling, or swimming for short durations at speeds faster than those used in competition will sometimes be helpful. Good flexibility allows motions to be more fluid and has an effect, although small, on speed. Muscle strength also plays a significant role, especially in those first few yards of acceleration. Finally, good anticipation can improve an athlete's total time. To develop anticipation you must constantly repeat game situations during practice time.

TRAINING TO IMPROVE MUSCULAR STRENGTH, POWER, AND ENDURANCE

Athletes who participate in contact sports like wrestling or football will assure you that only the strong survive. Coaches for these sports have always emphasized strength training in their athletic programs. Until relatively recently, however, coaches for other sports, such as track and swimming, often opposed such training, believing that it would make their athletes "musclebound," hampering joint flexibility and speed. Carefully controlled research studies have now laid these myths to rest, proving, in most cases, that proper strength training actually enhances speed, flexibility as well as strength and power. Most outstanding athletes now include at least some strength training in their routines.

Muscle strength is obvious. You see it when the wrestler lifts his opponent off the ground or when the weight lifter performs a bench press. Explosive strength, the muscle *power* that can be applied in a fraction of a second, is less apparent. It is required for the shot put, the discus throw, and the high jump, and it is used by baseball pitchers to put extra speed on their fast balls. Explosive strength spells the difference between two opposing linemen. Each wants to hit the opponent off balance and make him useless for the play. The player who generates the greatest force in the shortest time usually wins.

Muscle power can be improved by increasing either speed or strength. Speed can usually be improved to a degree, but after rather quick improvement, it tends to level off and added training will help little. On the other hand, the amount of force (strength) that an athlete is able to exert can almost always be improved. Thus, we recommend that you concentrate on increasing your strength and concern yourself less about your speed, which is apt to be close to the level of your genetic capability already.

In addition to muscle force and muscle power, muscle *endurance* is also important. It is required by athletic events that involve repeated short periods of all-out effort. For example, today's tennis style includes more hard hitting, baseline rallies. The player with less arm endurance will weaken first and hit the ball out or hopelessly short. Wrestling involves repeated exertion of maximal force, and the wrestler with the least endurance will be at a decided disadvantage.

Before 1970, training routines to improve muscle endurance consisted of a high number of repetitions and low resistance (30 to 40% of the maximal lift). But an experiment conducted in that year led to a change in the thinking. Two experimental groups were given endurance training, one performing the traditional endurance routines and the other working out with low repetitions and high resistance (80 to 90% of the maximal lift). The scientists concluded that the high resistance training technique was as good as the more traditional approach for

Training to Improve Your Athletic Fitness

developing endurance; and since it can be performed in half the time, most coaches now recommend its use.

The specific muscle lifts prescribed in this section were selected to ensure good general body strength training for athletes in a variety of sports. Again, however, it should be remembered that the more similar the lift is to the action used in competition, the more effective the training. So you are encouraged to add routines with movements specific for your sport. Many ingenious strength training devices that simulate actual performance are now available. Use those appropriate for you if available, in addition to the general program outlined below.

Two separate strength training programs are described here. Program A consists of five routines that do not require strength training equipment. Program B provides guidelines to use with weight machines, with a list of ten recommended lifts. Program A is convenient; it can be used wherever you are, at any time of year. Program B is less convenient but is preferred when feasible because of its greater selection of lifts and greater degree of sport specificity.

Strength Training Program A: without Weight Apparatus

Sequence   *Description*

1. *Push-up:* Keep your legs straight and fingers facing forward. Lower yourself until your upper chest touches the ground; return to the starting position for a complete repetition.
2. *Sit-up:* Either use bent knee position or, preferably, lie next to a chair or bed with your lower legs resting on the upper surface. With hands held behind your neck, curl forward until the stomach muscle cramps; return to the starting position for a complete repetition. (See page 53 for illustration.)
3. *Stationary Jump:* From a standing position, swing

Handbook for the Young Athlete

your arms and jump as high as possible. Each jump constitutes one repetition.
4. *Pull-up:* Grasp the bar with knuckles facing you. Without jerking the legs, slowly pull your chin up and over the bar; return to hang position for repetition. Note: Females may substitute fifteen seconds of hanging for one pull-up.
5. *Hill run:* Find a steep hill or use the rows of seats of a grandstand. At full speed, run up the hill for a total of five seconds; return to the starting position for one repetition.

Schedule for Strength Training Program A/Females

Progression	Number of Repetitions				
	Exercise 1	Exercise 2	Exercise 3	Exercise 4	Exercise 5
Level 1	1	5	9	1	4
Level 2	2	8	10	1	4
Level 3	3	11	10	1	5
Level 4	4	12	12	2	5
Level 5	5	13	13	2	6
Level 6	6	14	14	3	6
Level 7	7	15	15	3	7

Schedule for Strength Training Program A/Males

Progression	Number of Repetitions				
	Exercise 1	Exercise 2	Exercise 3	Exercise 4	Exercise 5
Level 1	10	10	9	4	4
Level 2	15	15	10	5	4
Level 3	19	19	11	6	5
Level 4	22	22	12	7	5
Level 5	25	25	13	8	6
Level 6	28	28	14	9	6
Level 7	30	30	15	10	7

Training to Improve Your Athletic Fitness

Strength Training Program B: with Weight Apparatus

There are several popular models of weight training machines, each backed by claims of superiority. However, unbiased research has concluded that all the units provide about the same results. The critical aspect of a good weight training program is not the machine, but the athlete and the effort he or she puts into the program. Therefore, select the apparatus that is the most convenient for you and stay with the program.

The following is a recommended list of fundamental strength training "lifts." It is important to follow the sequence as it is presented here. Before you begin your strength training program, you must first determine the maximum weight you can lift in each maneuver (this is not necessary with sit-ups). At each station, add weights until you can no longer perform the lift. The last weight is your maximum.

At each level of the strength training program, you should perform three sets consisting of ten repetitions (lifts) per set. Starting with one set of bench press, go all the way through the sequence before doing a second set of bench press.

At level one, lift only 40% of your maximum lift. As soon as you can perform all three sets "comfortably," increase the weight by the smallest possible increment for the next session. It is not necessary that you improve in each maneuver at the same rate. In fact this would be quite unusual. Moreover, strength improves at a different rate with different people. Do not move ahead until you have comfortably finished the last weight level. A muscle injury from advancing too fast would cause you to stop training and you would lose all the benefits previously gained.

Sequence *Description*

1. *Bench Press:* Lying on your back on a small bench, hold the weight above your chest with your

Handbook for the Young Athlete

hands about two feet apart. Slowly bring the weight down to your chest, and then push it up until the arms are once again fully extended (one repetition).

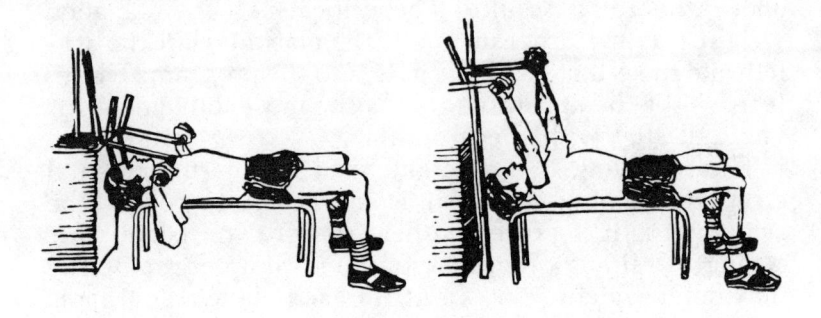

Bench Press

2. *Leg Press (requires special apparatus):* Sitting in the specially attached chair, place both feet on the pedals. To start, your knees should not be bent much more than ninety degrees. Press with both legs simultaneously until they are fully extended. Slowly release the tension until the weights are back at the starting position (one repetition).

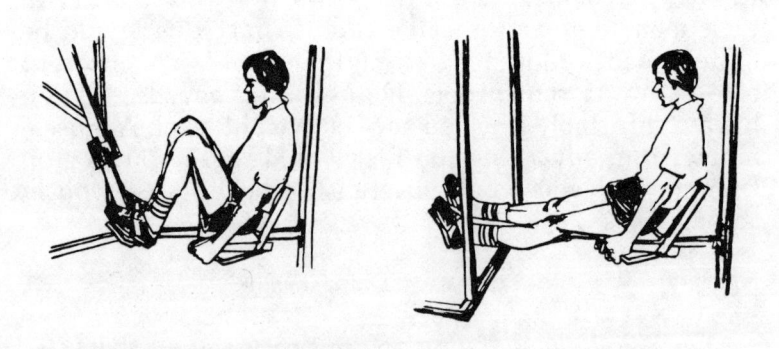

Leg Press

3. *Shoulder Press (requires special apparatus):* Using both hands, hold the weight just below your chin at shoulder level. Your hands should be about two feet apart with palms facing outward. Without using any leg muscles, push the weight above your head until the arms are extended. Slowly return the weight for one repetition.

Shoulder Press

4. *Sit-ups:* Either use bent knee position or, preferably, lie next to a chair or bed with your lower legs resting on the upper surface (same as strength training program A). With hands held behind your neck, curl forward until the stomach muscle cramps; return to the starting position for a complete repetition. For level one, perform ten repetitions per set. If small weights are available, hold one to five pounds behind your head during future levels of training. If no weights are available, increase the number of sit-ups per set by two until you reach a maximum of twenty-five.

Sit-up

53

5. *Pull Downs (requires special apparatus):* Using the overhead pulley apparatus, position yourself so that both hands are holding the bar and your arms are fully extended above your head. Your hands should be about two feet apart with palms facing outward. You may have to kneel to achieve this position. Pull the bar down behind your head until it touches your shoulders, and then release it slowly until your arms are once again extended (one repetition). Note: for heavy weights you may need a friend to hold you down.

Pull Down

6. *Leg Extension (requires special apparatus):* Sit on the special bench and hook your feet under the movable bar. Holding on to the bench with your hands, slowly lift the weight until your legs are fully extended; then slowly lower the weight to the starting position for one repetition.

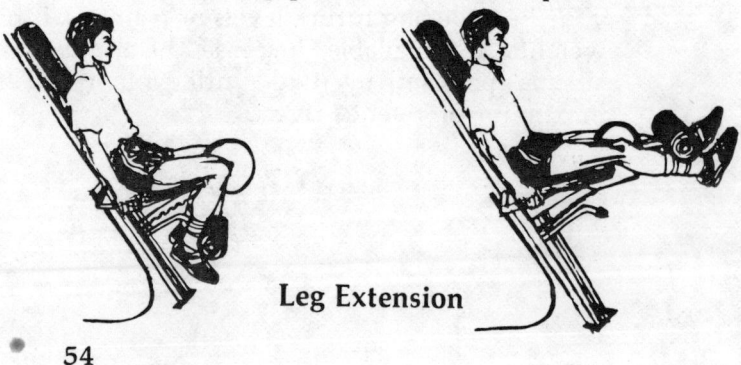

Leg Extension

7. *Bicep Curl (requires special apparatus):* Hold the weight in both hands (palms facing up) in front of your body with arms extended. Your hands should be about one to two feet apart. Without using any leg muscles and without leaning backward, lift the weight up to your chest. Slowly return the weight to the starting position for one repetition.

Bicep Curl

8. *Leg Flexion (requires special apparatus):* Lie face down on the same or similar bench that you used for leg extension. With your legs extended, hook your heels under the movable bar. Slowly pull the bar with your heels toward you until the knees are at ninety degrees. Then slowly return the weight to the starting position for one repetition.

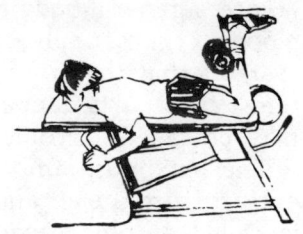

Leg Flexion

9. *Upright Rowing (requires special apparatus):* Hold the weight in both hands (palms facing down) in front of your body with arms extended. Your hands should be together in the center of the bar. Without using any leg muscles and without leaning backward, lift the weight up until your hands touch under your chin. Return the weight slowly to the starting position for one repetition.

Upright Rowing

TRAINING FOR CARDIORESPIRATORY ENDURANCE—
AEROBIC CAPACITY

The endurance needed for sustained periods (one minute or longer) of vigorous exertion, as in running, swimming, or cycling, is quite different from the muscular endurance we have just talked about. The latter depends mostly on the condition of the muscle fibers, whereas general body endurance depends on an adequate blood-oxygen supply to all the involved muscles. Living systems that require oxygen are defined as "aerobic" systems, and sports demanding sustained general endurance may be called "aerobic sports."

The maximum amount of oxygen that an athlete can extract from the air and transport to his working muscles is called aerobic capacity. As you might have already guessed, mother nature assigns your aerobic capacity the day you are born. Those athletes possessing high aerobic capacities will naturally perform better in sports requiring endurance or "good wind." Proper training techniques (discussed later) can improve aerobic capacity by 15 to 30%, depending on initial fitness level and genetic limit.

In a laboratory, aerobic capacity is measured by having an athlete breathe through a snorkel-style mouthpiece while running on a motor-driven treadmill. The expired air from the athlete is collected and analyzed to determine the amount of oxygen absorbed for each exercise intensity. The athlete continues with the test until he becomes exhausted and needs to stop. Toward the end of this treadmill test, there comes a point when a further increase in workload does not produce a further increase in oxygen uptake. This point is defined as maximal oxygen uptake, the single best measure of an athlete's endurance capacity. Even a well-motivated athlete will last only a short while on the treadmill after reaching maximal oxygen uptake.

To train for aerobic capacity, coaches formerly advocated continuous, moderate-intensity exercise over long distances. Studies have shown, however, that repeated short stints of moderate to high-intensity exercise bring just as good results. This is now called interval training. Although no one method is best for all, it appears that the most "fool proof" training program for aerobic capacity consists of repeated three to five minute bouts of exercise requiring an oxygen uptake that is 80 to 90% of maximum.

What you will need to know is the oxygen level at which you are exercising, in terms of percentage of your maximum oxygen uptake. How can you determine it without elaborate laboratory equipment? A simple technique has been developed that requires only a stopwatch (a wristwatch with a large second hand will do).

The first thing that you must know is that heart rate and oxygen uptake increase proportionally during large muscle dynamic exercise like running. This means that when heart rate is at its lowest level, oxygen uptake is also

Handbook for the Young Athlete

at its lowest level, and when heart rate is high, oxygen uptake is also high. Heart rate and oxygen uptake levels correspond so closely that we can estimate one by measuring the other—you can estimate what percent of your maximum oxygen uptake level you are exercising at by knowing your heart rate. If heart rate is at 75% of maximum, oxygen uptake is also at about 75% of maximum.

Before you can determine the oxygen level at which you are exercising, you must determine your maximal heartbeat rate. This is done by measuring heartbeat rate after heavy exercise. Locate the surface artery in your neck or in your wrist, as pictured in Figure 2-1, and gently feel for the pulses of blood. Each pulse is a heartbeat. Using your watch, count the number of pulses you feel in ten seconds and multiply this value by six; this will give you your resting heart rate in terms of beats per minute (BPM). Normal resting heart rates range from fifty to eighty BPM.

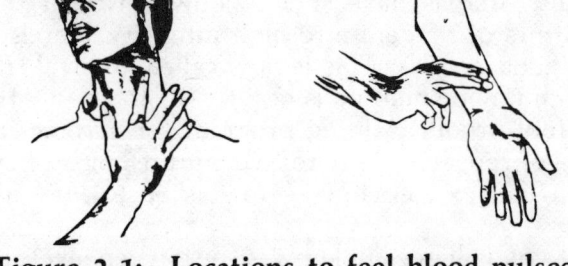

Figure 2-1: Locations to feel blood pulses for the measurement of heart rate. (Heart rate = beats per 10 seconds x 6.)

When you have mastered the technique of measuring heart rate, you are ready to determine your *maximal* heart rate. This can be done at the peak of or immediately after intense activity that has been performed at an intensity that produces limiting fatigue within two to six minutes, such as a ¼ or ½ mile run.

Test to determine maximal heart rate

> Step One — Get a wrist watch with a sweep second hand or a stop watch and go to your local track or a large field.
> Step Two — Perform some leg stretching exercises and jog slowly at an easy pace for several minutes or so to warm up.
> Step Three — When you feel well warmed up, begin running at a pace you think you can continue for the next two to three minutes. When you reach a point where you feel you cannot run much longer, prepare to slow down and count your heart rate.
> Step Four — Slow down and while still walking briskly, immediately take a ten-second pulse count (your heart will quickly slow down so be sure to do this immediately).
> Step Five — Multiply this ten-second count by six to determine your maximal heart rate (10 sec. count ____ x 6 = ____ your maximal heart rate).

Your maximal heart rate may be as low as 180 BPM or as high as 210 BPM, or somewhere in between.

Since heart rate and oxygen uptake increase proportionally, by determining what percentage of your maximum heart rate an exercise produces, you will know what percentage of maximum oxygen uptake (or aerobic capacity) the exercise requires. First, find your maximum heart rate on the left column of Figure 2-2. Next, perform heavy exercise, such as running hard for three to four minutes. Stop and immediately take your pulse for ten seconds. On the same row as your maximal heart rate, find the ten-second heart rate that you just achieved. The figure at the bottom of that column will tell you the percent of maximum. For example, if your maximum heart beat rate is 195, and your heart rate per ten seconds after heavy exercise is 26 beats, then you have exercised at 70 to 80% of your maximum heart rate level. This means that you have exercised at approximately 70 to 80% of your maximum aerobic capacity. If your exercise program calls for 80 to 90% of maximum, you then know that you must exercise at a greater intensity (for example, running faster or up a hill).

Maximum Heart Rate (BPM)	Beats Per 10 Seconds		
204–209	25–27	27–29	29–31
198–203	24–26	26–28	28–30
192–197	23–25	25–27	27–29
186–191	23–24	24–25	25–26
180–185	22–23	23–24	24–25
% Maximum:	60-70%	70-80%	80-90%

Figure 2-2: Ten-second heart rates: Percent of maximum.

You will find opposite a specific, aerobic training program, consisting of six progressive work levels. In general, working out three to four times each week will improve your aerobic capacity up to your genetic limit. Workouts of two to three times each week are necessary to maintain capacity.

Aerobic Training Schedule—Running or Swimming

Level	Work Description	Repetitions	Intensity	Total Time
Aerobic I	5 min. work – 5 min. recovery*	3	60–70%	30 min.
Aerobic II	5 min. work – 5 min. recovery	4	60–70%	40 min.
Aerobic III	4.5 min. work – 5 min. recovery	4	70–80%	38 min.
Aerobic IV	4 min. work – 4 min. recovery	5	70–80%	40 min.
Aerobic V	3.5 min. work – 4 min. recovery	5	80–90%	38 min.
Aerobic VI	3 min. work – 3 min. recovery	6	80–90%	36 min.

*During recovery period you should not totally rest, but continue to exercise at an easy intensity (walk slowly, cycle slowly, hang on pool edge and tread slowly, etc.)

The aerobic training program applies equally to males and females, and you can use running, cycling, swimming, or jumping rope for it, depending on which is closest to the movements of your sport. Be sure to measure heart rate after each exercise interval and adjust your exercise intensity to stay within the prescribed intensity limits.

You will soon discover that running or swimming speed is not directly related to work intensity. That is, you can run at about 50% of maximum speed and still achieve 70 to 90% of maximum aerobic capacity.

Before you start your workout, you may want to go through a three-minute test period of your training activity to discover the pace required to achieve the proper heart rates.

TRAINING TO IMPROVE FLEXIBILITY

An athlete should be concerned about good joint flexibility for three reasons: (1) to improve fluidity of motion, (2) to help prevent muscle or connective tissue injury, and (3) to reduce muscle soreness and stiffness. The need for fluid motion varies among athletic events; in some sports it is all-important. A high hurdler depends on his flexibility, and shoulder and ankle flexibility are essential for the competitive swimmer, particularly for short speed races.

After a muscle is vigorously exercised, it will remain in a partially contracted state for up to forty-eight hours. That is much of the cause of post-game muscle stiffness and tightness. The muscle has less elasticity and is actually shorter. This problem can be reduced considerably with proper stretching exercises before all practice games. These exercises "loosen" the muscles and connective tissue, and ready them for the upcoming action, often preventing a pulled muscle or a torn tendon.

There is a growing belief among respected coaches and trainers that stretching immediately *after* exercise as well will reduce the amount of muscle stiffness and virtually eliminate muscle soreness. The highly successful track coach of UCLA, Jim Bush, is one who demands complete flexibility routines both before and *after* each workout or meet. He knows that sore leg muscles decrease motivation and can dull performance.

Of all athletes, the track competitor probably has the greatest problem with tight muscles because of the tremendous amount of running required virtually every day. But stretching exercises can be important for all athletes who experience muscle tightness.

You can stretch muscles and gain flexibility in one of two ways: either with repeated bouncing or jerking motions, or by holding a stretched position for a few seconds (static stretching). Studies have shown them to be effective, but because bouncing often produces muscle soreness, the static method is recommended. To perform static stretching, slowly lengthen the appropriate muscle until the first signs of muscle tightness (or "pull") appear. Hold this position for five seconds and then slowly return to the starting position. This is defined as one flexibility repetition.

The basic training principle of specificity clearly applies to flexibility exercises: stretch those muscles that are used in competition. The following flexibility routines are designed to prepare all the major muscle groups used in most athletic events and training sessions. You are encouraged to perform these simple exercises completely, both before and after each workout. Your coach may point out other, more specific, flexibility routines. Feel free to include them in this general flexibility program.

Flexibility Routine Important: When stretching a muscle, do not bounce, jerk or otherwise force the movement. Move slowly until you feel the muscle pull, then hold for three to five seconds.

1. *Trunk Rotation:* With hands on hips and feet about shoulder width apart, twist to the right as far as you can and then twist to the left as far as you can (one repetition). Perform fifteen to twenty repetitions.
2. *Shoulder Rotation:* Extend the right arm and move it

around in the largest circle possible. Complete ten circles with the right arm and then ten circles with the left arm. Return to the right arm and repeat ten circles in the opposite direction. Do the same with the left arm.
3. *Side Stretch:* Place hands behind head and spread your feet wide apart (about three feet). Keeping your legs straight, lean sideways until you feel your muscles pull. Return to the starting position and lean to the other side. Return to starting position, all for one repetition. Perform ten repetitions.
4. *Hamstring Stretch:* With feet together and legs straight, lean forward until you feel your hamstrings (muscles in the upper back leg) pull. Hold this position for three to five seconds, and then stand up straight for one repetition. Perform ten repetitions.
5. *Quadricep Stretch:* Hold your right foot with your right hand behind your body (hold a chair or table with your left arm for balance). Pull your right foot up toward your back until you feel the quadricep (muscles in the upper front thigh) pull. Hold this position for three to five seconds, and then stand on both feet for one repetition. Perform ten repetitions. Perform ten repetitions with the left quadricep muscles.
6. *Calf Muscle Stretch:* Place your right foot about three feet behind your left foot with both feet pointing forward. Keeping your right heel on the ground, bend your left knee and lean forward until you feel the calf muscle (muscle in the back of the lower leg) pull. Hold this position for three to five seconds, and then release the tension for one repetition. Perform five repetitions. Repeat five more repetitions with the left calf muscle.

SPECIALTY TRAINING

A varsity cross-country runner may be able to run continuously for one to two hours, and yet find himself completely breathless after fifteen minutes of full-court

Training to Improve Your Athletic Fitness

basketball play. This is an example of the training principle of specificity. The runner's physiology is finely tuned for long, moderate-intensity workouts but is completely out of sync with the repeated all-out exertions demanded in basketball. Leg muscles in the distance runner are adapted for energy efficiency and contain larger than normal amounts of glycogen (muscle sugar stored for fuel—see pages 115-121 for a description of glycogen in terms of nutrition). In contrast, the basketball player's muscles are chemically adapted to his needs: he can endure repeated short bouts of maximal effort with little intervening time to "catch his breath." Most sports require at least some short, high intensity bursts. Therefore, practically all athletes should include specialty training in their total program of physical training.

The best form of specialty training is repeated all-out sprints lasting ten to thirty seconds each, with a three to five minute rest between each work interval. Specialty training is not designed to "burn out" the athlete, but rather, to train his muscles to withstand repeated high intensity work comfortably, without fatigue. Because the work periods are short and the rest periods relatively long, the heart rate may never reach maximum levels. You should try to maintain *body speeds* of 90 to 100% of your maximum.

Specialty training is difficult and requires a high degree of motivation. Thus, the above techniques are recommended only for the two month pre-season training period. Specialty training is introduced about midway into this period and should be increasingly emphasized up to the time official practice begins. The descriptions of each exercise are below and a weekly schedule is found in the pre-season training schedule, page 71.

The basic exercise modes for specialty training are running and swimming (if your major sport is swimming). You are encouraged, however, to develop your own specialty training drills; ones that precisely imitate your own competitive moves. Because straight-ahead running is common to so many sports, specialty drills using running

Handbook for the Young Athlete

will often be effective. A sample list of specific drills that can be used for specialty training is presented below. Use this list as a guide in developing your own drills specific to your sport and position.

Specialty Training—Pre-Drill Exercises

1. Flexibility routine, pages 63-64.
2. Two-minute run at 30% top speed.
3. Three-minute run at 50% top speed.
4. Ten five-second intervals of all-out running in place—lift knees as high as possible.

Specialty Training—Running or Swimming

Level	Performance Time	% of Top Speed	Recovery Time	Repetitions	Total Time
1	15 sec.	90–100%	5 min.	5	21 min.
2	15 sec.	90–100%	4 min.	8	23 min.
3	15 sec.	90–100%	3 min.	5	
	30 sec.	90–100%	5 min.	3	28 min.
4	15 sec.	90–100%	3 min.	5	
	30 sec.	90–100%	4 min.	5	31 min.

Suggested Specialty Drills for Selected Sports

Note: Your specific sport "moves" may only last a few seconds. If it is impossible to imitate competition-like actions for fifteen to thirty seconds, develop longer runs that combine moves or special footwork.

Football: A receiver (or defensive back) may practice long "down" patterns or string two or three short patterns together.

Training to Improve Your Athletic Fitness

Basketball: Full court speed dribbling with a lay-up at each end of the court. Conclude each thirty-second drill with a fifteen-foot jump shot.

Baseball: (a) All-out base running initiated with a bat swing and terminated with a slide. (b) Have a friend hit two to four fly balls continuously, about forty yards apart. The object is to keep moving for thirty seconds and to catch the balls.

Tennis: (a) Practice shadow tennis. First rush in to the net to retrieve a drop shot, and then run back to hit an overhead. Repeat continuously for fifteen to thirty seconds. (b) Have a friend at the net with a bucket of balls. Work on wide baseline shots alternating forehand and backhand.

Soccer: Play one-on-one the full length of the field, where the defensive man does not try to steal the ball. Upon reaching the end of the field, attempt a goal shot.

YEAR-ROUND TRAINING PATTERNS

Because of the world's keen interest in sport, the world of the once serene amateur athlete has changed dramatically—his achievements can bring him personal renown and win great respect for his country. This has caused tremendous pressure in sport competition and resulted in much more sophisticated training techniques. No longer can the athlete expect championship performance with just a few months of training and competition each year. Today, most world class athletes train throughout the year.

A few professional sports, like golf and tennis, have year-round seasons, so the athlete is constantly training and competing. But most sports, at both professional and amateur levels, have definite seasons of four to six months followed by long periods with no competition. Psychologically, it is impossible for an athlete to maintain a top competitive edge in the absence of competition.

Therefore, year-round training strategies for seasonal sports must be flexible to ensure peak physical condition for the season, and provide adequate training, without boredom, during the off-season.

There are four distinct training periods during a seasonal athlete's year. These require four distinct programs: pre-season (the months immediately before official team practice), the competitive season, immediate post-season, and off-season. The remaining sections of this chapter will be devoted to showing you the physiological basis of training, and setting out specific training programs for each of these four periods.

Figure 2-3 shows a comparison between the athletic fitness of a champion athlete and a non-athlete during one year. The 100% level is that of an outstanding athlete. The first important point to note is the basic difference in condition between the athlete and the non-athlete even during the off-season—a sign of the athlete's genetic superiority and generally more active life style. Next, we see that the good athlete comes into the pre-season period at 80% of top athletic condition and attains almost the full additional 20% during the following two months.

After official team practice begins, and for the remainder of the season, it is imperative for the athlete to keep himself in top condition. The post-season is a time for physical rest. Athletic condition declines rapidly, but the psychological benefits of resting far outweigh any negative aspect. By abstaining from his major sport for one to two months, the athlete feels rewarded for the past six months of hard work. Soon he will tire of inactivity and hunger once again for the excitement of competition. The post-season is the time when motivation is restored—crucial for top performance in the upcoming season.

The three to four months between the post-season and the pre-season are defined as "off-season." This is a period where training has to be delicately balanced; too much will destroy the desire for action, whereas too little will fail to bring the athlete up to the season at the important 80% of optimal condition.

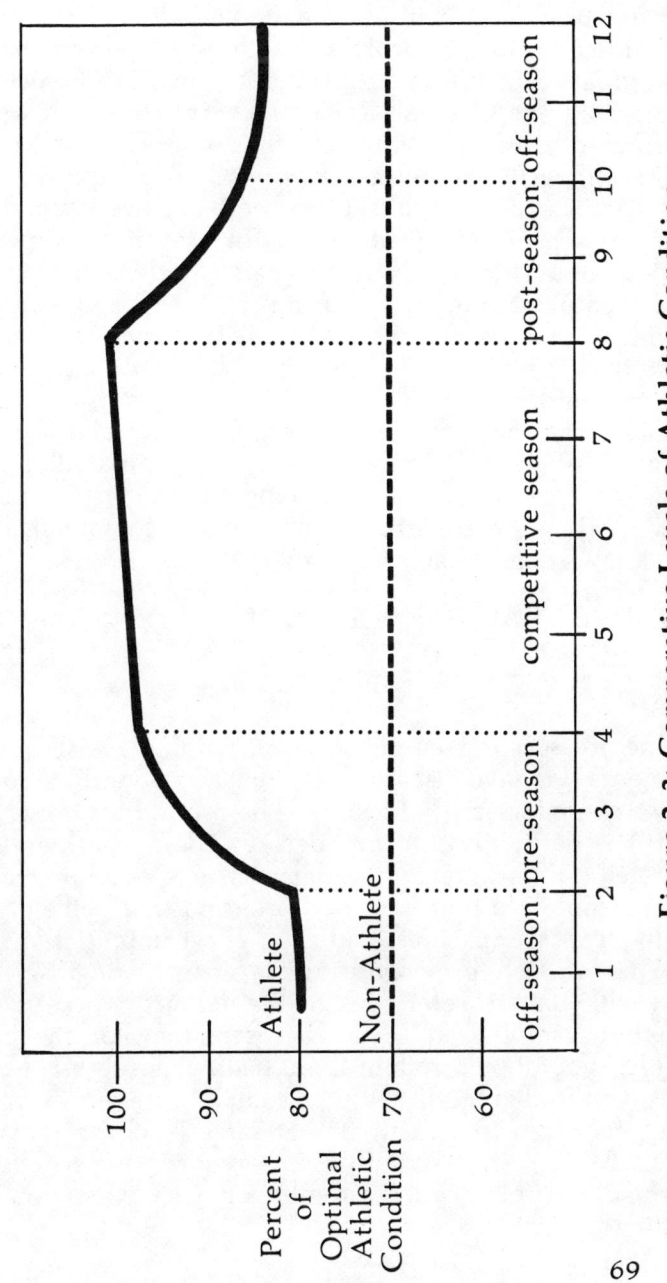

Figure 2-3: Comparative Levels of Athletic Condition during One Year.

It has been our fortune over the years to evaluate the athletic condition of professional football players from such great teams as the Los Angeles Rams, San Francisco 49'ers, and the Oakland Raiders. The tests, which were performed at various times during each year, confirmed the training pattern shown in Figure 2-3. When questioned about their training habits, these football players said that the post-season is indeed a time for rest and a time to forget about football. But they also told us that they remained physically active during the off-season, participating in moderate to heavy intensity activities such as basketball, tennis, and racquetball. Then two to three months before the start of training camp, most of them would start their own intensive physical training programs. Usually these programs were self-initiated on the basis of experience. These outstanding athletes have discovered the same basic training patterns recommended by the knowledgeable sport scientist.

ANNUAL TRAINING SCHEDULE

Pre-Season

The pre-season training schedule emphasizes all of the elements we have discussed: flexibility, strength, aerobic capacity, and specialty training. The program is not easy, and it is definitely not intended for the non-athlete interested only in "staying in shape." The pre-season training schedule is a high-powered program that will elevate your physical capacities to their highest potential levels.

What we have provided below is a composite program. You will want to refer back to the detailed workout descriptions set out in the earlier sections. For the best results, you should follow the schedule closely. If, however, you find great difficulty in completing some exercise level, feel free to remain at that same level for another week. Moreover, if something interrupts your schedule, like an illness or vacation, drop back a week when you re-enter the program.

Pre-Season Training Schedule

Week	Mon	Tues	Wed	Thur	Fri	Sat	Sun
1	Flexibility Aerobic I	Flexibility	Flexibility Aerobic I	Flexibility	Flexibility Aerobic I	Flexibility	Flexibility Aerobic I
2	Flexibility Strength I	Flexibility Aerobic II	Flexibility Strength I	Flexibility Aerobic II	Flexibility Strength I	Flexibility Aerobic II	
3	Flexibility Aerobic III	Flexibility Strength II	Flexibility Aerobic III	Flexibility Strength II	Flexibility Aerobic III	Flexibility Strength II	Flexibility Aerobic III
4	Flexibility Strength III	Flexibility Aerobic IV	[Flexibility Strength III [Flexibility Specialty I	Flexibility Aerobic IV	[Flexibility Strength III [Flexibility Specialty I	Flexibility Aerobic IV	
5	Flexibility Aerobic IV	[Flexibility Strength IV [Flexibility Specialty I	Flexibility Aerobic V	[Flexibility Strength IV [Flexibility Specialty I	Flexibility Aerobic V	Flexibility Strength IV	Flexibility Specialty II
6	Flexibility Aerobic V	Flexibility Specialty II	[Flexibility Strength V Aerobic V	Flexibility Specialty II	Flexibility Strength V	Flexibility Aerobic VI	Flexibility Strength V
7	Flexibility Specialty III	Flexibility Aerobic VI	Flexibility Specialty III	Flexibility Strength VI	Flexibility Aerobic VI	Flexibility Strength VI	Flexibility Specialty III
8	Flexibility Strength VI	Flexibility Specialty IV	Flexibility Aerobic VI	Flexibility Specialty IV	Flexibility Strength VII	Flexibility Specialty IV	Flexibility Strength VII

One final note: You should not neglect your sport skill training completely during the pre-season. As explained earlier, physical training is particularly important during this time, but basic sport skills should be maintained at a "familiar" level. At most, the required pre-season workouts last one hour each day. You are encouraged to set aside an additional three to four hours a week to practice specific sport skills.

COMPETITIVE SEASON TRAINING

If you check back to Figure 2-3, page 69, you will see that the two month, pre-season training program leaves you at the beginning of official practice at 90 to 100% of top physical condition. The following one to two months of team practice should provide the last refinements in conditioning that will ensure that you are at your absolute peak.

In most cases, especially with first string players, active competition combined with intervening practice sessions will provide more than adequate physical training. But what about the athlete who is not getting regular playing time because of illness or mid-season vacation, or because he is a second or third-string player, or in a poor league schedule? Assuming no other significant source of exercise, what is the minimal amount of training necessary to maintain top athletic fitness?

A scientific study was conducted in hopes of answering this important question. An athlete trained daily on a stationary bicycle for two months, bringing his aerobic capacity to peak levels. He was then able to maintain a high percentage of this peak aerobic capacity by reducing his workouts to two times a week. The investigators concluded that exercise should be performed three to four times a week to improve aerobic capacity and that two to three times a week was sufficient for maintenance. We recommend aerobic training at level six, two to three times a week to maintain aerobic capacity during the competitive season.

Training to Improve Your Athletic Fitness

Other aspects of physical conditioning require minimal exercise time during the season to maintain top levels. The flexibility routines can be completed in five to ten minutes, but they should become as much of a daily habit as brushing your teeth. Specialty training should be performed at level four at least three times per week. Muscle strength will usually be maintained through the vigorous workouts of competition. For extra insurance, however, you may wish to perform Strength Training Program A (level 7) or Strength Training Program B (weights set at 75% maximum), one to two times per week.

In summary, the athlete generally gets sufficient exercise during the competitive season to maintain the capacities previously achieved. However, flexibility exercises should be maintained on a daily basis and if the athlete is not getting enough playing time—providing at least two to three days of vigorous exercise a week—he should reactivate his physical training. And this supplemental training is critical for the second or third string athlete, who sees little competitive action yet wants to be ready to perform at his best when he does get a chance.

POST-SEASON TRAINING

The one to two months following the last game or meet of the year constitute the post-season period. For athletes participating in seasonal sports, this is a time to rest and be rewarded for the past six months of hard exercise. Figure 2-3 shows that in the absence of any physical training, condition regresses rapidly toward the 80 to 70% level of fitness. Many "hard line" coaches would shudder at a training philosophy that allows you to decondition. However, to force training year-round without any competitive stimulus can be psychologically damaging. Sport play and exercise would become boring, making the athlete stale and dull, and possibly affecting next year's performance. Two months away from competition or strenuous training will rest the athlete and leave him yearning for more competition. This mental attitude is necessary for good practices and for good athletic performance.

If deconditioning is distressing to you, try other sports to keep yourself active. Two to three days a week of moderate to heavy exercise will help retard the deconditioning process. Remember, the training protocol during the post-season calls for mental rest and relaxation. Make this your goal whatever you do.

OFF-SEASON TRAINING

The off-season training period includes the three to four months between the post-season and pre-season. As we said earlier, it must be delicately balanced: too much training will dull desire, and too little will provide insufficient conditioning. The primary objective of the off-season training program is to maintain an 80% level of peak fitness, where you want to be at the start of the two month pre-season program. If you are below 80%, it will be too difficult to reach your optimal level in two months.

During this period, then, you should exercise two to three times a week; it is important that these sessions be evenly spaced through the week. Training three days in a row with no activity for the next four days will not work. Common off-season training schedules call for exercise on either Monday-Wednesday-Friday or Tuesday-Thursday-Saturday. A good rule of thumb is to never have more than two or three days in a row without training.

Off-season training should be diversified, and moderate to heavy in intensity. If you want to use the pre-season training program, stay with levels one and two for the strength and aerobic programs (do not forget to include frequent flexibility workouts). Do not be concerned with specialty drills at this time; they are meant exclusively for the pre-season program. Participation in your major sport or in other sport games like basketball, tennis or soccer are encouraged for off-season training. Other activities that provide good training effects include swimming, bicycle riding, and racquetball.

three

Food for Sport

Nathan J. Smith

NUTRIENTS: THE BASIC BUILDING BLOCKS

Athletes make special demands of their bodies, and must be physically prepared to meet those demands. The starting point is sound nutritional knowledge and practice. Yet dedicated competitors, who will sacrifice so much to excel, often ruin their chances with inefficient, sometimes harmful diets. Reduced stamina and strength take their toll, and the effects on performance are clear.

With some basic knowledge of food, and how it supplies the body's needs, it is usually a simple matter to reverse the situation; the athlete who has competed at a disadvantage can in fact become the one with the advantage.

Foods And Nutrients

In physiological terms, food satisfies three fundamental body needs: (1) the need for energy, (2) the need for new tissue and tissue repair, and (3) the need for chemical regulators of the metabolic functions constantly taking place in the body. These three needs are provided for by specific components of food called "nutrients." There are six classes of nutrients, each with very precise chemical characteristics and each suited to meet very specific body needs. The six classes are: water, minerals, vitamins, proteins, fats, and carbohydrates.

Water Water is the most "essential"[1] of all nutrients inasmuch as it takes priority over all others in the need for a constant and uninterrupted supply. But because it is abundantly available and essentially free of cost, it is easily overlooked.

Minerals Mineral nutrients are considered in two groups: those present in relatively large amounts, and those needed in very small amounts (the "trace" minerals). The first group—all available in the foods we eat—are sodium, potassium, calcium, phosphorus, magnesium, sulfur, and various chlorides.

Sodium and potassium are widely distributed throughout nature, and in abundant supply in all foods. Sodium is the chief metallic ion in body sweat, and a significant amount may be lost in profuse and protracted sweating. Under any but the most extreme circumstances, however, the sodium lost in sweat will be readily replaced through the sodium content of the normal diet. In fact, given the usual abundance of salt in the American diet, the concern should be for too much, not too little.

Potassium plays an essential role in the function of muscle cells, and a deficit of potassium is associated with muscular weakness and fatigue. Fruit juices, bananas,

---

[1] "Essential" nutrients are those the body cannot synthesize. They must, therefore, be provided by food intake.

apricots, soybeans, and potatoes are excellent sources of potassium. Along with sodium, it determines the amount of water held in the tissues. This is an important factor in athletic performance and will be more fully discussed later.

Calcium, phosphorus, and magnesium are present in the body in relatively large amounts. Milk and milk products are the main sources of calcium and phosphorus. A variety of plant foods, such as broccoli, spinach, and other leafy greens, can provide calcium. Phosphorus and magnesium needs can be met by whole wheat cereals, red meats, and certain vegetables, such as kidney beans and lentils.

There are at least fourteen trace minerals that must be ingested by humans. Although the amounts required are relatively small, the need is very real. Iron, iodine, and fluorine are particularly important. Fluorine is essential for healthy dental and bone formation. In many parts of the United States, the concentration in water is very low, and adding fluorides to community water supplies has greatly improved dental health by reducing dental caries.

Iodine is obtained primarily from water supplies; and in certain areas in the United States, the level of iodine concentration in the water is very low. These areas once had widespread problems such as "goiter," but because of the general use of iodized salt, iodine should no longer be a problem.

Zinc is a trace mineral which many nutritionists believe is particularly important. It is required for normal growth, tissue repair, blood cell formation, and reproductive function, and may not be present in adequate amounts in the small diets of inactive people. Whole grains and most meats are the principal sources.

Iron is the trace mineral present in largest amounts in the body. Frequently athletes do not get enough, and it is particularly important for them because a shortage hurts energy production and reduces endurance. Iron-rich foods—such as meats, meat substitutes, leafy vegetables, dates, and raisins—should be a regular part of any diet.

Vitamins Vitamins function as chemical regulators, and are necessary for growth and the maintenance of life. Because they are needed in such small amounts, they were the last "essential" nutrients to be discovered. Contrary to popular belief, active people eating a variety of foods generally get all their bodies can use.

In fact some of them are required in such small amounts (vitamin E, pantothenic acid, and biotin), that even the most irregular and poorly selected diets provide sufficient amounts.

Vitamin C and the B-complex vitamins are soluble in water and thus are not stored to any significant degree in the body; therefore, the diet must constantly replenish the supplies. The daily requirement for vitamin C can be met with the natural sources of leafy vegetables, most raw vegetables, and citrus fruits. Sources for the B vitamins are listed in the accompanying table. If one does not get enough of the water-soluble vitamins, problems will develop after a few weeks. When intake is greater than body needs, the excess is excreted in the urine.

Excess fat-soluble vitamins (A, D, E, and K) are stored in the liver and, to a lesser extent, in the fatty tissues of the body. If stores have accumulated during a period of excess, one may get along on too little for many months, even years.

Vitamins are widely distributed in the foods that make up the typical American diet and, as a rule, are eaten in proportion to the total caloric intake. Therefore, people eating the generous amounts called for in times of growth and active exercise will be receiving an adequate supply of nearly all the vitamins. Vitamin C and folic acid (a member of the vitamin B group) are exceptions. The foods in which they are found in highest concentration are foods which make minimal contributions to caloric intake. In order to provide these vitamins, an uncooked or lightly steamed vegetable or some fresh fruit should be included in the daily diet.

Vitamin Functions It is important for the athlete to under-

VITAMINS: DIETARY SOURCES AND PRINCIPAL FUNCTIONS

Fat-soluble Vitamins

VITAMINS	SOURCES	FUNCTIONS	DEFICIENCY STATES
Vitamin A (Provitamin A)	Liver, egg yolk, milk, butter (Vitamin A) Yellow vegetables, greens (Provitamin A)	Adaptation to dim light Resistance to infection Prevents eye and skin disorders	Night blindness Xerophthalmia (softening of eye structures—blindness)
Vitamin D	Sunlight, fish, eggs, fortified dairy products	Facilitates absorption of calcium	Rickets
Vitamin E	Vegetable oils, greens	Prevents oxidation of essential vitamins and fatty acids	
Vitamin K	Greens, liver	Blood clotting	Hemorrhage disease

Water-soluble Vitamins

VITAMINS	SOURCES	FUNCTIONS	DEFICIENCY STATES
Thiamine (B_1)	Meat, whole-grain cereals, milk, legumes	Energy metabolism Formation of niacin	Beriberi
Riboflavin (B_2)	Milk, fish, eggs, meat, green vegetables	Energy metabolism	Mouth and lip lesions and loss of vision

VITAMINS	SOURCES	FUNCTIONS	DEFICIENCY STATES
Niacin	Peanut butter, whole-grain cereals, greens, meat, poultry, fish	Energy metabolism Fatty acid synthesis	Limitation of energy production Pellagra
Pyridoxine (B_6)	Whole-grain cereals, bananas, meats, spinach, cabbage, lima beans	Protein metabolism Hemoglobin synthesis Production of energy from glycogen	Convulsions Anemia
Folic Acid (Folacin)	Greens, mushrooms, liver	Blood cell production, growth	Anemia
Cobalamin (B_{12})	Animal foods	Blood cell production Energy metabolism Central nervous system function	Pernicious anemia, neuro-muscular weakness
Ascorbic Acid (Vitamin C)	Citrus fruits, tomatoes, strawberries, potatoes, papaya, broccoli, cabbage	Formation of supporting tissues particularly in capillaries Metabolism of vitamins; i.e., folic acid	Scurvy

stand what vitamins do, and particularly what they do not do. Vitamins function primarily as regulators, governing the hundreds of biochemical reactions involved in organ function, growth, and energy metabolism. *They do not contribute significantly to body structure nor are they a direct source of body energy.* Thus, the vitamin needs of an active athlete are generally no greater than those of the most sedentary individual—and the unfortunate tendency toward taking excess vitamin supplements for athletic performance is a real problem.

One B vitamin, thiamine, is an exception, since it is required in proportion to carbohydrate intake (and very active athletes as a group may be expected to eat more carbohydrate). Fortunately thiamine is also present in primary carbohydrate sources, such as breads and other foods made with whole-grain or fortified grain products. It is thus abundant in the typical American diet.

No one food contains sufficient levels of all the vitamins needed by man, but a varied diet selection from different groups of food provides an adequate supply and eliminates any need for supplements. After infancy vitamin supplements are needed only by those with very specific disease-related health problems, or by those who, for any reason, have been deprived of an adequate diet for a prolonged period of time.

Vitamins and minerals do not contribute significantly to the bulk of the diet. It is mainly composed of water and the remaining three classes of nutrients: fats, carbohydrates, and proteins. These provide the body's energy and contribute the structural components for growth and tissue repair.

Fats Fats are essential in our diet. They are greasy substances, not soluble in water. They are the most concentrated source of food energy, containing twice as many calories per unit of weight as either protein or carbohydrate. They are, therefore, uniquely well suited for storage of excess energy.

Fat adds palatability to our food, and is often abundant

in foods desired for flavor; as a result, it is easy to get an excess. The well-marbled steak, the whipped cream on the strawberry shortcake, the lemon butter brushed over the broiled salmon, and the sour cream on the baked potato are all foods high in fat. They are eaten because "they taste good." But fat is not only flavorful, it also has a high satiety value. Some of the feeling of satisfaction and fullness after a fine dinner is due to the fact that fatty foods leave the stomach slowly—an important concern in planning pre-game meals.

Fats may be "visible," as when surrounding an expensive steak, or dressing a salad with oil. Other forms may not be so apparent, but nonetheless contribute significantly to fat intake: in the marbling of the steak between the meat fibers, the oil and salami in the pizza, the avocado slices on the salad, the chocolate in the dessert, and the margarine or butter used in an unending variety of foods.

Carbohydrates The most efficient (and generally the most inexpensive) sources of food energy are the plant-source sugars and starches which comprise the group known as "carbohydrates." The sugar in carbohydrate food provides the most efficient and readily available source of energy. Fats are a more concentrated energy source, appropriate for long-term storage of energy. But the conversion process involved in energy utilization is more complicated, and consequently the energy is not so readily available. (Protein is the least efficient energy source.)

The simple sugars from digested carbohydrates are absorbed from the intestinal tract and taken via the bloodstream to the liver, where they are converted to glucose. Much of this glucose then reenters the bloodstream and is transported to body tissues, principally the brain and muscles. A relatively small amount is converted to "glycogen," a form of carbohydrate which is readily stored in either the muscles or liver. (The importance of glycogen

Food for Sport

storage, as an important source of energy in athletic performance, is discussed later.)

In addition to supplying the muscles and brain, glucose must be constantly transported to other vital organs, such as the heart and kidneys. The constant glucose supply, particularly to the brain, is essential for an optimum sense of awareness and for the quick reflexes necessary for top athletic performance. An inadequate supply of glucose, particularly to the central nervous system, results in feelings of weakness, hunger, nausea, and dizziness.

It is important to note that this primary source of energy, carbohydrate, cannot be stored in significant amounts by the body. An average well-nourished man has only enough glucose and glycogen in his bloodsteam and tissues to meet his energy demands for about half a day of sedentary activity. This should come as no surprise to the student who has missed breakfast and lunch and can recall the symptoms of glucose depletion he felt by late afternoon. He probably felt hungry, unable to concentrate and lethargic. Since the body cannot store significant amounts, it is obvious that an active person should take some form of carbohydrate at regular intervals throughout the day. A very large, active athlete may function best with occasional high carbohydrate snacks in addition to the contribution from the regular daily meals.

There was a recent case of a college freshman basketball player whose afternoon practice performance had been deteriorating. He was found to be in good health and his eating habits were not unusual. He was living in a dormitory, where he regularly ate a large breakfast before going to class at 8:30 and a generous lunch three hours later when the dining room first opened at 11:30. He would have nothing more to eat until the evening dinner hour.

It was apparent that he was exhausting his energy stores midway through the afternoon practice session, and was lacking endurance and unable to concentrate. He was advised to eat a sizable high carbohydrate snack just

SOME PRINCIPAL NUTRIENTS: THEIR SOURCES AND FUNCTIONS

Nutrient	Rich Sources	Functions
Protein	Meat, fish, eggs, legumes, nuts, and cereal	Growth and repair of tissue Synthesis of hormones, antibodies, and enzymes Milk production during lactation Energy source (expensive and inefficient)
Fats	Oils, margarine and butter, well-larded meats, mayonnaise and salad dressing, nuts, chocolate, and peanut butter	Concentrated source of energy Efficient storage of energy Carriers of fat-soluble vitamins (A, D, E, and K) Satiety value Flavor
Carbohydrate	Cereal grain products, sugar and honey, pastries, dried fruits	Economical and efficient energy source Flavor

Important Minerals

Calcium	Dairy products, green leafy vegetables, legumes	Bone formation Enzyme reactions Blood coagulation

Iron	Liver and lean meats, soybeans, dried fruits	Hemoglobin formation Muscle growth and function Various energy-producing enzyme systems
Zinc	Shellfish, oysters, grains, and meats (fruits and vegetables are poor sources)	Growth Blood cell production Tissue healing Enzyme reactions Reproductive functions
Fluorides	Water supplies, plants and animal tissues (depending on water supplies)	Formation of teeth and bones
Iodine	Fresh seafoods, water supplies in certain regions, iodized salt	Production of thyroxine
Water	All beverages, foods (vegetables and fruits), water	All bodily chemical reactions Excretory function Cooling function

before the dining room closed at 2:00 p.m. The new diet schedule with the added midday intake allowed him to maintain a sense of well-being throughout the afternoon practice sessions. His performance improved and he played varsity basketball during his freshman year.

Foods That Provide Carbohydrate for Energy Americans now eat more than one hundred pounds of common table sugar, or "sucrose," each year. Most sugar-rich products are relatively expensive.

Less expensive but still readily available sources of carbohydrates come from the starches contained in cereal grains such as wheat, rice, and corn. Bread, spaghetti, pies, waffles, pancakes, doughnuts, etc. are made primarily from wheat flour and contribute wheat starch as a common source of carbohydrate. Potatoes, beans, and various kinds of tuber or root foods are dietary staples throughout the world. Fresh and dried fruits also contribute significant carbohydrate in the form of sugar.

Leafy vegetables, like lettuce and cabbage, and stem vegetables like celery are high in "cellulose," a large, complex carbohydrate, which represents roughage in the diet. Cellulose is generally not digested by man and therefore contributes no usable energy; but it does provide important bulk to the diet.

Many of the dietary contributors of carbohydrates, such as bread, spaghetti, and pastry, are relatively inexpensive, and there is a popular notion that they are of low nutritional value. In fact they are important sources of energy and highly desirable for active sport participants. Carbohydrate from such cereal grain products, along with other sources, should contribute well over fifty per cent of the athlete's total calories.

Proteins The last of the six major classes of nutrients is protein. Throughout most of the world, protein is in short supply, and there are various American myths about protein superiority as a food. Actually high-quality protein is abundantly available to most Americans and they generally get far more (two or three times as much) than their bodies need.

To be sure, some protein is essential in our diet. But in general, proteins are inefficient sources of energy, and are used for energy only when the more efficient sources, carbohydrates and fats, are not available.

Sources of Protein Protein is generously available in nature, both in animal tissue and in the seeds (grains) of plants.

Although most Americans, and particularly active athletes, place a high priority on animal protein, one does not have to look far to find large numbers of people, even champion athletes, who are meeting their protein needs from predominantly vegetable sources. A varied diet limited to vegetables, grains, and fruits can very adequately meet human needs for protein. The needs will be met somewhat less efficiently when there is no animal protein in the diet, and larger amounts of vegetable protein will be needed. But just a small amount of animal protein added to a predominantly vegetable diet will enhance the protein efficiency of the vegetable proteins in the diet. A large number of people take advantage of this fact by adding egg, or cheese, or other dairy products to an otherwise strictly vegetarian diet, and thus satisfy their protein needs with a so-called "lacto-ovo-vegetarian diet."

Protein Requirements of the Athlete It is important for athletes to recognize that their athletic activity, even though vigorous, will not significantly increase their need for protein. Growing young athletes have significant protein requirements, but it is in direct proportion to their needs for other essential nutrients. If they eat a varied and widely selected diet—adequate to meet their needs for energy, the essential vitamins, minerals, fatty acids, etc.—they will get all the protein they can use.

Excess protein, particularly animal protein, should be avoided. Foods such as meat, whole milk, eggs, and most cheeses tend to be expensive, and often are high in fats. In addition, they are an immediate handicap to athletic performance because they contribute to dehydration. More about that later.

THE BASIC DIET

Haphazard eating habits exact their toll eventually. At some point almost all athletes run into problems which better food choices might have prevented: insufficient stamina, difficulty concentrating, impaired strength, and unwanted weight loss (or gain), etc. And their immediate solutions are not highly specialized diets, but a well-balanced diet.

In truth, there is no *one* diet for the athlete. Every sport makes individual energy demands that call for specific dietary plans. But there are nutritional essentials common to all such diets. This section discusses those essentials and how they constitute a "Basic Diet."

The Importance of a Well-Balanced Diet

The importance of an adequate diet was recently dramatized by the experience of a high school junior. John was an all-around performer: he was a member of the cross-country team, vice-president of the student body, and an excellent student. However, by the end of the fourth week of cross-country training, his running performance had notably deteriorated and he had lost eight pounds. He was 6'2" tall, weighed 147 pounds, and his estimated body fat composition was 6 percent of his total body weight (a very low level).

John would start the day with an hour's running before school, leaving him with no time for breakfast. His brown bag lunch consisted of a sandwich, an apple, and occasionally some cookies, all or part of which frequently did not get eaten because of his busy schedule. Returning home to dinner after a strenuous afternoon workout, he had little appetite, and what he did have was further dulled by parental urging to "eat a good dinner." His most significant and regular food intake came at night while doing his homework: typically, a peanut butter sandwich and milk.

His weight-loss problem was easily explained. A growing sixteen-year-old boy cannot run ten miles every day and participate as a highly effective student on the energy and nutrient intake provided by such an unpredictable and casual diet. He, like many athletes, needed to know what constituted an adequate diet, and he needed to know the priority a good diet deserved.

Specific recommendations for John were relatively simple. He was told the importance of "walking himself down" at the end of each run, providing continuing muscle movement after intense exercise. This would enhance

Food for Sport

his recovery from fatigue and help restore his appetite. And he would be expected to have more interest in his evening meal if dinner were delayed for thirty or forty minutes after his arrival home.

The advantages of eating breakfast were discussed, but it was apparent that a sit-down breakfast at home was not in the realm of reality. Instead, a small can of fruit juice or a piece of fruit was added to his lunch bag, along with a breakfast roll or additional sandwich to be eaten between classes during the morning. His lunch was expanded, and an extra dessert was provided before the mid-afternoon workout. The evening meal consisted of generous servings of whatever the family was having for dinner; this, together with his earlier eating, provided all the essential nutrients. The balance of his energy needs were satisfied by late-evening snacks.

During the early weeks of school John's caloric intake had been erratic, as low as 1500 Calories per day. After two weeks on the new diet plan it had increased, to as much as 4500 Calories per day. He felt energetic, was running better, and had gained four pounds. (Later in the season he was instructed on how to modify his normal diet in preparation for performing in district and state cross-country meets.)

John's experience is all too common. There are few teams without at least one or two members with such problems—deteriorating performance and accompanying weight loss. The solution must begin with the personal schedule of the athlete.

The starting point for sound diet planning may be called a Basic Diet. It is based on a system for choosing foods from different food groups, and is known as the Four Food Group Plan.

THE FOUR FOOD GROUP PLAN

The Four Food Group Plan can readily be used to advantage by athletes. It has almost limitless flexibility and is particularly well suited to the American food supply.

Each of the four food groups is composed of common food items that have been grouped together because of the common nutrient contributions they make to the diet. The four food groups are:

1. Milk and Milk Products
2. Meat and High-Protein Foods
3. Fruits and Vegetables
4. Cereal and Grain Foods

The Milk and Milk Products Group Each adult should receive the equivalent of two servings from the milk group each day—either drunk directly as a beverage, included in the preparation of other foods, or as alternate milk products (such as cheeses and ice cream). It may be desirable for some adolescents to have as many as three servings, depending on their age, growth rate, and the food choices that make up the remainder of their diet.

With all its virtues, milk can be drunk to excess. Young athletes drinking more than two glasses of milk each day would be well advised to drink skimmed, fortified milk.

The Meat and High-Protein Food Group This group includes meat, fish, poultry, eggs, and such alternate vegetable items as dried beans, peas, and nuts. Two or more servings from this group should be eaten each day. (A basic serving of meat is 3.5 ounces of the edible portion of the meat, a delicate serving for many hungry athletes.)

Because of concern over the saturated fat content of many meats and meat products, a "prudent" diet for Americans would limit intake of red meats to three or four servings per week, and eggs to three or four per week. The remainder of the week's servings from this group should come from fish, chicken, and high-protein vegetable alternates such as beans, peas, and nuts.

Fruit and Vegetable Group As the name indicates, this group consists of fruits and vegetables, including the potato; they are generally highly nutritious. Four or more servings of fruit and vegetables should be included in the daily diet.

The Cereal and Grain Group Bread, cereals, flour, and baked goods are relatively inexpensive carbohydrate sources of energy. They also contribute protein, minerals, and a number of vitamins. (Whole-grain cereal and cereal products, if prepared with enriched flours, provide significantly larger amounts of vitamins and minerals.)

Most people have little difficulty getting the recommended four daily servings from this group.

THE BASIC DIET PLAN

The recommended daily servings from the Four Food Groups are then: two servings each from the milk group and from the meat and protein-rich foods group, and four servings each from the cereal group and the fruit-and-vegetable group. These servings will of themselves supply essentially all necessary nutrients (except the exceptional iron needs of young women), no matter how large the athlete or how rigorous the training program. But such a Basic Diet will *not* meet the energy (caloric) needs of a moderately active athlete, even a small one.

What foods should be added to satisfy the needs for additional energy? Once the needs for essential nutrients have been satisfied, there's ample room for individual choice. An old axiom holds true: "First eat what you need and then eat what you want."

Most athletes respond by making their servings from the Four Food Groups much larger than the so-called "normal" servings. They also eat second and third helpings. The word of caution is to limit the intake of animal fat. When high-calorie density foods (such as desserts) are used, the athlete should turn to items made with vegetable shortenings, to sherbets, and to milk drinks such as shakes and malts (which are usually made with fat-free dairy solids).

Lastly, the importance of water must be emphasized

again. Available in abundance in this country, water is often overlooked as a most essential part of a daily diet. Yet few things can compromise athletic performance as effectively as an inadequate intake of water. Participation in even moderate exercise demands a minimum of a quart of fluid for every 1000 Calories of food. For a moderately active young person expending 3000 Calories per day, approximately three quarts of water are required. A large, very active athlete may need two to three times as much. The problem can become critical in warm and humid weather. It is therefore essential that the athlete develop water-drinking habits; soft drinks and milk are inadequate substitutes.

NONTRADITIONAL DIETS AND DIETARY SUPPLEMENTS

Can an athlete perform well on a meatless diet? We know, from the experiences of many cultures over the centuries, that meat is not a dietary essential. Vegetarian diets can and do support good health and active exercise if selected with proper care. But in recent years, rigidly restricted diets have been advocated which have been the cause of real nutrition problems.

Vegetarian and Other Meatless Diets

A very small number of people in the world eat a true vegetarian diet, restricted completely to fruits and vegetables. More commonly milk and milk products are also eaten in a so-called "lacto-vegetarian" diet. If eggs are included (a "lacto-ovo-vegetarian" diet), there is an even wider choice of foods to meet nutritional needs. The addition of milk and eggs is a particular advantage when the total amount of food eaten is limited, as in the diets of inactive young women.

Anyone living on a meatless diet should follow a variant of the basic food selection principles described earlier with respect to the Basic Diet, i.e., the daily selection of food

ADDITIONAL SUGGESTIONS FOR NON-MEAT EATERS

Use a combination of beans; this will improve protein value. Add cooked beans to salads and soups; mash and combine with cheese for sandwich or taco filling.

Also eat a variety of cereal grains, for one protein complements another, increasing the value of both.

Four large mushrooms give ¼ of a day's allowance for niacin; slice them raw in salads.

One cup of prune juice supplies 55% of an adult woman's RDA for iron.

Sesame seeds can be made into candy squares. Prepare a thick syrup of brown sugar, margarine and water, add seeds, let cool and cut.

Eat sunflower seeds as a snack. They are a good source of protein and vitamins.

Brown sugar, honey, and syrup add calories and small amounts of minerals.

Sprinkle brewer's yeast, a vitamin B-complex source, in soups and cereals.

Add wheat germ to cooked cereal or sprinkle it over other foods. One-half ounce (2½ tablespoons) contains approximately three grams protein, plus iron and niacin.

from designated food groups. The following shows a food group plan for the lacto-vegetarian diet, based on six food groups of vegetables, fruits, and milk and milk products. Eating one to three daily servings from each of these food groups will satisfy essentially all nutritional requirements.

As indicated in relation to the Four Food Group Plan, some young women may not satisfy their needs for iron, unless their energy demands are unusually large and they take several servings of selected vegetables and fruits rich in iron. Young women with greater than normal iron demands, because of menstrual iron losses, often will require a medicinal iron supplement.

As with the Basic Diet, the meatless Six Food Group Diet is designed to provide essential nutrients, but it does not necessarily satisfy the energy needs of an active individual. These needs can be more easily met with the use of certain meatless supplements—such as salad oils, nuts, and nut spreads—that have high caloric density.

There is one essential nutrient which is available only in food of animal origin. Unless milk, milk products, or eggs are included in the meatless diet, there will be no source of vitamin B_{12}. When this vitamin is lacking for a period of many months, anemia and muscle weakness may develop. A relatively small amount of milk, cheese, or eggs will satisfy the normal need for vitamin B_{12}.

Daily Food Groups for Lacto-Vegetarian Diet

I. *Fruit Group*   Include daily three servings:

At least one serving of citrus or other fruit rich in Vitamin C.

¼ cantaloupe ½ cup orange juice
½ grapefruit 1 cup red raspberries
½ cup grapefruit juice 1 cup strawberries
1 orange 1 cup tomato juice

Food for Sport

At least one serving of fruit rich in iron.

½ cup dried uncooked apricots
¾ cup dates
7 large dried figs
½ cup dried uncooked peaches

¾ cup cooked prunes
½ cup prune juice
¾ cup raisins
¾ cup dried cooked peaches

II. *Vegetable Group*   Include daily three servings:

At least one serving (½ cup) green or yellow vegetable.

Beets greens, cooked
Carrots, raw
Collards, cooked
Kale, cooked

Pumpkin, canned, cooked
Mustard greens, cooked
Spinach, cooked
Squash, winter, baked

At least two ½ cup servings of other vegetables. Some suggestions:

Bean sprouts
Beets
Broccoli
Brussels sprouts
Cabbage
Cauliflower
Celery
Cucumber
Eggplant
Green beans

Lettuce
Macaroni
Mushrooms
Noodles
Onions
Potato
Rice
Spaghetti
Tomatoes
Turnips

III. *Milk Group*   Include daily three servings of milk and milk products:

1½ oz. American cheese
1 cup buttermilk
½ cup cottage cheese, creamed
2 cups ice cream
1 cup milk (skim, low-fat or whole)
1 cup plain yogurt made with low-fat milk

IV. *Peas and Beans* Include daily at least one serving
(½ cup):

Fresh:

Black-eyed peas   Lima beans
Green peas   Sprouted mung beans

Dried:

Black-eyed peas   Soybeans
Great Northern beans   Split peas
Lima beans   Red kidney beans, canned
Navy beans

V. *Nuts* Include daily at least one serving (½ cup) of nuts or peanut butter:

Almonds, shelled whole   Pecans, shelled halves
Cashew nuts, roasted   Walnuts, black
Peanuts, roasted

VI. *Breads and Cereals* Include daily at least three servings of bread (1 slice/serving) and cereals (¾ cup/serving).

Can an athlete compete optimally on a meatless diet? He can, as long as he follows the rules laid down above, choosing from a wide selection of foods each day, and, if the diet includes no foods of animal origin, adding a periodic supplement of vitamin B_{12}. Several world class athletes have competed very successfully on such meatless diets.

NONCONVENTIONAL DIETS THAT WILL NOT WORK

Several recently popular diets limit food choice to one or two food groups, and therefore exclude many essential nutrients. Perhaps the best known is the Zen Macrobiotic Diet. It involves a series of ten diets, progressing from the lowest level, minus 3, which allows 30 per cent animal products, to the highest level, 7, which consists entirely of cereal and restricted amounts of fluids. Not surprisingly, disciples of this diet have developed a whole spectrum of nutritional problems, from mild starvation to death. Such extreme dietary practices among young athletes usually call for medical (and perhaps psychiatric) consultation.

Less immediately threatening is a Fruitarian Diet, which is limited to raw and dried fruits, nuts, honey, and olive oil. These foods are highly nutritious, but they do not contain all essential nutrients. And athletic performance (as well as general health) will suffer, if specific provision is not made to supply missing nutrients through a broader selection of vegetables and grains.

Now and then a question arises regarding the advantages of periodic fasting. Fasting limited to twenty-four or forty-eight hours need not be damaging to a healthy individual, but an athlete cannot expect to compete effectively if he is deprived of energy sources for such periods during his training. There is no evidence to suggest that periodic fasting provides any competitive advantage.

It is obvious from what has been said that good health and top athletic performance do not require a "traditional" diet. But basic needs must be met. And this is best accomplished by following a food group guideline, and thereby eating foods which supply essential nutrients and sufficient energy.

Organic Foods Growing interest in nutrition, new diets, and food safety has prompted a widespread use of so-called "organic" and related "health" foods. Of course all foods are organic in a chemical sense, but the term "organic food" is now commonly used to mean foods grown and processed without the use of "chemicals." Proponents claim health, flavor, and ecological advantages.

There is no sound scientific evidence that either taste or nutrient quality of food is affected by the nature of the fertilizer used in its production. And although eating adventures with so-called "health" or "natural" foods may add interest to the diet, there is no justification in terms of nutrition or safety; there is no need to part from conventional food sources.

Weight Control Diets Millions of dollars are spent in the United States each year on schemes alleged to insure quick and effortless loss of weight. Most of them say nothing about increasing exercise. They simply recommend bizarre and severely restricted diets. Nutritionally, they are grossly inadequate. The only saving grace is that their potential harm is limited by their unattractiveness; most often people can't stay on them long enough to develop serious nutritional deficiencies.

A book published in 1972, *Dr. Atkins' Diet Revolution*, has been used by some athletes in attempts to lose weight. Dr. Atkins' diet allows an unrestricted intake of calories from protein and fat, and in fact encourages a high intake of saturated fats and cholesterol-rich foods. Carbohydrates are rigidly restricted. This very unusual diet is particularly hazardous for the athlete and warrants particular mention.

Metabolizing a large amount of fatty acids will produce ketosis, which in turn can produce fatigue, dehydration, nausea, and alterations in heart rate, and can contribute to dehydration. Physically active people are most susceptible. Several groups of high school wrestlers have tried to control their weight with Dr. Atkins' diet, jeopardizing their health and athletic performance.

VITAMIN SUPPLEMENTS

It has been said that American athletes have the most expensive urine in the world. The reason is their tendency to use massive doses of vitamin supplements which far exceed their needs. The water-soluble vitamins that the body cannot use are rapidly excreted in the urine. (As pointed out below, fat-soluble vitamins taken in mass are retained in the body.)

Is there a need for vitamin supplements in the diet of

the competitive athlete? The answer is no, not if the diet includes a proper variety of foods. Nevertheless, the widespread use of such supplements by well-nourished American athletes has reached ridiculous proportions.

Take the recent example of a varsity crew in intense training for the rowing season. All the oarsmen weighed over 200 pounds, all were over six feet tall, and all were eating at a training table. During the training period, they each consumed between 5000 and 6000 Calories per day. Their diet was ample, professionally supervised, and actually contained several times the amount of vitamins and protein their bodies could use. Yet each of the oarsmen was taking five different nutritional supplements each day. More than once a day each took a high-potency multi-vitamin capsule, a rose hips vitamin C capsule, a "High Energol" capsule, a vitamin E capsule, and a vitamin B-complex capsule. The supplements were completely worthless and represented (over the season) several hundred dollars of needless expense.

A disturbing level of nutritional ignorance supports the market for such things as the "High Energol" capsules, taken, as the name implies, for energy. According to the label, the recommended dose of six capsules each day provides a total of 84 kilo-calories. This is equal to the energy contribution of a small glass of Coca-Cola and less than that of a piece of buttered toast.

Not only are the supplements worthless, they can conceivably prove harmful. The fat-soluble vitamins (A, D, E, and K) provided by the multi-vitamin capsule cannot be excreted in the urine and are instead stored in body fat, principally in the liver. Over a significant period of time, this build-up of excess vitamins can produce serious toxic effects, particularly through an accumulation of vitamins A and D.

Vitamin supplementation is often abused by athletes under the misconception that if a little is good, more will be better. As mentioned earlier, vitamins function in regulating metabolic body processes; they do not contribute energy. Increasing energy demands and energy expenditure does *not* increase the demand for vitamins (with the exception of thiamine, which is adequately supplied in the normal diet). To put it simply, a large, active man does not require significantly more vitamins than a small, sedentary woman.

As stated earlier, a diet providing no more than 1200 to 1500 Calories, if properly selected from traditional American foods, will provide all the vitamins and protein anybody needs.

Vitamins E and C Two vitamins deserve special consideration since they are commonly taken as supplements in very large amounts. The first of these is vitamin E. In an earlier chapter it was pointed out that certain of the vitamins, including vitamin E, are required in such minute amounts that even the worst of diets ordinarily supplies all the body can use. Yet millions of people, and especially athletes, spend enormous amounts of money on vitamin E capsules, solutions, fortifiers, skin lotions, etc.—all unnecessary and useless. Supplements of vitamin E do *not* increase stamina, do *not* improve circulation or delivery of oxygen to muscles, do *not* lower blood cholesterol, do *not* prevent graying of hair, and, perhaps of most interest, do *not* enhance sexual potency or cure infertility.

Vitamin C is also commonly taken in large amounts. The Basic Diet supplies the very generous RDA of this vitamin, and accordingly, supplementation is not needed by anyone on a well-selected diet.

PROTEIN SUPPLEMENTS

Hoping to increase body size and strength, many athletes have been attracted to high-protein diets and concentrated protein supplements. This blind belief in protein goes back well before the advent of modern nutritional science. The theory persists today. The use of high-protein diets, supplemented by high-protein drinks and powders, is widespread among certain groups of athletes, even though their diets ordinarily contain three or four times what the body needs for optimal performance.

It is worth repeating that the Basic Diet provides abundant protein. In addition, many foods preferred by athletes as energy supplements to the Basic Diet, particularly dairy products, soy products, and nuts, contain large amounts of high-quality protein. There are drawbacks to uncontrolled protein intakes in the diet, in addition to the needless expense. It is the least efficient source of energy; and, as mentioned earlier, high-protein diets are dehydrating because they demand large amounts of water for urinary excretion of the metabolic by-products. When taken in excessive amounts, protein supplements may also cause loss of appetite and diarrhea.

Typical of many of the popular protein supplements is a product called "Super 96 Protein," which one conscientious football player took while attempting to gain weight. Instead, it ruined his appetite and produced severe diarrhea, resulting in actual weight loss. The label of Super 96 Protein indicates that it contains animal protein from, among other sources, "undenatured liver, pancreas, heart, spleen, mammary, ovarian and testicular substance." This long list of slaughterhouse refuse certainly has no place in the diet of any individual, especially a healthy athlete trying to maintain a good appetite and a sound level of hydration.

GAINING OR LOSING WEIGHT

Conceptually, nothing could be more simple than gaining or losing weight. To lose weight, you have to expend more energy (calories) than you ingest. Gaining weight requires just the opposite. It all seems an easy matter of energy balance. But if that's true, why the difficulty?

Weight problems among athletes are common, and with a better understanding of the principles involved, they can be solved. This can't be done with the sudden starvation or glutting that so often precedes the ceremonial march to the scales. Weight-change programs must be carefully planned and developed from a clear recognition of how and why the body loses or gains weight. A basic understanding of energy, and its relationship to body input (food) and output (energy expenditure), provides an excellent starting point.

How Energy Is Measured

The energy sources in food, as well as the body's energy expenditure, are conventionally measured in units of heat expressed as "calories." This is a very small unit of heat, and when dealing with energy in food and in human energy expenditure, a more suitable unit is the kilo-calorie. One kilo-calorie is equivalent to 1000 calories; and common usage has been adopted in this book, with "Calorie" (with a capital "C") referring to the kilo-calorie.

The Body's Use of Energy

Man gets his energy in chemical form, through the food he eats. It is utilized to meet a variety of body needs, including physical work and the physical activity associated with athletic performance.

Man's Energy Expenditure

When we are completely at rest and have not eaten for at least twelve hours, we are using energy only to keep internal organs functioning and to maintain body temperature. This so-called "basal" energy expenditure, or "basal metabolism," goes on day in and day out, throughout the entire twenty-four hours of the day. And in order to maintain a given weight, our energy intake (from food measured in calories) must equal our basal energy expenditure *plus* that expended through physical activity.

The basal energy needs of a man six feet tall and weighing 175 pounds are approximately 1800 Calories a day. His age, sex, size, and his degree of fatness, all influence his basal rate. Since fat tissue is metabolically much less active than muscle and organ tissue, a muscular person

Food for Sport

will expend more energy when at rest than a person of the same weight with a larger proportion of body fat. As a result, women (with a larger percentage of fat) generally have a lower rate of basal metabolism. The effect of age on basal metabolism is also important. There is a significant decline in basal energy expenditure with increasing age. Consequently, a person with very large energy and food needs during adolescence may have rather modest needs when middle-aged.

ENERGY EXPENDITURE IN VARIOUS SPORTS

In estimating total energy needs, we must add to the basal energy expenditure the calories that are used up in various forms of physical activity. The size of an individual and the speed and vigor with which the activity is

RECREATIONAL ENERGY EXPENDITURE[1]
(in Calories per minute)

Sitting—bridge	1.5-2
Walking level (3 mph)	3-5
Canoeing (4 mph)	3-7
Volleyball	3-10
Playing with children	3.5-10
Cycling (13 mph)	4-11
Golf	5
Archery	5
Dancing	5-7
Swimming	5-10
Tennis	7-10
Touch football	7-10
Squash	10-12
Cross-country	10-15
Skiing	15
Climbing	11-12
Running (10 mph)	18-20

[1] Astrand, P.O., and Roclabl, K., *Textbook of Work Physiology* (New York: McGraw-Hill, 1970), p. 439.

pursued all affect the amount of energy expended. For example, a 187-pound man walking at two miles an hour may burn approximately 200 Calories in an hour's walk. If he walks a brisk four miles an hour, his caloric expenditure will double to nearly 400 Calories in the same period of time. A larger man walking at the same rate will expend more, a small man less.

The preceding table shows approximate energy expenditures for a variety of activities. Since two individuals may expend greatly differing amounts of energy while participating in the same game, this table can give only rough estimates.

THE ENERGY CONTRIBUTION OF VARIOUS FOODS

Each gram of fat contributes about 9 Calories of energy. Each gram of protein contributes only about 4 Calories of effective energy (the same as for carbohydrates). Alcohol is absorbed completely, and each gram contributes 7 Calories of energy.

The 9 Calories per gram of fat represent the most concentrated form of food energy. In practical terms, 3500 Calories of energy, the amount that may be needed daily by an active young athlete, would be found in almost a full pound of pure fat. Recognizing this fact, the fraud of the high-energy capsules, often marketed specifically for athletes, becomes quite obvious. Since one teaspoon of fat weighs approximately 5 grams, it contributes no more than 45 Calories. Assuming that a high-energy capsule weighed 5 grams (certainly gargantuan for a capsule), its caloric contribution would also be 45 Calories. And that is the energy available from about half of a typical cola drink.

The athlete with high energy demands may find it helpful to include in his diet generous amounts of fatty foods. This is particularly true for the young competitor in energy-demanding sports, like basketball, soccer, and distance running, who can reduce the total bulk of his diet by including larger amounts of fat and still meet his energy needs. Margarine, nuts, and nut-spreads such as peanut butter and vegetable oils all add concentrated calories without an unnecessary addition of bulk or saturated animal fats.

As indicated, carbohydrates provide 4 Calories of energy per gram, less than half that of fats. Nonetheless, starches and sweets may contribute a lot of calories to the diet and are often considered "fattening." They do provide a significant amount of energy, because they are made from refined carbohydrate sources like table sugar and highly milled flour. They also have minimal water and fiber content, and are, therefore, relatively concentrated sources of calories. Popular desserts like pies, cakes, and pastries, which are customarily thought of as being carbohydrate foods, actually contain large amounts of shortening, which is fat and accounts for much of their caloric contribution. Other carbohydrate foods, like spaghetti, noodles, potatoes, and rice, contribute fewer calories, unless eaten in very large amounts or in combination with fatty foods.

Certain vegetables, such as celery, lettuce, and cabbage, contain large amounts of carbohydrate in the form of cellulose, but provide very little energy. Humans cannot digest cellulose, and it only adds bulk to the diet. In fact, foods high in cellulose are excellent for people who must restrict their caloric intake. But, because of their high bulk and low caloric content, they are inefficient for those who have high energy demands.

As mentioned earlier, protein is the least efficient of the three energy sources in the diet. Although protein provides 4 Calories of energy per gram, the manner in which it is metabolized greatly reduces the availability of the energy it supplies.

Alcohol is a poor source of energy under any circumstance. It has a depressing effect on the central nervous system, has a dehydrating influence, and must be converted into glucose by the liver before its energy can be made available for muscle work. It's important to recognize that the conversion of alcohol to glucose takes place very slowly. Muscles cannot use alcohol as a direct source of energy. And the practice of exercising to hasten the metabolism of alcohol ("walking off" an intoxicating dose) is of no help and may actually be dangerous.

ALTERING ENERGY BALANCE

Food energy taken in excess of that required for basal metabolism and physical activity must be stored, usually as fat. One pound of fat represents a storage of about 3500 Calories of energy. Lean body tissue, such as muscle, represents approximately 2500 Calories of potential energy.

These estimates are very approximate, but they can be useful in diet planning. For example, *to gain one pound in the form of muscle mass, an excess of approximately 2500 Calories will be needed. To lose one pound of fat, on the other hand, approximately 3500 Calories of energy must be expended in excess of that taken in the diet.*

Gaining Weight For many athletes, gaining weight is a real and difficult problem. There are obvious contact sports, such as football and hockey, where added weight is often valued. But the problem of gaining or maintaining weight is rather widespread. In swimming and basketball, for instance, where training and competitive seasons are long and arduous, many athletes have difficulty reaching or maintaining their "ideal" weight, to the detriment of their performance.

The difficulty is often one of underestimating just how many calories are required by the active competitor, in terms of the kinds and quantities of food which must be eaten. When one thinks of "fattening" foods, something like beer or potatoes comes to mind. These foods provide considerable energy, but they will not help an athlete gain weight, because they are not high in caloric density—bulky in relation to the number of calories they represent.

Take the recent experience of a young man who decided

to gain weight by drinking beer. Every evening he managed to get down about fourteen bottles of beer. Yet in spite of the popular images of beer-bellied folks in Milwaukee, he was not gaining weight. As a matter of fact, it was an inefficient way to get his calories. He was burning up approximately 6000 Calories a day; and the 1700 Calories represented by the beer (which eliminated his appetite for the day) were clearly not enough.

The amount of energy expended by a typical young male athlete in training, up to as much as 5000 to 6000 Calories per day, represents the energy contribution of a large diet. If he is trying to gain weight, his caloric intake must become very significant indeed. At a rate of 2500 Calories per pound of muscle mass, an athlete must exceed his caloric expenditure by nearly 1000 Calories per day if he wishes to gain as much as two pounds per week (figuring five effective training days in a week). For a large active athlete, this could add up to a total requirement of 6500 to 7500 Calories per day. And that takes both knowledge of the principles involved and a well-devised diet program.

The starting place is a careful record of all food eaten for one week. By analyzing the record, the athlete can determine his regular caloric intake, which usually will be the amount necessary to maintain his present weight. Often he will be amazed to discover how great a caloric requirement he has. The food record will also show individual likes and dislikes. And these are important. As is true with any diet program, but perhaps most critically true in setting up a high-calorie diet, desired foods must be emphasized or the diet can't be maintained.

A realistic time schedule is important in any weight-gaining program. Since 2500 Calories in excess of needs are required to gain one pound of lean body weight, an active athlete, one, for example, who expends 4000 Calories a day, can gain approximately two to three pounds each week if he is able to ingest a 5000-Calorie diet. *(It is important that caloric intake not exceed expenditure by more than*

1000 to 1500 Calories per day, if accumulation of excess fat is to be avoided.)

The athlete usually wants to make sure that any added weight is primarily in lean body mass, not fat. The high-calorie diet must therefore be accompanied by a vigorous training program. This will insure that exercise is sufficient to build body muscle and that the increase in weight is not merely in the form of fat.

Promoting Weight Gain With Androgen Hormones It has been repeatedly demonstrated that the administration of male sex hormone, testosterone, and of synthetic anabolic agents such as Dianabol, will result in an increase in muscle tissue—if accompanied by a vigorous conditioning program and a high-calorie diet. There is no agreement as to whether strength, endurance, or athletic performance will be improved. In any case, these hormone agents and their derivatives are frequently used by athletes, particularly those involved in such sports as weight-lifting, football, and wrestling. In the opinion of most, diet management and training, without the use of hormones, can produce essentially the same results.

But the question of whether or not these hormones have positive effects is academic. Anyone who takes anabolic steroids before he or she stops growing will have growth stunted (through the premature fusing of the growth zones at the end of long bones). Many who take them for as long as a few weeks develop acne, deepening of the voice, excessive body hair, and enlargement of the breasts (because some of the hormones are converted to the female hormone, estrogen). And, in cases where anabolic agents are administered to males after growth has stopped, generally after the ages of eighteen to twenty, the most serious problems relate to testicular structure and function. In studies in which these agents were administered for periods of from eight to twenty-five weeks, there was uniform evidence of diminished testicular size, loss of potency, and marked decrease in sperm production.

Even after recovery from the other side effects, evidence of altered sperm production persisted.

It is obvious that the use of these hormones by healthy individuals is never justified and is contrary to the goals of any sports program. It is encouraging to note that newly developed methods for hormone detection by urine analysis are currently in use in Europe and in international competition. These methods may help bring this dangerous form of "doping" under effective control.

Losing Weight The basic principles of energy balance applicable to weight gain also govern weight loss. The elimination of one pound of body fat requires the expenditure of approximately 3500 Calories more than are consumed. 3500 Calories can represent the total daily caloric intake of an active young man. With this amount he will utilize the energy stored in only one pound of body fat, if he pursues his normal daily activities and eats nothing for an entire twenty-four hour period. (Anyone attemping this brief period of starvation will note weight loss somewhat greater than one pound because of the water excreted with the metabolic waste products of fat and protein.)

Who Should Lose Weight? The skin-fold measurements of high school boys have indicated levels of body fat averaging fifteen to eighteen percent of body weight. A level of eight to ten percent would probably be a better upper limit for a male in his late teens. It would make sense therefore for a large number of American athletes to reduce to improve their general fitness and, most particularly, their athletic performance.

Weight reduction programs are often requested by twelve- to fourteen-year-old girls who wish to participate in gymnastics, figure skating, or other sports. This particular group warrants unusual care. Some girls with relatively large skeletal frames are apt to seek weight levels which are completely unrealistic. Their excess weight loss will have to come from reduction in muscle mass, hurting their athletic performance. There is a similar danger for athletes in weight-controlled sports like wrestling, lightweight crew, and boxing, where it is too often assumed that a participant will be most effective in the lightest weight class he can possibly reach.

Planning a Weight Reduction Program A successful weight-loss program for an active athlete must involve: (1) a realistic time schedule; (2) an appropriate training program; and (3) a diet which limits caloric intake, yet provides sufficient energy to allow effective participation in training and other daily activities.

Circumstances will often dictate the rate at which weight loss can be programmed, but four pounds per week would ordinarily represent the maximum healthy rate. A loss of no more than two pounds per week is usually better. Remembering that each pound of lost fat requires a deficit of 3500 Calories, it is simple arithmetic to calculate the necessary combination of exercise and dieting required.

The energy expenditure tables for various forms of exercise often discourage the would-be dieter. He or she may lose interest upon learning that it will take several hours of bicycle-riding to expend the energy equivalent to one pound of body fat. But when viewed in the context of two one-half-hour bicycle rides each day, representing a lost pound of fat each week, twelve pounds in three months, the program becomes more appealing.

Such a program was set up recently for a promising young figure skater, in the form of a half-hour bike ride each way to and from her daily workouts. At the same time, she reduced her daily intake by 500 Calories, to a level of 1800 Calories, creating a diet deficit of 3500 Calories each week—the equivalent of one pound of fat. With the additional energy expenditure of the two one-half-hour bike rides added to the modest diet reduction, she had a caloric deficit equivalent to two pounds of fat loss per week. In little more than a month she lost ten pounds.

Attemping to create a caloric deficit through diet alone, or through exercise programs alone, is usually unsuccessful. A reduction of 6000 to 8000 Calories per week below customary intakes would essentially be a starvation diet, and few people could stay on it for long. On such minimal intakes, daily academic and training demands could not be met. Similarly, an exercise increase equivalent to 6000-8000 Calories, without added food, would be physically impossible for most people.

Most active athletes need at least 2000 Calories per day; and with appropriate physical activity, a 2000-Calorie diet can result in significant weight loss.

The importance of a reasonable time period for weight loss cannot be overemphasized. However, time is sometimes not available. The football player reducing for wrestling competition after the football season may wish to lose fifteen to twenty pounds in four or five weeks. His conditioning and weight reduction program must be very carefully supervised; and strict adherence to a well-planned diet is essential. A four- to five-week period should be the minimal length of time for losing this amount of weight.

THE ENERGY DEMANDS OF THE ATHLETE

Until recently, accepted nutrition dogma held that all athletes perform at their best on a "well-balanced" diet. However, we now know that different types of activity depend on different energy-producing systems. And considerable evidence suggests that what is appropriate food for one sport may not be best for another.

The Sources of Energy

In one sense, the body is an energy-transformer, taking in fuel and converting it to energy to build or replace its parts and to keep it mobile. This last function, actually physical exercise, requires the conversion of chemical energy into mechanical energy for muscle movement. In order to do this, the body relies on certain internal sources, which ones depending on a number of variables: how quickly the energy is needed, how strenuously the muscles must work, and how long the activity lasts. In the case of the athlete, another factor becomes extremely important—his capacity to introduce oxygen into his bloodstream and deliver it to body tissues, particularly working muscles. This has a significant influence on which energy system his body will primarily utilize, and its effect will be more clearly understood as the section develops.

In approaching the energy sources, keep in mind that the biochemical reactions which take place in the body are part of an intricate network of interlocking energy cycles. We are not certain about the precise nature of these cycles and how they interact. But we do know some simple facts: The body does not switch in and out of sequential energy systems, permanently turning off one source as it moves on to the next. There occurs rather a smooth phasing with overlapping from one energy source into another, as the energy demands increase during any given athletic event.

For the purposes of explanation, however, it is helpful to divide the energy sources into three separate categories.

The ATP-PC System The immediate source of energy for muscle work is a compound called "ATP" (adenosine triphosphate), the ultimate fuel which all muscle cells need in order to do their work. It can be called upon rapidly to meet the needs of sudden outbursts of activity in intensive, short-term exercise, such as shot putting, pole vaulting, or track and swimming sprints.

Since the body is able to metabolize ATP without the need for oxygen, the reaction is classified as "anaerobic" (occuring in the *absence* of oxygen). This is important in strenuous exercise, where the heart and lungs cannot deliver oxygen quickly enough to the muscles. Under such circumstances it is easy to see why a dashman, for instance, who may not even take a breath during a 50-yard dash, would basically depend on an anaerobic energy supply.

If the energy demands last for more than brief spurts, the muscle cells contain a high-energy back-up compound, phosphocreatine, or "PC," which can almost instantaneously provide the energy required to regenerate ATP. But within a matter of minutes of vigorous exercise the small stores of ATP-PC are used up. And the body must turn to a second line of energy supply in order to recharge the ATP-PC system.

Glycogen The second energy source is "glycogen," a storage carbohydrate found only in animal tissues, which the body makes from glucose (a simple sugar) and stores in limited amounts in the liver and muscles. When ATP-PC energy has been exhausted through exercise, glycogen can be metabolized within the muscle cells to restore ATP. Again, this metabolism is primarily carried out in the absence of oxygen, so it is also designed as anaerobic.

As will be shown, a well-designed nutrition program can supplement proper conditioning to insure maximum glycogen storage. This is very important for athletes like middle-distance runners, since glycogen is a major source of energy for heavy exertion lasting more than a few minutes. It may have even more impact in long-distance events, where endurance appears to be measurably improved when competitors' muscles are "loaded" with maximal stores of glycogen.

Fats and Carbohydrates As continuing exercise progressively depletes the stores of ATP-PC and muscle glycogen, the body increasingly resorts to a third source of energy. This last fuel comes from the "aerobic" (occuring in the *presence* of oxygen) metabolism of carbohydrates (more specifically, glucose) and fats.

Although fats can be stored in body depots in virtually inexhaustible supplies, their slower rate of metabolism makes them a less efficient source of quick energy, particularly for the casual athlete. This is not necessarily true for the highly conditioned competitor, and a prime object of conditioning is to improve oxygen-burning capacity. With intensive training the athlete can appreciably increase his or her efficiency in utilizing fat as an energy source. This is especially helpful in endurance events. It means, quite simply, that one can delay the glycogen depletion by burning fat instead. This is called "glycogen-sparing," and it appears to enhance endurance performance significantly. In the context of the strenuous exercise demanded by intensive competition, glucose metabolism makes a relatively minor contribution. The illustration on page 117 gives a graphic outline of the energy sources for various athletic events.

The Importance of Training and Diet

The illustration shows the sources of energy and when they are needed to meet the demands of muscle work in a wide range of athletic events. But one must remember that the anaerobic and aerobic systems are not entirely distinct. For that reason general conditioning programs are crucial to maximize oxygen utilization capacity, even when training for events where the exertion must be largely explosive. (The additional significance of specific muscle group training will be discussed later in the chapter.)

Diet Management for
All-out Effort of Short Duration

Getting ready for the short-term contest requires two preparatory steps: (1) Adequate nutritional intake during the days prior to the competition and (2) measures to ensure that muscle sources of ATP-PC and glycogen have not been exhausted by muscular work immediately before the actual event. During track and swimming meets, for example, where competitors are often involved in several daily events, time should be allotted between contests for

Food for Sport

PRINCIPAL ENERGY MECHANISMS IN COMPETITIONS OF VARYING DURATION

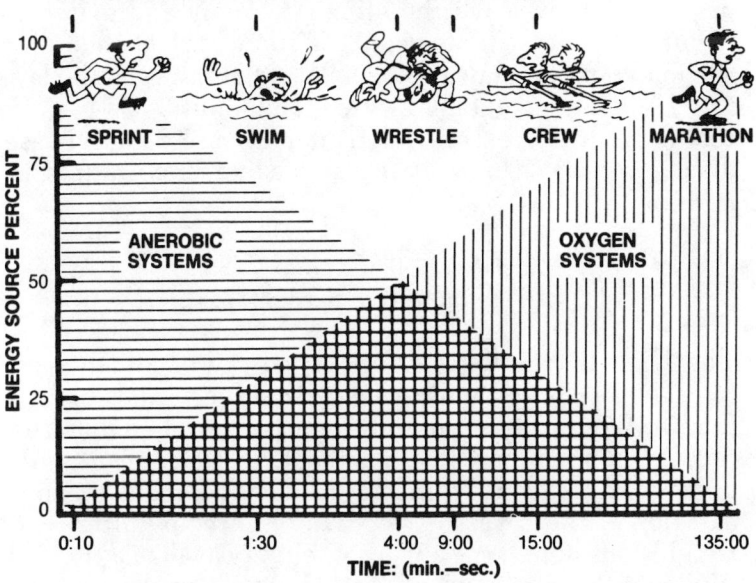

[Chart showing energy source percent vs. time for SPRINT (0:10), SWIM (1:30), WRESTLE (4:00), CREW (9:00–15:00), MARATHON (135:00), with ANEROBIC SYSTEMS dominating short events and OXYGEN SYSTEMS dominating long events.]

Source: Mathews, D.K., *Physiological Basis of Physical Education and Athletics*, Philadelphia: W. B. Saunders Co., 1976.

replenishing optimal levels of glycogen and ATP-PC. Such periods will also allow time to clear the muscles of the by-products of anaerobic metabolism, such as lactic acid. Energy depletion and the accumulation of lactic acid both contribute to fatigue.

Throughout the day of the meet, the competitors in short-term events will have particular need for an adequate supply of carbohydrate and water. Successful athletes have often met these needs by limiting food intake on the day of competition to frequent but modest drinks of fruit juices or water. Hard candies and water are preferred by some athletes, while complete liquid meals are becoming increasingly popular with others.

Many athletes value a feeling of lightness, particularly as they enter major competition. This can be enhanced by a pre-competition diet that restricts foods high in fat, in particular; they leave the stomach slowly and may contribute to a persistent feeling of fullness. Depending on the individual, it may also be helpful to limit such foods as raw fruits and vegetables, dried fruits, nuts, whole-grain cereal products, berry and fruit pies, milk, and cheese, during the days immediately preceding important competition.

MEETING THE ENERGY NEEDS FOR INTERMEDIATE LENGTH EVENTS

The High-Performance Diet A variety of athletic contests demand intense muscle exertion for periods of from four to five up to ten minutes and longer. The mile run, the wrestling match, the middle-distance swimming events, and rowing contests all demand truly maximal exertion without rest. After two or three minutes (very roughly speaking), the anaerobic energy available through ATP and PC is exhausted. And in these events, even the most highly-conditioned athlete cannot provide enough oxygen to his muscles to supply the needed energy through aerobic metabolism alone. The other potential source is stored glycogen; performance may be helped significantly, if muscle glycogen stores have been built up prior to competition.

In recent years it has been found that glycogen stores can be greatly increased when a high-carbohydrate regimen is introduced during the week preceding competition, and increasing numbers of athletes are utilizing this glycogen-loading "High Performance Diet." For many, but not all, it has proven successful in improving performance in the mid-length contests mentioned above, and also in the long-term events, like the marathon and cross-country skiing.

Assuming a six-day period of preparation, the High Performance Diet is initiated (Phase I) on the Sunday or Monday prior to a Saturday contest. For the first two and one-half days, the diet consists mainly of proteins and

The High Performance Diet
Food Groups & Daily Amounts

	Phase I	Phase II
Meat	20 to 25 ounces	8 ounces
Breads & Cereals	4 servings	10 to 16 servings
Vegetables	3 to 4 servings	3 to 4 servings
Fruit	4 servings	10 servings
Fats	8 to 9 ounces	4 to 6 ounces
Desserts	1 to 2 servings (only fruits & unsweetened gelatins)	2 servings (include ice cream, cookies, etc.)
Beverages	Unlimited (no sugar)	Unlimited (assuming proper calorie control)

fats. The essential feature of the diet is the limitation of daily carbohydrate intake. This period must accompany a vigorous training schedule, exercising the specific muscles to be involved in the competition in order to deplete their glycogen stores.

By Wednesday most athletes find that they tire easily in their workouts. Because of the glycogen depletion, they experience unusual fatigue and poor workout performance. These adverse effects on training must be recognized as the inevitable results of the low-carbohydrate phase of the diet, and taken into account in judging the limitations and advantages of this regimen.

Beginning with dinner on the third day, the athlete switches to a diet high in carbohydrate (Phase II). The diet still contains adequate protein and fat, but also unrestricted amounts of carbohydrate. The only limitation in this phase of the diet is the general restriction on both salty and high-residue foods.

The high-carbohydrate, low-salt, low-residue diet is then maintained until the day of competition. During this stage we have found that a portion of the necessary high-carbohydrate intake can be effectively provided by fruit-flavored drinks rich in glucose. These provide a high concentration of readily available carbohydrate, without the detrimental residues of bulky foods. Commercially available through pharmacies[1] and reasonably palatable, they can be taken as a supplement to the Phase II diet, up to and even during the day of competition.

Caloric needs can also be met (less expensively) by a daily quart of Kool-aid and a bag of jelly beans or raisins.

The High Performance Diet requires considerable insight and dedication. Phase I is most demanding, with its restricted carbohydrate intake during a period of intensive training. Less demanding is the high-carbohydrate, low-residue diet later in the week.

For most athletes, it is advisable to limit the High Performance Diet to important competitions. For more casual contests, a limited version can be followed, simply utilizing Phase II, the high-carbohydrate intake late in the week. This modification will be better for those who don't wish to compromise their training on Tuesday or Wednesday.

Dietary Considerations for Endurance Contests

The High Performance Diet seems particularly helpful when intensive output is required for more than ten or fifteen minutes without rest. When competition is at hand, of course, other considerations should affect the choice of diet.

On the morning of competition, athletes should avoid high-bulk and fatty foods like pancakes, fried eggs, bacon, and sausages, choosing instead such carbohydrate sources as toast or muffins with jam or honey. Lightly sweetened fruit juices throughout the day are popular. (Their carbohydrate content helps prevent hunger, but contributes only minimally to energy needs.)

---

[1]Such products as Poly-cose® (Ross Laboratories).

Food for Sport

In preparing for a lengthy afternoon competition, the best eating program will usually be a light lunch of low-residue, nonfatty foods, at least two and one-half hours before the contest. Within such limits, the athlete should eat those foods he likes and which he feels contribute to his best performance. The preferred foods should always take precedence; an athlete should eat the foods that he thinks will make him win.

Some care must be taken in choosing high-carbohydrate foods during the day of competition. If carbohydrate is taken in too concentrated a form—as in undiluted honey, glucose tablets, or syrups—it can cause stomachaches and diarrhea. The tense, nervous athlete is apt to have a poorly functioning stomach anyway, and may be particularly vulnerable to high concentrations of carbohydrate.

Diluted sweetened fruit juices, or fruit-flavored noncarbonated drinks are best. Honey-sweetened tea may produce undesirable side effects in the very young athlete who is not accustomed to caffeine; in particular, the stimulation from caffeine can be followed by depression.

A Word of Warning

Do not introduce new dietary plans or new foods shortly before an important competition: You may be inviting a last-minute encounter with an unexpected food intolerance.

The athlete should do his experimenting early in the season, not when preparing for important events, and this is particularly true of the High Performance Diet. Any foods planned for the day of competition should certainly be investigated long beforehand. On that day especially, the tense and sensitive gastrointestinal tract should not be challenged by new and strange foods.

THE ATHLETE'S NEED FOR WATER AND SALT

Obviously, no one "essential" nutrient can be more essential than any other. But the constant need for water makes it particularly important from the standpoint of time. Most essential nutrients may be absent from the diet for periods of several weeks to months without serious deficiency symptoms. Not so with water. It must be regularly available, for without it we cannot survive for more than a few days.

The Importance of Adequate Hydration

The role of water in regulating body temperature is of particular importance. The excessive heat generated by exercise must be dissipated—and the most effective way is through the evaporation of sweat. This mechanism fails to function effectively, however, if the water supply is inadequate to meet the needs of the sweat glands. (Loss of body heat by sweat evaporation will also be hampered if the body is too completely covered or if the environmental humidity is too great to allow effective evaporation.)

The Distribution and Regulation of Body Water

Daily losses of body water are relatively large, even under circumstances of moderate temperature and light physical activity. The entire mass of water (again, approximately sixty percent of adult weight) must be replaced every eleven to thirteen days. Vigorous exercise, or high temperatures and low humidity, will further increase the need for water. A normal adult in an average environment requires approximately 2.5 liters of water every day (a little more than 2.5 quarts). This water comes from the water in food, as well as from drinking water and other beverages.

Moisture loss from the skin through sweating is often obvious during exercise, but there is also a constant loss of water which is not obvious, from the normally moist skin to the less moist air. The losses of water through breathing and from the skin (without obvious sweating) are referred to as "insensible" water losses. The lower the level of humidity in the environment, and the more rapidly air is moving over the skin and lungs, the greater the insensible water loss will be.

Air travel by athletes has substantially increased in recent years. The very dry air of airplanes, combined with the rapid circulation of air in airplane ventilation, cause large insensible losses of water. In a recent case, team members taking a three and one-half hour flight in a standard commercial jet liner were found to have lost as much as two pounds, more than a full quart of body water each. Such water losses should be compensated for by increased drinking prior to and during the flight or be promptly replaced afterward. The insensible water loss from long airplane flights can contribute to so-called "jet-lag."

Regulation of body water through the rate of urinary excretion is obvious to everyone. What is much less widely appreciated is that thirst is not a sensitive indicator of the need for additional water. An athlete preparing for a contest may be suffering from a significant lack of body water and still not be thirsty. It is particularly important that a healthy supply of water be assured during the intensely emotional periods prior to competition, most effectively by precise scheduling of fluid intake. *Don't depend on thirst to tell you when water is needed.*

THE WATER REQUIREMENTS OF THE ATHLETE

Following a period of exercise and resulting dehydration the average thirst response will not in itself call for complete replacement of body water for a considerable period of time, often up to three days or more. This lag period can be cumulative. As a result, after two or three days of dehydrating workouts, water deprivation can reach serious levels. Again, the need for a prescribed schedule of water intake to maintain body weight is extremely important.

The athlete who is well conditioned and acclimatized to exercise in high temperatures will voluntarily drink more often than one who is not as well trained. The acclimatized athlete will also sweat more profusely and will thus more effectively dissipate his body heat. But even the well-conditioned athlete, who drinks more, and more nearly compensates for his water losses, may spontaneously replace only one-half to one-third of his sweat losses within twenty-four hours of a vigorous workout in warm weather.

All athletes should weigh in before and after each practice session during warm seasons or when temperatures are unseasonably high. The difference in weights before and after a practice or competition represents water loss, and the proper amount of water can be calculated.

The Athlete's Need for Salt

As mentioned earlier, sodium and potassium are widely distributed throughout the foods we eat, with sizable amounts of sodium in the common table salt (sodium chloride) used in flavoring and preserving foods. Avoiding too much salt is critical to assure optimum availability of water where it is needed during vigorous exercise. Except under extreme environmental conditions, we normally get more salt than we need. This is particularly true in the contemporary American population, where, increasingly, much of our food is pre-packaged and pre-salted.

When is additional salt needed to replace salt lost in sweating? As was pointed out earlier, specific salt replacement is rarely needed during athletic activity, even if heavy sweat loss is involved. Americans eating a varied diet generally get more than enough sodium in their daily foods to meet even the extraordinary needs of vigorous athletic activity. But as a general guideline, if the rates of water loss exceed five to ten pounds in a given contest or workout, specific salt replacement may be needed.

This replacement is best made by adding salt to the normal diet, or it can be provided by very dilute salt-containing fluids, whose concentration should not exceed 1/3 of a teaspoon per quart. (Commercially available salt-containing drinks taste good and have known salt concentrations. But they should not be used for all the water replacement, because they provide excessive concentrations of salt.) *Taking additional salt without abundant water can be very hazardous;* and the danger is greatest when a high concentration of salt is taken, as in the form of salt tablets. Many of the commercial salt-containing beverages contain potassium salts as well as sodium salts. Potassium losses in sweat are negligible, under any but the most extreme conditions, and potassium depletion is not a primary concern. Nearly all potassium ingested in the average diet is quite promptly excreted in the urine.

The Critical Role of Water in the Prevention of Heat Disorders

Life-threatening situations are fortunately rare in athletics. But nothing is more tragic than the deaths that occur each year due to heat stroke, most commonly during early-season football training. They are completely preventable and absolutely needless.

Necessary loss of body heat takes place if the environmental temperature is lower than the body temperature. It almost always is, since normal body temperature is 98.6°F. As previously indicated, the major avenue of heat loss during exercise is through heat evaporation of sweat from the skin. The athlete can, through exercise, generate considerable body heat, and he needs to dissipate that heat in order to maintain normal body temperature. Sweat evaporation from the skin surfaces is the necessary cooling process.

If the humidity is too high, and sweat merely falls to the ground without evaporating, the cooling effects of evaporation are lost. Other factors can also hamper the sweat-cooling process: inadequate supply of body water for sweating; a layer of fat underneath the skin of the obese athlete, which insulates and thus helps retain body heat; or too much clothing, interfering with the evaporation of sweat.

It is obvious that an adequate supply of water is the

most important factor in preventing heat stroke. It is easy to identify those who are at greatest risk: They are the athletes in poor condition, who are not acclimatized to high temperatures and who are apt to be obese, with thick layers of insulating body fat. The risk is greatly increased if a full uniform covers much of the skin surface.

This description most typically fits the middle lineman in the early days of late-summer football practice. His eagerness to make the team and "to get in shape" will lead him to extreme efforts; and he is apt to take faulty reassurance from the weight loss which is really dehydration. By the third or fourth day of practice, he begins his practice session having accumulated a significant deficit in body water. Further water loss limits his ability to lose body heat during practice, the sweat mechanism fails, body temperature climbs rapidly, and he is in a serious situation.

The general guidelines for prevention of heat stroke cannot be repeated too often:

1. Be concerned about the level of general conditioning before attempting exercise in hot weather.
2. Follow a well-devised plan of progressive exercise and rest while becoming acclimatized.
3. Maintain as much skin exposure as possible. In track and field events, competition without shirts can be helpful. In football, early drills in shorts and tee shirts, and later drills and competition with knit jerseys with exposed abdominal areas and no stockings, may all be advisable.
4. In early football drills, humidity and temperature may reach levels which are unsafe for any strenuous exercise. With humidity greater than ninety percent and temperatures of 84°F. or higher, practices should be postponed.
5. All athletes should begin their practice or competition well hydrated and take care to replace fluid losses with a combination of clear water and diluted saline drinks, served at cool temperatures (50 to 55°F.). Any athlete

Food for Sport

who has a persisting weight deficit of more than two or three pounds from a workout should be regarded as a high risk and excused from practice.
6. If heat stroke occurs, undress the victim and cool him with any means available: a bucket of ice water, a hose, or a cold shower. Get him to a hospital immediately. This is a true medical emergency.

IRON NUTRITION

Growth imposes extraordinary demands for iron. During the adolescent years the normally larger needs of the female system are matched by the extraordinary needs of adolescent boys for their lean mass growth. During adolescence over eighty-five percent of male growth is in lean body tissues, compared to sixty percent for the average girl. As a result, the need for adolescent boys is about the same as for the adult female.

Adolescent girls are more apt to be iron-deficient than boys. As indicated, their iron needs are comparable, but they don't eat as much food. The growing boy, requiring and usually eating a large diet, will ordinarily get enough iron. Girls, on the other hand, who are generally more concerned with their silhouettes and exercise less, tend to eat less.

Iron in the Diet

Iron is found throughout a range of animal and plant tissues, and is widely distributed in the earth's crust. Animals often meet their own iron needs by ingesting substantial amounts directly from the soil (as when pigs and wild animals "root," or domesticated animals drink from muddy pools of water). Since the sanitary American diet has had the soil washed out, we are dependent upon the iron in the plant and animal tissues themselves.

For reasons not yet clear, humans absorb the iron in animal tissues (meat, fish, and poultry) more readily than

Sources of Iron

Food	Measuring Unit	Iron (mg.)
*Liver—Pork	3 oz.	17.7
*Liver—Lamb	3 oz.	12.6
*Liver—Chicken	3 oz.	8.4
*Oysters, fried	3 oz.	6.9
*Liver—Beef	3 oz.	6.6
Dried apricots	½ cup (12 halves)	5.5
*Turkey, roasted	3 oz.	5.1
Prune juice	½ cup	4.9
Dried dates	½ cup (9 dates)	4.8
*Pork chop, cooked	3 oz.	4.5
*Beef	3 oz.	4.2
Dried prunes	½ cup (10 prunes)	3.9
Tostada, bean	1	3.2
Kidney beans, cooked	½ cup	3.0
Baked beans with pork & molasses	½ cup	3.0
*Hamburger	3 oz.	3.0
Soybeans, cooked	½ cup	2.7
*Beef enchilada	1	2.6
Raisins	½ cup	2.5
Lima beans, canned or fresh cooked	½ cup	2.5
Refried beans	½ cup	2.3
Dried figs	½ cup (4 figs)	2.2
Spinach, cooked	½ cup	2.0
*Taco—Beef	1	2.0
Mustard greens, cooked	½ cup	1.8
Corn tortilla, lime treated	8" diameter	1.6
Peas, fresh cooked	½ cup	1.4
Enchilada, cheese and sour cream	1	1.4
Egg	1, large	1.2
Sardines, canned in oil	1 oz. (2 medium)	1.0

*Foods of animal origin. Iron in foods of animal origin (except milk, which has little iron) is absorbed twice as efficiently as iron in foods of plant origin.

Food for Sport

the iron from vegetable sources. Furthermore, twice as much vegetable iron will be absorbed if it is eaten at the same meal with meat. Consequently, anyone on a vegetarian diet has to be particularly careful about getting enough iron. And supplementation with milk and milk products is not especially helpful, since they are poor sources of iron.

The table, "Sources of Iron," shows the iron content of a list of common foods, organized in decreasing order of concentration.

In recent years the food industry has initiated the practice of adding iron to certain staples, notably wheat flour. These additional amounts are nutritionally significant, particularly in view of the popularity of baked products.

THE PREVENTION OF IRON DEFICIENCY

Iron deficiencies in females are usually the result of either (or a combination of) their efforts to avoid high-caloric foods, simply not eating enough, or extraordinary menstrual losses. Those using intrauterine contraceptive devices which increase menstrual blood loss are at particular risk.

THE PRE-GAME MEAL AND EATING DURING COMPETITION

Athletes have lots of excuses for losing. They may feel unprepared, badly coached, short-changed by the officiating, or handicapped by some injury or illness. But they seldom have a clear explanation for why they win. They usually end up with generalities, like, "I had a good day...," or, "things sure felt good today...."

Out of this has grown a mythology about pre-competition eating, which has little basis in fact. Many runners regard pizza as a "fast" food, while soccer players the world over demand bacon and eggs before a game. In this country, numerous athletes, particularly football players, feel unprepared for competition without a game-day ceremonial steak dinner, with baked potatoes, dry toast, and tea.

Important Factors in Pre-Game Eating

There are endless bizarre stories of pre-game eating practices. Most of them not only reflect confusion, they add to it. Take the well-known account of a young lady swimmer who broke the world's record for the 200-meter butterfly after a pre-race meal of two hamburgers with onions, french fries and catsup, a root beer, three brownies, and a candy bar. It is usually told as a nutrition horror story. Actually the meal wasn't all that bad, and it was considerably better than some of the eating practices which have become traditional. Her meal was relatively low in fat and high in carbohydrate; it was eaten well before the race, and it was food she enjoyed and was familiar with. She could have done worse.

There was the much worse example of three varsity swimmers who went to their apartment during the noon break of a conference swimming meet, and ate steaks, potato chips, french bread, and ice cream. In the early afternoon events, one swimmer won and set a new conference record, one swam his worst time of the season, and the third never finished. What accounted for their varying reactions? Obviously, different individuals react differently to any one diet. Nevertheless, it is possible to set general guidelines which should be helpful to all athletes.

One factor that will always be present, and a primary consideration, is the nervous tension. The more important the competition, and in many cases the more successful and intense the competitor, the greater is the tension leading up to and surrounding the actual event. Women are no less affected than men. Appetites are often finicky and stomachs unsettled.

Individual likes and dislikes are apt to become more accentuated. People who generally eat almost anything suddenly develop pronounced feelings about what foods

Food for Sport

they can and cannot tolerate. The fact that these are purely psychological factors makes them no less real, and any pre-game diet must take such personal preferences into account.

THE GOALS OF THE PRE-GAME DIET

The following goals should be considered in planning the pre-game diet:
1. Energy intake should be adequate to ward off any feelings of hunger or weakness during the entire period of the competition. Although pre-contest food makes only a minor contribution to the immediate energy expenditure, it is essential for an adequate level of blood sugar, and to avoid hunger and weakness.
2. The diet plan should ensure that the stomach and upper bowel are empty at the time of competition.
3. Food and fluid taken prior to and during prolonged competition should guarantee an optimal state of hydration.
4. The pre-competition diet should offer foods that will minimize upset in the gastrointestinal tract.
5. The diet should include food that the athlete is familiar with, and is convinced will "make him win."

The traditional steak breakfast or mid-day banquet fails to meet many of these goals. Its high protein content will tend to dehydrate, the high fat content will delay the emptying of the stomach and upper intestinal tract; and the low carbohydrate content will fail to support the glycogen and glucose stores necessary for immediate energy and a good level of blood sugar.

All too often the steak "brunch" has represented the only game-day meal. One varsity football player said recently that the best thing about making the first team was that it kept him busy on the field. Sitting on the bench, he had had the chance to think about how hungry he was; and by the fourth quarter he was usually so famished that he got headaches.

Except for this one day in the week large and active

young football and basketball players are used to a regular schedule of eating every two to four hours. Their bodies are not about to agree that there is something special about game day that makes food unnecessary for seven or eight hours.

FOOD INTAKE BEFORE COMPETITION

For most competitors the best diet plan provides modest amounts of high-carbohydrate foods, taken at regular intervals up to within two and a half hours of the competition. As stated earlier, the carbohydrates will provide the quickest and most efficient source of energy, and have neither the slow gastric emptying problem of fats nor the dehydrating tendency of protein.

Some competitors will prefer soup and light sandwich meals, others cold cereal eaten with sugar, skimmed milk, and perhaps fruit. Large meals with fatty meats are usually a poor idea. And again, it is essential that athletes not skip meals, particularly the early meal on the day of competition. The fewer the deviations from regular eating schedules, the better.

FLUID INTAKE BEFORE COMPETITION

The third goal of pre-game eating is avoiding dehydration. Fluids are important—not only before and during the contest, but for two or three days beforehand. The immediate pre-game diet should include two to three glasses of some beverage (and "beverage" includes water). Whole milk is not recommended because of its high fat content (and many cannot tolerate large milk intakes). Caffeine-containing beverages, such as coffee and tea, may present problems for the very young athlete, who is unaccustomed to the effects of caffeine. Non-carbonated, fruit-flavored drinks are generally good. They are liked by most athletes, and they provide some sugar; and they are particularly helpful during those competitions which go on for a prolonged period of time.

Travel

Most teams, particularly high school teams, do not have to worry about jet travel and hotel eating. Budgets usually call for car pools and school buses, and food is taken from home or the school cafeteria. The pre-event meal needs can be met very adequately, at times superlatively, with the foods planned and prepared at home or at school. Sandwiches, fruit juices, fruits, and hard candies can be provided in a "brown bag" meal.

Of course, simple principles of good nutrition must be kept in mind. It is important to avoid mayonnaise and spreads which may be high in fat and susceptible to spoilage without refrigeration. It is advisable to stay away from high-salt snack foods, such as chips and salted nuts, and to have an abundant supply of non-carbonated drinks available prior to competition. Once again, the "brown bag" meal should cater to individual food preferences. The trip itself is no time to experiment with new and strange concoctions, regardless of their theoretical merit.

Wrestling and Other Weight Control Sports

"You can always spot the members of our wrestling team by the middle of the season. Their clothes don't fit and they fall asleep in class."

The above was heard recently from a high school chemistry teacher. With no minced words, he neatly summarized exactly what's wrong with the majority of wrestling programs in high schools and colleges all over the country. During the competitive season, wrestlers often have severe nutritional problems.

The Effects of Inadequate Weight Programs

It is an article of faith that wrestlers perform most effectively at their lowest possible weight. But do they? There is some evidence to the contrary. And there is nutritional common sense which says that you cannot seriously dehydrate the body and deprive it of food, and expect it to perform most effectively. The weight that is lost during the typical crash period at the end of the week, when the team members can no longer study because they feel "thickheaded," is water loss. And that can mean severe dehydration.

One of the outstanding members of a university team provides a typical example of the weekly weight ordeal. Wrestling at 128 pounds, he has competed regularly for six years. He was a state champion in high school and is now a strong contender for national honors at the college level. As a first step in helping him establish a sound weight-control program, he was asked to keep careful records of his food intake for one week during the season. It looked like this:

College Wrestler—
Weight and Food Intake, Before Counseling

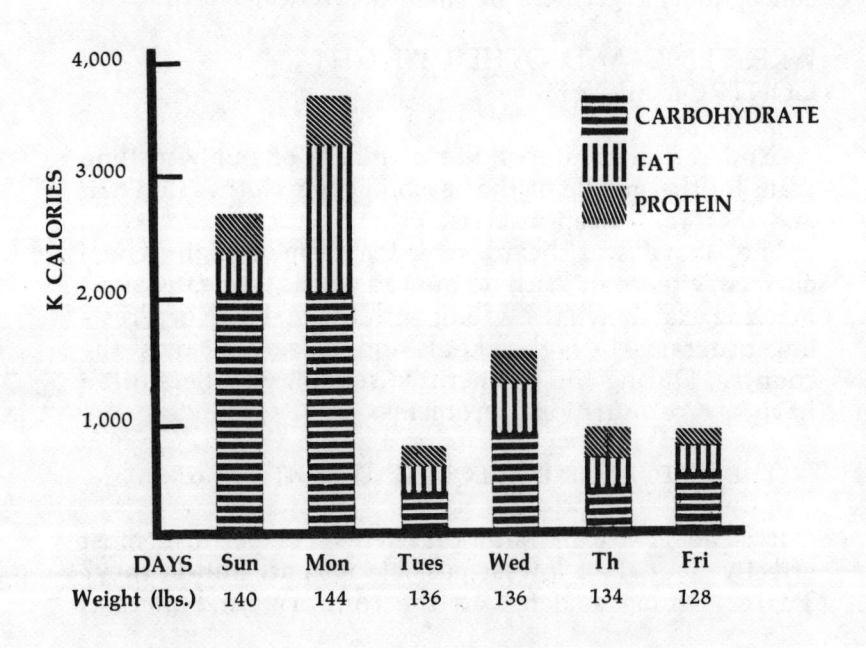

DAYS	Sun	Mon	Tues	Wed	Th	Fri
Weight (lbs.)	140	144	136	136	134	128

Food for Sport

After making weight and wrestling at 128 pounds on Saturday, this wrestler and his equally dehydrated and hungry teammates headed for a nearby drive-in. There they consumed large quantities of soft drinks and drive-in quality barbecued sandwiches with potato chips. On Sunday, he ate one meal in the middle of the day which included chicken, a vegetable, a salad, and dessert. During the remainder of the day, he studied, ate thirty-eight Ritz crackers, drank forty ounces of lemonade, and snacked on rolls, jam, and apples. His caloric intake for the day was 2685 Calories.

On Monday he ate three meals: a breakfast of milk and cereal, a lunch of a soft drink and tamales, and a steak dinner. With candy snacks throughout the day, his caloric total came to 3661 Calories. By Tuesday he weighed 144 pounds and was suddenly confronted by the fact that he had to lose sixteen pounds by Saturday.

So he reduced his eating sharply. On Tuesday his diet contained only 630 Calories—from one meat pie, a cherry cola, and an apple. His weight was 136 pounds on Wednesday morning. He avoided breakfast and lunch, but on Wednesday evening he met a friend and had a ham dinner, containing 1580 Calories. His weight stayed at 136 pounds on Thursday. He ate a small fish dinner on Thursday and drank no fluids. By Friday his weight was down to 134 pounds. On Friday he had one can of soft drink and twenty shortbread cookies, which contributed a total of 826 Calories. By Friday afternoon he was still six pounds overweight.

As was his custom, he spent Friday afternoon in the sauna, remaining there until he could no longer sweat. Then he put on two sweat suits and a rubber suit and ran until he had lost five of the last six pounds. He lost the last pound in the traditional manner: by spitting into a mason jar. He went home and refrained from eating or drinking anything until the weigh-in on Saturday morning.

This wrestler's regimen was frightening enough. But at least it did not involve laxatives or diuretic "water pills," which have become all too common. Nonetheless, he went into his match badly depleted of water and the carbohydrate stores necessary for the desired level of energy, strength, and endurance. He won this particular match, but as had happened quite consistently in the past, he was out-pointed in the last period.

The wild fluctuations in this wrestler's weight were due mainly to changes in his body water. He was expending approximately 3000 Calories a day, and even if he had eaten no food between Tuesday and Saturday, he would have lost less than three or four pounds of body fat over the four-day period. Since he actually took in about 4000 Calories in that period, even on his restricted diet, his net loss of body fat could have been no more than three pounds. The remaining thirteen pounds, which were lost between Tuesday and Saturday, were entirely made up of body water.

An important factor was the salt in the diet. The barbecued roast beef sandwiches and chips on Saturday, the Ritz crackers on Sunday, and the mid-week ham dinner were all high in salt content, accentuating water retention and weight gain. (The emphasis on salt in his eating was not surprising, after the induced sweating and salt loss at the end of the preceding week.)

There is a better way to control weight. The first step is to determine the ideal competing weight for each wrestler. (Methods of calculation are discussed later in this chapter.) Once the competing weight is reached, a diet program for weight maintenance can be readily devised.

THE HIGH PERFORMANCE DIET

The wrestler described above required about 3000 Calories a day. His needs were met through a combination of the Basic Diet and, for important competition, the High Performance Diet. (The High Performance Diet is particularly well suited for wrestling, because it provides the glycogen stores and carbohydrate necessary to meet the very strenuous energy demands of a wrestling match.) He

Food for Sport

was told to eat as much as he wanted to satisfy his appetite early in the week, as long as he restricted his carbohydrate intake to approximately 110 grams per day. Towards the end of the week the restriction on carbohydrate foods was removed, and the diet was supplemented with a high-carbohydrate glucose drink. To help him make weight, he was instructed to avoid the high

---

High Salt-Containing Foods The following foods should be limited in the diet for 72 hours prior to competition or weigh-in in weight control sports. Very modest intakes are permissible, but large servings will result in water retention. Water intakes should be generous during this period: no less than eight full glasses each 24 hours:

Anchovies	Luncheon meat
Bacon and bacon fat	Meat tenderizer
Bologna	Mustard
Bouillon cubes	Olives
Bread and rolls with salt topping	Peanut butter
Catsup	Potato chips, corn chips
Celery salt, onion salt, garlic salt	Pretzels
	Relish, pickles
Cheese (all kinds)	Salt, Monosodium glutamate
Chili sauce	Salt pork
Chipped and corned beef	Salted nuts and popcorn
Cottage cheese (salted)	Salty and smoked fish
Crackers	Salty and smoked meats
Dry cereals	Sardines
Frankfurters	Sauerkraut
Ham	Sausage
Herring	Soups (canned)
Horseradish	Soy sauce
Kosher meat	Worcestershire sauce

salt-containing foods listed in the box, and bulky foods with high residue; it is helpful if food residues in the bowel are minimal for weigh-in and competition.

The chart, "Weight and Food Intake, After Counseling," reflects the dramatic changes in his diet and weight fluctuations: The wrestler was able to satisfy his appetite, meet his energy needs, and stabilize his weight for competition. He had a highly successful year, both in wrestling competition and academically. And he particularly impressed the coaching staff by becoming a strong third-period performer.

Most competitors will not want to follow the High Performance Diet all the time. It should be limited to periods immediately preceding the most important competitions, particularly the tournaments and critical events toward the end of the season.

College Wrestler—
Weight and Food Intake, After Counseling

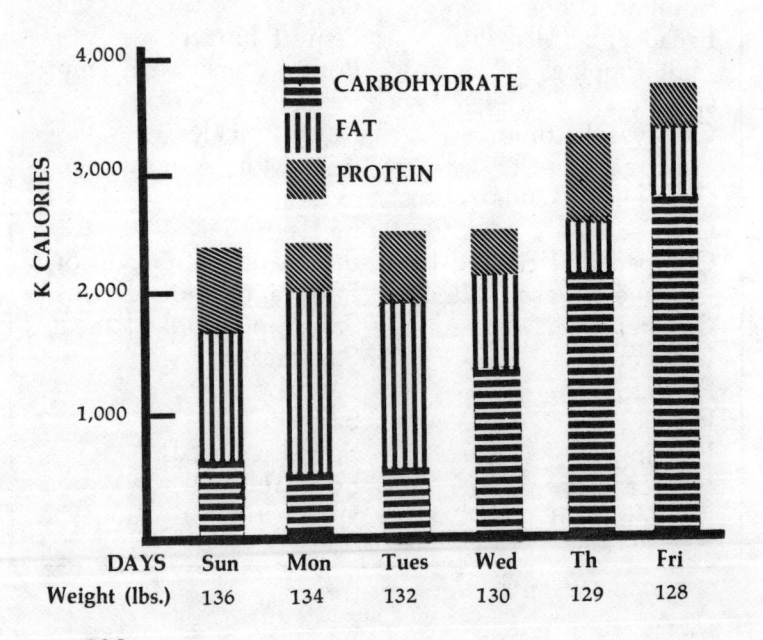

Food for Sport

THE IDEAL COMPETING WEIGHT

How does one determine ideal competing weight? We have discussed the popular belief that a competitor will wrestle most effectively at his lowest possible weight; the emaciated participants found on many wrestling teams (seldom the champions) bear witness to this fallacy. The most effective weight for competition is one where there is a healthy and effective level of hydration, optimal muscle mass, and no excessive body fat.

What is the recommended level of body fat? Several recent studies approached this question by evaluating the body composition of wrestling champions. Their average body fat was approximately five to seven percent.

The simplest method of estimating body fat is through measurement of skin fat fold thickness. This simply requires a pair of skin-fold calipers and a conversion table with which to estimate the percentage of total body weight represented by fat tissue. (Hopefully this can generally be found locally, either through one's own athletic or school health department, or perhaps at a neighboring college.) These measurements can be effectively utilized to establish the minimum (and most effective) weight for each wrestling team member. A wrestler may wish to compete in a heavier weight class, but if he attempts to wrestle below a minimum based on his skin fat fold estimate, his wrestling will probably suffer—and possibly his health.

A typical sixteen-year-old American high school boy who weighs 156 pounds can be expected to have a body fat composition of fifteen to seventeen percent of his total body weight. The ten percent he would have to lose in order to reach an optimum level of five percent would be approximately 15 pounds (ten percent of his 156 pounds). If this estimate is made at the beginning of the school year, a necessary allowance should also be made for an increase in muscle mass from the regular wrestling conditioning program. In all, he should lose approximately 15 pounds of body fat and gain 3 to 5 pounds in muscle mass, a net loss of 10 to 12 pounds. His optimal wrestling weight would be 145 pounds.

As is true of all weight reduction programs, the critical factors are, first, sufficient time, and secondly, increased energy expenditure—along with reduced caloric intake. No program should require a loss in excess of four pounds per week; two pounds is generally more desirable. Since each pound of fat lost requires a caloric deficit of 3500 Calories, the active athlete who can raise his daily caloric expenditure up to 3500 Calories can follow a Basic Diet of 2000 Calories and lose two to three pounds per week. *An intake of 2000 Calories each day should be the minimum allowed for an athlete involved in a vigorous training program.* This will provide the necessary nutrients and minimal energy needed for academic performance, daily activities, growth, and training.

Special attention must be paid to members of the football team who expect to participate in wrestling. They will generally be among the heavier members of the team, and will often end the football season with a higher than desirable percentage of body fat and a relatively brief period of time for weight loss. Since they should get at least 2000 Calories a day, they will often need special training programs (often two-a-day workouts) to insure sufficient weight loss.

Holidays present particular problems for weight control programs. It is traditional to eat more, to eat more foods with high caloric density, and to avoid the regular schedule of workouts over the holidays. (In many states weight certification takes place in early December, and a sudden weight gain over the Thanksgiving recess can seriously jeopardize weight qualifications for the season.) In many states, if a high school wrestler competes at a higher than certified level in one match, he must continue to compete at that weight during the remainder of the season. Therefore, it may be important to continue scheduled workouts and have weigh-ins during the holiday season. If weight loss is required immediately after the holidays, there may be a need for a special program of vigorous exercise and dietary restriction (limited caloric intake, and avoidance of bulky and high-salt foods).

GROWTH DEMANDS OF THE HIGH SCHOOL WRESTLER

The high school years are, of course, a time of vigorous growth, and any weight control program must allow for the needs of that growth.

Cutting weight through crash dieting and erratic eating arrests growth during the wrestling season. After the season the participants generally appear to "catch up" in growth, but whatever else happens, athletic performance is bound to suffer.

DIURETICS AND CATHARTICS

Wrestlers are often tempted to resort to the use of diuretics and cathartics—to increase urinary water losses.

Both diuretics and cathartics cause water loss and consequent dehydration, which can directly inhibit the production of energy. In addition, they both remove significant amounts of potassium from the body. Potassium is necessary for muscle function; and the "washed out" feeling of weakness following an attack of diarrhea is due in large part to the loss of potassium and body water.

The adverse effects of the cathartics are usually obvious and one experience is frequently enough. The results of the diuretics are not so apparent, and the urinary losses of water and potassium can actually result in life-threatening shock. These agents have no place in weight programs, and their abuse can result in serious muscle weakness and total collapse.

four

Taking Care of Injuries

Nathan J. Smith

As the athlete strives for optimal performance, muscles, tendons, ligaments, etc. can often be stressed to the point of injury. In contact sports, such as football, ice hockey, and lacrosse, collisions result in a variety of bumps and bruises and occasional lacerations. Competition and training with all-out effort can be expected to be associated with occasional injuries and it's important to know how these injuries may be prevented, or cared for when they do occur.

In a recent survey of high school sports injuries in Seattle high schools, different sports were studied to determine their level of risk. Injuries occurred most commonly in contact or stressful sports, such as football, wrestling, and girls' gymnastics, and were least common in sports such as swimming, tennis, and baseball. Those with a moderate number of injuries included basketball, field hockey, and soccer.

Fortunately, most sports injuries are not severe, and do not cause the athlete to miss more than three to five days of practice or competition. The injured athlete must always assume the primary responsibility for proper injury management, initiating and following a management plan that will assure return to competition as safely and as quickly as possible. Prompt treatment and effective followthrough on a sound treatment plan are most important. Postponing care or failing strictly to follow the prescribed treatment plan will prolong discomfort, reduce effectiveness, and will markedly increase the chances of experiencing another injury.

You should inform your coach or trainer about any or all injuries so that you can get prompt treatment and return to the game as soon as possible. Attempting to "tough it out" and play with a painful injury can harm both the player and the team. It's better to stay out of practice two or three days while having an injury properly treated, returning to practice only when fully recovered.

The Management of Common Sports Injuries

The common injuries encountered in sports training and competition are bruises, sprains of ligaments that support bony joints, and strains of muscles and the tendons that attach the muscles to bones. Lacerations (cuts) occur commonly in some sports. Broken bones (fractures) and dislocated joints are not uncommon in sports such as skiing and wrestling. These injuries are not generally life threatening and certainly minor bruises, sprains, and strains can often be managed by the athlete.

Things Not to Do If Injured

1. Don't try to hide your injury. Report it to your coach or trainer.
2. Don't treat an injury if you don't know what's wrong. See your trainer or doctor.
3. Don't apply any source of heat to an injury without orders from your doctor or trainer.
4. Don't use an injured part if it hurts. More "hurting" means more injury.
5. Don't take any drugs unless prescribed by your doctor.
6. Don't tape or splint an injured part without a doctor's supervision.
7. Don't go back to practice or competition until you have a full range of motion, full strength, and full function of the injured part.

The above "don'ts" are to be modified only under the direct care of a doctor or a certified, professional athletic trainer (not student trainer). The quickest way to return to effective participation is to limit activity as long as there is still pain and swelling and to follow rigidly the prescribed rehabilitation program including any schedule of planned exercise.

What to Do When Injured

Your first responsibility when injured is to get out of the game or practice. Continued participation may make the injury worse, and because you may not be able to move normally and protect yourself, may place you at risk of another injury. A healthy substitute is better for the team than an injured star.

When leaving the practice or game, avoid using the injured part. Don't walk on the painful leg or ankle (use crutches); support the injured arm (use a sling).

The only treatment for a sports injury without professional advice is the important *I — C — E*. Remember the word *Ice;* I for ice, C for compression, and E for elevation.

Never apply heat to a sports injury unless ordered by a physician.

The ICE treatment is easily applied and should be applied immediately on the sidelines. All that is needed are plastic bags (from the supermarket produce counter), crushed ice (from the school cafeteria ice machine), and a two dollar styrofoam picnic cooler containing the bags of ice and wet four-inch elastic bandages.

Remove the clothing from around the injury, elevate the arm or leg, apply one layer of wet elastic bandage on the skin over the injury, put on the plastic bag of ice and firmly apply the remainder of the elastic wrap. Keep the ice and compressed wrap on the elevated, immobilized part for twenty-five to thirty minutes. ICE treatment may be repeated three or four times a day for a couple of days following an injury. If pain and swelling persist, call a doctor.

You've probably seen injured football players on TV sitting on the sideline with bags of ice wrapped onto their legs or shoulders. This is the ICE treatment being used by the team's doctor or professional trainer.

Why Does ICE Work?

When the basketball player's ankle is sprained (and its supporting ligaments torn), when a quarterback's thigh muscle is bruised, or when a sprinter strains and ruptures fibers of his hamstring muscles, a sequence of events occurs that is common to all such injuries.

Blood vessels are damaged and some will break, allowing blood and fluid to accumulate in the injured area. This causes increased pressure, swelling and pain, which can result in further damage to surrounding tissues.

The pain of the initial injury causes the muscles of the injured area to go into spasm. This is nature's attempt to limit all movement of the injured area and prevent further injury. Muscle spasm is painful.

Applying ice chills the bruised or injured area, causing blood vessels to contract and reducing the circulation to the injury. Applying pressure with the elastic bandage prevents much of the accumulation of blood and fluids in the area, minimizing painful, damaging swelling. Elevating the injury puts the part at rest, reducing painful muscle spasm, and encouraging the draining away of blood and fluid from the injury. When applied promptly and conscientiously, ICE treatment will significantly reduce the discomfort and period of limited activity resulting from an injury. When applied properly it can do no harm to any type of injury. Almost anything else you may do can cause harm in some instances.

The Management of an Injury—A Case in Point

Howard was a guard on the FHS basketball team. In a game in early December, he broke free for a lay-up. As he came down from the basket, his extended foot came down on the foot of the trailing opponent. Falling with his weight on the outer edge of his foot, it collapsed under him, painfully stretching and rupturing portions of the tendons on the outside of his left ankle.

The team physician diagnosed a moderately severe second-degree ankle sprain, and the student trainer, properly equipped with plastic ice bags and chilled, wet elastic bandages, applied ice and compression to the injured ankle and had the player elevate it on the bench. Thirty minutes later at the end of the game, using crutches brought from the trainer's room, Howard showered quickly and was driven home. At home ICE was again applied for thirty minutes and he slept with the foot of his bed elevated twelve inches. He remained home for the weekend using crutches for minimal essential movements around the house and applied ICE for thirty minutes three to four times each day. On Monday, he used crutches, applied ICE during his free period at school, and when seen by the physician at practice time, was found to have no pain on walking and only slight swelling and discoloration around his ankle. Without pain he was allowed to walk without crutches and to begin graduated ankle exercises three times a day. He was running in five days and back in full competition in two weeks.

This was an excellent recovery from a moderately severe ankle sprain. The rapid, complete recovery was due to preventing marked swelling by repeated ICE, using crutches to avoid further injury, and conscientiously following the rehabilitation exercise program. His ankle was taped for each practice and game for the remainder of what proved to be a very successful season.

Preventing Injuries

We are continually seeking practical ways to minimize the risk of sports injury. Here are some things the athlete can do to reduce sports injuries:

1. Compete with persons of similar level of proficiency, size, and strength. This is especially important in collision sports such as football and ice hockey. The poorer and smaller players get more than their share of injuries.
2. Get in condition before turning out for practice or competing vigorously. Most sports require good endurance and strength and these can be developed by proper conditioning programs specific to particular sports (see Chapter Two). If possible, talk to the coach about conditioning two or three months before the season starts. The unconditioned athlete gets injured, sometimes seriously.
3. Warm up properly before each practice and game. Muscle strains and tendon sprains are common in sports. A good stretching sequence in your warm-up can reduce the chances of these injuries.
4. Use the proper equipment. Protective equipment has been developed and provided for a good reason. Be sure it fits, that it doesn't need repair, and that you wear and use it properly.

Most sports are played on our feet. Be certain that shoes and socks fit and that all socks are clean and without holes.

Taking Care of Injuries

5. Don't wear jewelry in active sports. Neck jewelry can be dangerous; rings can produce serious finger injuries getting caught on baskets and so forth.
6. Practice good hygiene. Skin infections are particularly common among athletes and can put you out of competition for a week or more of treatment and may spread to other team members. Showering with an antibacterial soap daily and after every workout reduces the risk of skin infection. Keeping all uniforms and equipment laundered and clean is also helpful. Keep fingernails trimmed shorter than the tip of the finger to prevent painful scratches and serious eye injuries (it's a rule in the NBA).
7. Never play with a fever. Some common viral infections can become serious generalized illnesses lasting all too long following a hard workout or game. You also want to avoid any chance of giving your illness to the rest of the team. A good rule is "with a fever over 100° stay home and get well."
8. When playing in an unsupervised playground or gym, take a minute to be sure that anything a player may run into and get injured from is well away from the game area. Bicycles, cars, benches, lawn mowers, sprinklers, score tables, and other obstacles can cause serious injuries.

BE PREPARED FOR EMERGENCIES

Most injuries occuring in sports are minor; but on rare occasions serious injuries occur, that may threaten life and may have to be managed on the scene before any medical help is available. In professionally supervised school sports, at practice or during games, the coach or trainer will be responsible for having a plan of action to be followed in such an emergency. But what do you do at the unsupervised, weekend pickup game, at the afternoon basketball game on the neighbors' driveway, or in the Boys' Club gym without a coach or a trainer on hand?

One thing that you can do before the start of any

practice or competition is to take a course in CPR (Cardiopulmonary Resuscitation). Such training may be available at your school, through your Fire Department, Red Cross, or Scout program. You can learn the simple lifesaving techniques that can keep a seriously injured athlete alive until emergency medical help arrives.

An accident or injury that results in any of the following presents a serious medical emergency:
    An injured athlete who is—
        not breathing,
        unconscious,
        bleeding, or
        in shock.

These injured athletes can die before any medical help can arrive on the scene if someone isn't prepared to initiate thoughtful action.

CALL FOR HELP!

Before you start that fun, pickup game with your friends, take ten seconds and think through exactly how you would get emergency help if one of those rare life threatening injuries should occur. You must know—
    Where is there a telephone?
    Who has the change needed to make it work?
    Whom do you call?
    What is the location of your playfield or gym?
    Can an emergency vehicle get on the field?
    Is there a locked gate? Who has a key?

If you don't know these things, you may be helpless when the crisis occurs.

SOME IMPORTANT DON'TS

Don't move an unconscious player any more than is needed for CPR.

Don't use ammonia capsules to revive an unconscious player. (They can complicate a neck-spine injury and may cause face burns.)

Taking Care of Injuries

Don't remove a football helmet from an unconscious player. (You may seriously compound any spine injury.)

IN CONCLUSION

Much of the satisfaction and fun of participation in sports comes from extending ourselves to maximum performance. Such stresses may on occasion result in injury, rarely serious, but often interfering temporarily with the ability to compete. Be prepared to act effectively if the rare instance of a serious injury should arise. Know how to manage the more common, less severe injuries to avoid making them worse than need be, causing another injury, or prolonging the period of disability.

five

The Young Woman Athlete

Bruce Ogilvie

Until recently, very few women seriously played basketball or baseball, threw a javelin, or drove a race car. In the last ten years, however, we have seen women enter almost every type of competition, and women's sports have blossomed—with more players, more fans, and more money for the top players. It is difficult to remember that it was just a few years ago that Billie Jean King instigated the campaign to improve facilities and increase prizes for women tennis players. Virginia Wade earned about $250,000 in tennis in 1977.

But this does not mean that the woman athlete no longer faces obstacles. Women still have a difficult time earning a living through sports. It is only the tennis players and golfers who command top prize money. The female basketball or baseball player receives far fewer rewards than her male counterpart, and women are still excluded from one of the richest sports in the country—football. Federal legislation (Title IX) requires that universities must now provide equal sports facilities for men and women, and has begun to help the woman athlete in college. But the professional future of most female athletes is still very limited.

The female athlete faces not only financial, but also psychological hurdles. As a counsellor to women athletes at the California State University at San Jose, I have seen strong social pressures working against the ambitions of many women who want to participate in sports. This social pressure comes from both within the athlete herself and from outside sources, such as her family and friends.

But before looking at the psychology of women in sports, let's first look closely at whether there is any physical basis for the prejudice.

MALE-FEMALE PHYSICAL DIFFERENCES

Up to about age ten, boys and girls have similar body contours and are roughly equal in strength and endurance. In fact, because girls often mature earlier than boys, they tend to have a slight physical advantage.

However, after the onset of puberty, the picture changes. At this time, the level of sex hormones in the body increases sharply, and these hormones trigger development that is markedly different. Males generally become taller, gain more muscle mass, and develop wider shoulders. They develop longer legs and arms in relation to their trunk size, and have a lower ratio of fat to muscle.

The chart below compares world records set by men and women in various sports as of 1978. As you can see, top male athletes exceed top female athletes by as much as 30%. Male champion athletes have more endurance, are faster, stronger, and more powerful than their female counterparts.

But the reason for the higher performance of men is not entirely clear. We can identify physical differences between males and females, and we know that these physical differences all contribute in some way to differences in performance, but we do not know exactly how they contribute. The relationship between physical attributes and performance is a very complex one. For example, although height is generally considered an important attribute for high jumping, one of the best male high jumpers in the world, Franklin Jacobs, has jumped 7'8", but is only 5'7" tall. Many other high jumpers, male and female, are taller.

Figure 5-1. Differences in World Records for Men and Women Competitors (1978)

Event	Men	Women
Track		
60-yards	6.54 s	6.72 s
440-yards	46.20 s	53.50 s
1000-yards	125.10 s	143.80 s
1-mile	234.90 s	268.50 s
Field		
High-jump	7'7¼"	6'4½"
Long-jump	27'2¾"	22'2¼"
Javelin-throw	308'9¼"	216'10½"
Swimming (free-style)		
100-metre	49.44 s	55.65 s
200-metre	110.29 s	119.26 s
400-metre	231.56 s	248.91 s
1500-metre	902.40 s	984.60 s

Although we do not know how each physical characteristic independently contributes to the performances of men and women, we *do* know that women respond to training at the same rate as men do. They receive comparable benefits from a similar amount of training. Top female athletes are as concerned with conditioning as their male counterparts. For example, the training program set out in Chapter Two is as useful to women as to men.

In the next few pages we will explore the physical differences between men and women. Keep in mind that there is no ultimate standard for physical capacity. Top female athletes do not look to men to set the standard for achievement; rather, they strive to reach their own potential.

CARDIORESPIRATORY ENDURANCE

As we saw in Chapter Two, cardiorespiratory endurance primarily depends on the amount of oxygen that can be utilized by the body. Some people are able to transport oxygen more effectively than others—they get more "fuel" from each breath of air they take. The average female athlete has a lower capacity for transporting oxygen to her working muscles than the average male at similar levels of training. Nevertheless, women can train to improve their capacity and in fact, some have attained a maximal oxygen uptake expressed in terms of lean body mass almost identical to the well-trained male.

Nevertheless, men generally have more endurance. They are able to pump more blood with each beat of the heart and thus are able to transport more oxygen through their bodies during maximal exercise. Moreover, males have more hemoglobin per unit of blood, giving them a slightly higher oxygen-carrying capacity (hemoglobin "carries" oxygen to the muscles). But most importantly, females almost always have a greater proportion of their weight in fat. Even thin females tend to have a considerable layer of fat beneath the skin, and this extra fat

The Young Woman Athlete

reduces their endurance capacity. Female athletes who are in sports that demand high endurance strive to reduce their proportion of fat to muscle, and some are able to almost match the fat/lean ratios of men. This greatly improves their endurance capacity.

Strength The average male is thirty to forty percent stronger than the average female. This is because of his higher level of the sex hormone, androgen, which promotes muscle development. With training, women can increase their muscle strength in a manner similar to men. They seem to have the same *quality* of muscle, but because of their lack of androgen, they do not develop as much muscle *mass* in their arms, shoulders, or trunks. No amount of weight training will change this fact.

Because men have wider shoulders and longer arms and legs in comparison to trunk length, they also have a mechanical advantage over females. In other words, their bodies are better levers for lifting and throwing. Looking at Figure 5-1, you probably noticed that the greatest difference between male and female records was in the javelin throw. This is not surprising since that event requires not only upper body strength but also leverage on an unwieldy object.

One of the prevalent myths about women and sports is that strenuous exercise and weight training will result in a heavily muscled, unfeminine appearance. This is not true, not only because the lack of androgen prevents development of muscle bulk, but also because the female layer of fat tends to hide muscle definition.

Recently, many female athletes and their coaches have begun to realize the importance of weight training. Although females cannot match the strength of males, improving their strength to the extent of their potential will provide them with the same kinds of benefits—increased speed and power, and resistance to injury.

Injury Vulnerability With the expansion of women's sports, trainers have noticed that young women tend to receive an inordinately high number of injuries, especially "stress" injuries such as muscle sprains, strains, and stress fractures. It is believed that this is owing to the fact that females tend to enter competitive sports comparatively late. Thus, they often begin training for a sport at a relatively low level of fitness, and being out of condition is a major cause of injury. In addition, because many females did not participate in sports during their growing years, they are often inexperienced in the management of injuries. They will often ignore a minor strain or bruise and continue intense training, thus aggravating the original injury until it becomes much more serious.

Women new to sport should seek instruction on how to care for early training strains, contusions, and other minor injuries. With such instruction, and with adequate conditioning, women should have no more injuries than men. In fact, the female is in some ways better equipped to withstand contact and to resist injury even during the most vigorous activity. For one thing, the fat beneath her skin provides a padding for protection of bony joints and other bony protrusions.

Also, the female's sex organs are internally protected by bone and muscle and are practically invulnerable to injury. Until recently, there was considerable concern about harm to breasts during athlete activity, but we have found that significant injury is extremely rare, even in contact sports. Breast tissue is soft and easily displaced by pressure and can withstand considerable impact. Metal breast cups should be worn by female fencers to avoid a direct, confined blow, but such protection is not needed in any other sport.

Menstrual Cycle Many women believe that their menstrual period will adversely affect performance. This question has recently been studied extensively through analysis of the times of female swimmers, and by looking at the achievements of women athletes in the Olympic games. Both sources provided precise measures of performance, which were correlated with the menstrual cycles of the participants. It was found that women have set world records and won gold medals during every phase of the menstrual cycle, with little significant variance in relation to the cycle. For some women, there may be some minor physical decline resulting from premenstrual tension, but there is no effect during the actual flow. Variations at any time during the cycle are extremely slight, if they occur at all.

One effect of menstruation, however, is to deplete the body of iron. As many as fifteen to twenty percent of the young women participating in a given athletic program may be somewhat deficient in that nutrient and may need a dietary supplement each day. Some time during adolescence after the onset of menstruation, female athletes should have a medical assessment made of their iron status. It is important to develop and maintain proper levels of iron because even a mild deficiency may significantly interfere with athletic performance.

Many young women athletes entering advanced training programs have been concerned about cessation of menstrual periods—a condition that is not uncommon. Perhaps as many as twenty percent of women involved in endurance sports like running, swimming, skiing, and gymnastics have found that their periods have stopped altogether for as long as three to four years. Often, but not always, it follows significant weight loss as a result of dieting in preparation for a strenuous sport such as gymnastics. It is also associated with psychological stress caused by intense competition.

There is no need to worry about such irregularity which, as a matter of fact, often occurs among young women who are not athletes as well. When the training and competition are over, normal menstruation and obstetrical function return. In fact, research shows that female athletes have fewer difficulties with pregnancy than non-athletes.

Sports Activity Having looked at the physical capabilities of women, what can we say about their participation in athletics? Are some sports too strenuous or dangerous for them?

As we have seen, the answer to this is a resounding *no*. There is no physical reason for a woman to be excluded from any sport, not even football, as long as she is in good condition and plays with others of approximately the same size. She must learn how to take care of her body and how to avoid debilitating over-exertion, but this is no different for her than it is for a male athlete.

If there is no objective reason for a woman not to participate in sport, however, what about emotional and social barriers?

INTERNALIZED STEREOTYPES

Studies show that before the age of three most children show no boy-girl differences in their behavior. Girls are just as happy to play with trucks as with dolls; boys will cry and ask to be cuddled. But gradually, by copying their parents and other role models, most children develop "masculine" and "feminine" behavior patterns. Boys are taught to express their needs for self-assertion and the will to dominate, and not to show feelings of vulnerability or dependence. Girls are often told that it is unfeminine to strive for autonomy and to be aggressive. Many girls learn to set relatively modest goals for themselves, and to seek approval at every turn.

From the age of five to thirteen, many girls begin to shy away from competitive sports, preferring not to stand out as the aggressive competitor in any game. They have learned not to want to smash an ace or charge in for a layup or whack a home run.

This is the typical case—the early environments of many exceptional women athletes, on the other hand, have been far different. Their fathers and older brothers have encouraged them to express themselves openly, to push themselves to the limits of their physical abilities, and to want to win without worrying about the feelings of the opposing competitors. A high percentage of exceptional women athletes describe themselves as having been "tom boys," with no apology.

A SELF TEST

The following questions will help you compare yourself with top women competitors in terms of emotional and psychological attitudes and habits.

Circle each statement as objectively as possible in terms of the degree it describes your behavior. Each question can be answered on a four point scale from Never to Always.

Never True	Rarely True	Often True	Always True	
I	II	III	IV	
1	2	3	4	I strive to do things better than others.
4	3	2	1	I take instructions, suggestions, and advice from others.
1	2	3	4	I like to be the center of attention.
1	2	3	4	I like to do things that are unconventional.
4	3	2	1	I like to form strong attachments to others.
4	3	2	1	I like others to show me sympathy and listen to my problems.
1	2	3	4	I am elected to leadership roles.
4	3	2	1	I like to do small favors for others.
1	2	3	4	I like to participate in new fads and fashions.
4	3	2	1	I keep at a job until it is finished.

Handbook for the Young Athlete

I   II III IV

1 2 3 4	I like to tell others off when I disagree with them.
4 3 2 1	My emotions and feelings are difficult to control.
4 3 2 1	I follow rules and regulations with little conflict.
1 2 3 4	I enjoy participating in activities where there is high physical risk.
1 2 3 4	Others describe me as outgoing and warm-hearted.
1 2 3 4	I have the need to accomplish something of great significance.
4 3 2 1	I adjust easily to the leadership of others.
1 2 3 4	I will do most anything to make others attend to me.
1 2 3 4	I avoid situations where one is expected to conform.
4 3 2 1	I enjoy participating in groups and being a member of organizations.
4 3 2 1	I seek understanding and emotional support from others.
1 2 3 4	It is easy for me to settle the disputes and arguments of others.
1 2 3 4	I enjoy change and to experiment with the new and different.
4 3 2 1	I work hard on a single job before I take on another.
1 2 3 4	I seek revenge for insults.
4 3 2 1	I am easily upset by what others think about me.

I II III IV

4 3 2 1   It seems natural for me to be humble and conforming.
1 2 3 4   I often take chances where there is unusual emotional risk.
1 2 3 4   I am easygoing and attract others to me.
1 2 3 4   The thought occurs that one day I will make an important contribution to society.
4 3 2 1   It is easy for me to follow directions and the demands of superiors.
1 2 3 4   I like to talk about myself and have others notice me.
1 2 3 4   It is easy for me to criticize those in positions of authority.
4 3 2 1   I try to make as many friends as possible.
4 3 2 1   I like others to feel sorry for me and make a fuss over me.
1 2 3 4   I seek to supervise and direct the actions of others.
4 3 2 1   I get satisfaction out of listening to others' problems and taking care of them.
1 2 3 4   I would prefer to move about and live in different places.
4 3 2 1   I will stick at a problem even when no progress is being made.
1 2 3 4   I can get angry easily and express it towards others.
4 3 2 1   I get depressed and anxious whenever I feel threatened.
4 3 2 1   I tend to be socially shy and withdrawn.

I II III IV

1 2 3 4   I often participate in activities that could be dangerous in terms of my physical well-being.

1 2 3 4   I would be described as basically an extrovert.

Total Added Score

1-45 You express very different attitudes from those of the competitive woman.
46-70 You are considerably below the response style of the competitive woman.
71-95 You are starting to respond as the competitive woman responds but you have a way to go.
96-120 You are turning the corner and are beginning to have a number of the attitudes of the competitive woman.
121-145 You are well on your way and should be almost totally free to express your talents.
146-180 You are a member of a very special club; all that can be said is, "Go get 'em, tiger."

This test indicates some of the attributes common to the women who have excelled in athletics. They need and seek high goals and high achievement. They have strong desires to accomplish something of significance. They thrive on being in the spotlight, and enjoy being the center of attention. They have a strongly developed sense of independence and autonomy, and an ability to express aggression without feelings of guilt.

Such women tend to be tough minded, self-assured, self-confident, very trusting, and self-assertive. They measure slightly above average in terms of emotional maturity, and rarely experience feelings of depression. They have a strong need to express themselves in some physical way. They tend to enjoy social or psychological risks. They are strong non-conformists. In short, they are emotionally indistinguishable from their male counterparts who succeed in athletics.

But there can be moments of doubt. Many of the women athletes whom I have counselled have experienced painful internal conflicts at one time or another. Although they may consciously feel free to assert themselves in athletic competition, they may still have some unconscious inhibitions. Such parental admonishments as "nice girls don't hit back" may stir in the back of their minds as they pound a tennis volley back at an opponent's body or elbow their way in for a lay-up. This may cause them uneasiness that may grow as they encounter other prejudice during their growing years. Competing aggressively may come to be experienced as emotionally dangerous, even when the ongoing feeling during the sport is positive and self-fulfilling. It is as if some female athletes begin to escape, in terms of emotional freedom, only to become enmeshed once again in the judgment of their past authorities.

Such conflicts come out in various ways. One sprinter was dismayed to find herself winning easily one week and coming in last the next. Through psychological tests and discussion, I found that she was essentially beating herself. She felt so guilty about defeating her competitors that in the next meet she would make up for her "unseemly" aggressive behavior by virtually letting her opponents win. Every time she beat someone, she felt the loss of love or loss of support from her teammates. She had an unconscious fear of rejection through achievement, a fear that even she was not aware of. As we talked, she began to understand her feelings of guilt, and gradually she became a consistently excellent performer.

Although this kind of problem arises for some male athletes too, most men have been conditioned all their lives to compete. Although this can have some harmful effects (some men can't *stop* competing), they generally learn to separate competition from the arena of personal interaction. As more and more women gain early experience with competition, they too will feel more at ease with the aggressive sides of their personalities.

Top women athletes are quite comfortable with aggression. Chris Evert and Billie Jean King are close personal friends. After beating King 6-1, 6-1 at one meet, Chris Evert was asked how she felt. "Great," she replied, "but I would have preferred to win 6-0, 6-0."

HISTORICAL ORIGINS OF PREJUDICE

In her book, *Moving and Knowing: Sport, Dance and Physical Education* (1975), Eleanor Methany describes instances of ignorance, prejudice, and social denial in the world of female sports competition over a period of at least two thousand years. She traces the historical social environment which produced the psychological obstacles we just examined.

There are distinct categories of athletic activity from which women have been implicitly banned in most western societies. They can be defined as sports where:
(1) an opponent is subdued by force:
(2) there is body contact;
(3) the body is projected over a distance (such as the long jump); or
(4) there is face-to-face encounter.

One might logically ask, what is left?

If you think of the activities in which women have been depicted through the ages in great (and not so great) art, you will see how complete the stereotype has been. As Sheila de Brettevelle, co-founder of The Woman's Building, an artists' cooperative in Los Angeles, has said, women are most often shown reclining in a luxurious position or, if they are sitting up, it is much more often on a couch rather than a chair. The assumption seems to be that men are dynamic creatures ready to rise and conduct the business of the world, whereas women are passive and must wait for the world to come to them.

The Young Woman Athlete

The one major exception to this has been the implicit agreement that women may dance. You can probably recall paintings of Greek women dancing, of female folk and ballet dancers. Dancing was considered an acceptable form of feminine physical recreation and this has affected attitudes toward sport. Those sports which contain elements of the dance, such as ice skating, tennis, swimming, skiing, and gymnastics, gained acceptance as women's activities much earlier than sports which do not.

The contrast between two typical American sports provides a case in point. Basketball, which has many dance-like movements, is gaining wide popularity as a women's sport—about 10,000 fans turned out to watch the 1978 women's championship between UCLA and Montclair. But baseball, with its discontinuous, nonrhythmic action, has never caught on as a female sport. Many would say that women should stay out of baseball altogether, that the men should be left in peace to hit their home runs and chew their tobacco!

Even women who have overcome potential internal obstacles have often run into discouraging prejudice from others, even in this enlightened age. Many find that their friends or relatives object to their commitment to sport. Some boyfriends or husbands find it difficult to share the limelight with an aggressive woman eager to reach the top, and they resent the time commitments of training and competing. There are subtle pressures which can make athletic dedication seem "unfeminine."

When a young woman interested in sport comes to me with problems of this sort, I try to get her to consider four important questions:

(1) Is your commitment to the sport based on positive motives? Is your athletic experience personally enhancing? Do you do it for the joy of it, or is your commitment based on something negative, such as the desire to show up your boyfriend?

(2) How secure do you feel about yourself as a feminine person? Will you violate your physical self-image if your body becomes hard and lean through intensive

training? Do you think a strong feminine body is beautiful?

(3) Do you have the capacity to withstand rejection? Are you secure enough to shake off whatever prejudice you may encounter, even from someone very close to you?

(4) Can you pay the emotional and physical price for excellence? Are you truly aware of the sacrifices required for superiority in athletics? Are you prepared to make hard choices about the priorities in your life? Will you be able to spend hours and hours at practice, and not resent the sacrifice of other activities, such as socializing?

More and more young women are beginning to answer these questions in the affirmative, and the entire world of sports is becoming richer for their participation. In the last several years, the media have been covering more women's sport events and this exposure has helped give outstanding women athletes the recognition they deserve, providing incentive for other young women to strive for athletic excellence. Gradually, prejudice against the woman athlete is declining, and this presents fewer internal conflicts for her as well.

But the change *is* gradual and it may take another generation before women feel as free to compete aggressively as men do now. Until that time, any young woman interested in sport should take an introspective look at her motives, ambitions and the obstacles she may face. Understanding oneself and one's relationships with others will help make it possible to participate in the full joy of sport. It's there for the taking.

six

Recruiting and How to Handle It

Bob Gaillard

You've been training well and eating right. You've stayed healthy. All that discipline has paid off and you've scored big in high school competition. Now you're a senior and you're being recruited for college.

Recruiting is not a single, one shot matter. It's a total process whereby recruiters try to find and sign up the best athletes for their teams. The athletes in turn try to discover which college will best suit their athletic and academic needs.

In my eight years as the basketball coach for the University of San Francisco, I have been involved in a lot of recruiting. Let me show you the recruiting process first from the standpoint of the schools doing the recruiting and then from the perspective of the recruited athlete. Since basketball is my sport, I'll often use it for examples, but most of what I say applies just as well to other sports.

THE RECRUITER'S PERSPECTIVE

EVALUATING PLAYERS

The first step in recruiting is to analyze talent. And the first quality we look for is quickness. This has become the most important factor not only in basketball, but in about eighty percent of all competitive sports.

In addition, of course, size is very important. There's a saying among basketball recruiters that if you're going to make a mistake, make a big one: when in doubt, go for size.

Another key factor—one which the young athlete may overlook—is attitude. This has become more and more important. With the increasing number of recruits available, we find that often the top ratings for athletic ability level out. And what we have to look for is the intangible that is going to separate the very good athlete from the great athlete: the willingness to take the coaching and to spend the extra time in practice, and the ability to make the extra effort that separates winners from losers.

Some young athletes try to emulate the personal mannerisms of the pros. This can definitely hurt their chances of attracting recruiter interest. Phil Smith of the Golden State Warriors and I run a basketball camp for junior high and high school athletes and sometimes we see these antics reach a ridiculous level. There are kids in the sixth and seventh grades who make fools of themselves trying to look like the highly-paid professional "star" they've seen on TV. They always throw the ball down when called for a foul, risking a technical. When they're replaced in the line-up they seem to feel they have to throw a towel or kick a chair.

When playing man-to-man defense, as most teams do, it's customary for the player leaving the game to tell the

Recruiting and How to Handle It

player who's coming in which man he's guarding. But I've seen kids say, "_____ you, go find him yourself." Or they may walk to the far end of the court hoping their substitutes will give up and not pursue them.

Things like this became so prevalent at our camp that Phil and I decided to show the players just how silly they looked. When Phil came in for me, I turned my back so he couldn't get my attention and get me out of the game. Then I stealthily tiptoed over to the corner, crouched down, and hid. When the players cracked up, I knew they'd gotten the point.

Being temperamental is not professional. No professional is going to risk a foul except in extraordinary circumstances. And he's certainly not going to hold his job for long if he makes things difficult for the other players on his team.

If you watch even the most hotheaded pros, you'll see that they spend most of their time on fundamentals. But we think there is a serious ignorance of fundamentals even in some professional basketball.

What we're looking for during the recruiting process is talent that can be coached in the way which will allow a player to realize his full potential, and this usually means teaching fundamentals. When young athletes have a lot of ability and are tempted to take shortcuts, it is difficult to know how much they will allow themselves to be taught. We aren't interested in hotshots. We want to find those athletes who continually want to improve their game by learning the basics.

In order to evaluate fairly an athlete's ability and attitude, we must see him over a long period of time. An athlete will often play an untypical game when we're watching—sometimes better, sometimes worse—especially if he knows we're there. Our experience tells us not to base our report on one or two shots of scouting, so it's best for you not to put too much emphasis on it either. If you blow one game, don't worry, we'll be back to watch you again.

Some athletes go wrong by trying to show us what they

think we're looking for, or what a competing player can do. Don't try to be somebody else for us. Play your own game. We want what you can produce, not an imitation of something else.

Despite all our efforts to find the most talented athletes, recruiters can make mistakes. Since I'm from USF, I'll tell you of two examples where we recognized potential in players that other schools missed. Bill Russell was certainly one of the greatest players of all time, in both college and in professional basketball. We were the only school in the United States that recruited him. The other example is Phil Smith, currently one of the top guards in the National Basketball Association. He too was recruited only by USF, and not really very hard. No one dreamed he was going to develop into our leading scorer for three years and go on to star in the NBA.

The Scouting Process

The scouting process can be initiated in any of several ways. One way, of course, is for the coaches to come across an athlete themselves. The coaching staff is always checking on games that are being played—in summer league, varsity league, or wherever—and occasionally we see a good athlete who we decide should be recruited. Another way is through friends of the university, including alums who have contacts in different areas. They see someone who is a fine athlete and notify us to follow up.

Another method, perhaps the most common, is through scouting services. Many people involved in athletics or who have retired from athletics become involved with scouting services. There are several around the country, some regional and some national, and they can be very reliable. It is their job to contact summer camps, preseason camps, any place around the country where top athletes are performing, and to evaluate. They try to make an evaluation that is as complete and as accurate as possible, and they publish their conclusions for the uni-

Recruiting and How to Handle It

versities which subscribe to their services. The cost ranges from $25 to $100. The following is an example from one of the reports:

```
                        B C  Scouting Service


Vol. 9, No. 65            LOUISIANA WRAPUP              April 7, 1978

RANKING LOUISIANA'S TOP 25 SENIORS ...

Mike            6-6      F       DeRidder
Sanders         ... your ideal small forward  B/C All-Star excels offensively--can handle/
                shoot/score ... consistently in the high 20's (26.4 ppg) ... makes NO mistakes!
Micah           6-9      F       Metairie East Jefferson
Blunt           ... Tulane-bound ... can play the wing at 6-9--real good moves to the hoop,
                big-league shooter to 20 feet and exceptional passer ... needs to board better/
                195.
Dean            6-9      C       Metairie Archbishop Rummel
Carpenter       ... headed to Virginia ... key here is POTENTIAL ... garbage-style player who
                fills his role--very smart and plays aggressively ... good m/m D, sound,
                winner.
Bobby           6-4      G       Pineville
Tudor           ... definitely second-guard material ... can stroke it at 20', has improved
                his handling, decent passer ... great attitude! ... half-step tardy, ? strength.
Wade            6-5½     F       Metairie Archbishop Rummel
Blundell        ... no finer prep shooter in nation--67 FG as a forward (high of 48) ... MVP
                of state tourney as team won 4A second time in row ... full step slow/SCORER!!
Sean            6-1      G       New Orleans Newman
Touhy           ... signed Ole Miss ... unanimous state tourney pick with 58 points in 2 games
                ... deluxe floor general--handles/makes pass/chews out mates ... super HUSTLE!
Fred            6-5      F       Monroe Carroll
Chaffould       ... somewhat overrated since limited in what he can do away from the basket
                (inbetweener) ... shot selection shakey ... superior athlete, leaper, rebounds.
Jimmy           6-8      C       New Orleans Holy Cross
Carter          ... came on fast! .. big, strong, tough kid has added consistency ... still
                limited offensively, but gets the ball off the boards ... suspect hands and
                speed.
Robert          6-2      G       New Orleans Booker T. Washington
Jordan          ... excellent scoring tools--filled it up 23.6 ppg worth, second in city to
                Blundell's 24.8 ... quality shooter, but ? putting it on floor and lacks savvy.
Kenny           6-3      F       Shreveport Fair Park
Simpson         ... came out of the woodwork to emerge as mid-major swingman ... his 26.9 ppg
                scoring ranked No. 1 in 4A ... played very well in state tourney, ? G exposure.
Sammy           6-7      F       Hammond
Brumfield       ... ineligible entire season after brief trip to BR McKinley, then back to
                Hammond ... dandy shooting touch, runs well, strong, hard-nosed ... needs JC.
Alvin           6-1      G       Lake Charles Marion
Jackson         ... state's SLEEPER OF YEAR! ... No. 2 scorer in Cajun country at 31.2 vs.
                Class AA (third-highest) competition ... quality ball-handler, so seems #1G.
Michael         6-4½     F       Lafayette Northside
Robinson        ... never made the progress expected--the reason in part is he's a true
                'tweener ... good strength at 195, can stick it nicely from wing range, smart,
                slow.
```

Handbook for the Young Athlete

Darryl Ward	6-5	F	Metairie West Jefferson
	... shooting forward who had to play in the middle much of his time here ... flat can stroke the J! ... outscored Blunt in same district ... enough quickness.		
Barry Barocco	5-11	G	Metairie Archbishop Rummel
	... No. 2 run-your-show guard in state (to Tuohy) ... had 9 assists in state tourney game, 17 during Houston visit vs. Strake Jesuit ... smart, few mistakes at LM.		
Jeff Haisley	6-6	F	New Orleans Abramson
	... comes out of the Public League without much fan-fare, yet capable of getting it done for some lower-majors (top SC best) ... shoots in/out, OK speed/195.		
Chris Jennings	6-2	G	New Orleans Jesuit
	... outstanding scorer tools--averaged 23.2 ppg in city's most intense district (Rummel/Holy Cross) ... but problems: not an athlete and a step-plus slow.		
J. Brian Bergeron	6-2	G	Port Allen
	... this season's "mystery player" ... committed to LSU ... supposedly already tuned in to backcourt play ... scores well and known for hustle, consistency.		
Larry Coney	6-5	F	New Orleans Cohen
	... we could be far underrating this kid--gets no play, yet earned his points (19.1) in above-average competition ... positioning the big ? ... SLEEPER!		
Cherokee Rhome	6-7	C	Springhill
	... we gave you this kid as an unknown some time ago ... well, all he did was make first team all-state 3A with the likes of Tudor/Howard Carter ... 24.5 ppg.		
Willie Hey	6-8	C	Marthaville
	... if you're in the market for an unpursued big man, try this fella ... plays Class C, so needs time to develop, but shook folks with inspired tourney play.		
Kenny Williams	6-5	F	Baton Rouge McKinley
	... this program traditionally turns out the studs, going back beyond the Don Chaney days, and while this kid doesn't have much ink, a PLAYER! ... 15.2 scorer.		
Keith Richard	6-0	G	Baton Rouge Redemptorist
	... setup man for super junior Howard Carter ... made first-team all-state 3A off 22 ppg/6 assists ... will take the charge all night! ... quality D, size hurts.		
Kenny Johnson	5-11	G	Metairie Bonnabel
	... overlooked pointman called a 4* by some--doubt that, but plays top small college anyway ... average-plus sub-6-foot quicks, smart, strong body, intense.		
Terry Woods	6-4	F	Shreveport Byrd
	... No. 2 senior in the city to Simpson ... what does that mean??? ... in-betweener who'll fall into that old "wing" category ... shoots it enough and smart player.		

Scouting is a very specialized field. A national scouting service may come out with a special report on the top six-foot guards in the country, indicating which will probably emerge as team leaders. Another report may give the rundown on the really big forwards who can rebound but do not have all-around skills. The scouting services evaluate both special talents and the relative abilities of all the complete players in the country playing particular positions.

Often they use a star system, like a restaurant guide. Five stars will indicate a blue chip athlete, someone who absolutely can't miss in college. Two or three stars will indicate someone who is very questionable, who may be better for a small college scene, or who at best could perhaps make the team as a junior or senior.

Mass Recruiting

The initial step by most institutions is what we call "mass recruiting." This starts with a letter. A given school may send out 150 to 200 letters to the top prospects around the country. Many players are deceived by these letters and think they represent a concentrated recruiting effort. In fact, this is an early attempt for us to find out whether there is any reciprocal interest—or to get our foot in the door in case we decide to recruit actively later on. We're trying to make initial contact as early as most of our competition has.

Preliminary steps can be fairly extensive. We may send three or four personal letters to a prospect, and put him on our mailing list for everything that comes out of our sports information department—releases to the press, our press book, etc.—so that he is constantly seeing the name of our institution and the names of our coaching staff.

Many schools believe in this. They believe that getting as much information as possible into the home of the athlete is a good way to start recruitment. The problem arises when youngsters who receive many letters and are on a number of mailing lists don't get actively recruited by the schools. Many of these kids assumed they were getting the big rush and are dismayed when there's no follow up. It's a good idea not to get your hopes up at this stage.

Specific Recruiting

Once we learn of a player we might want, we try to have our staff, or someone extremely reliable and knowledgeable about our needs, analyze him. We go out, and if we like what we see, we try to get back for at least one more look. We try to catch him in a game, hopefully a big game where we can see him under the strongest competition available.

The problem is that most of the blue chip athletes, and those just a notch down from that category, never really have the competition needed for reliable evaluation. Many players look great against mediocre competition. They may have many of the necessary skills, but when they get up to the next level their physical deficiencies begin to show. For example, they may be half a step slow, and not able to do the things that first attracted attention. This is why we emphasize quickness and general physical ability. If you don't have these qualities when you run into a more consistent level of competition, you're going to have a real problem competing.

At this time we find out whether any recruiting guidelines have been established. For example, the coach may say that there will be no recruiting contact during the competitive season. If the season is a month away, we know that we have just that long to try to do as much as we can actively. Or there may be what we call an open door policy: we can drop in at any time and watch the young man play, but we can't talk to him. Whatever they may be, the coach generally sets his guidelines at this stage.

It is important to learn whether there are going to be any problems contacting the athlete at home. In most cases there are not, but coaches may want to screen the calls, or have someone else do it, so that the athlete can go through his senior year without too much distraction. Normally, however, we have the go-ahead, and we will contact the mother and/or father at home and tell them of our interest. We tell them we have talked to the coach and we want to know if they have set any guidelines of their own. If agreeable, we set up a house visit, normally as soon as possible.

THE THREE-VISIT RULE

We are allowed only three visitations with each athlete and/or his family under NCAA rule adopted in 1976. Prior

Recruiting and How to Handle It

to that we could see the mother, the father, the athlete, and coach, as many times as we wanted.

The three-visitation rule is probably the strongest change affecting recruiting adopted in the last decade. From the personal standpoint of USF, we feel it is the most detrimental rule because it allows us only three times to assure the parents, the young person, and anyone else associated with him that we are truly interested in his welfare and his potential at USF—his future as a basketball player, as a student, and his general development as a person.

I think the rule change was pushed through by the big schools. The point was to stop the zealousness of the smaller schools who were trying to make as many contacts as possible. That was about their only way to compete. Their strength lay in developing personal relationships since they could not offer the impressive display of a campus visit to a major university.

The one thing that is left out now is the personal contact: with so little time to spend with the athletes and their families, the recruiter will have little chance to establish credibility about his interest in the young person and about the athlete's personal potential at his college, little opportunity to assure the parents that their son or daughter will be in a good environment.

We feel that there is no way to show in three visits that you are that much different from any other recruiters around the country. We just cannot give the attention to detail that we could in the past. James Hardy, one of the best athletes in the country, went to Jordan High School in Long Beach, California. I personally made approximately twenty-five trips to Long Beach to visit with him or members of his family during the recruiting season. James Hardy's stepmother, Willie Mae Hardy, looks upon me as one of the family. She invited my wife, Sally, and me to her home for Sunday dinner and taught Sally how to cook soul food properly. Later, when James ate at our house in San Francisco, we were able to offer him something close to home cooking.

What school could really compete with the close association we had built up through the rapport with the entire family? I came to realize that James Hardy was concerned with many facets of life—he was not a typical Basketball Benny, thinking only of the game twenty-four hours a day. Everyone else who came to talk to him stressed only basketball; we talked about almost everything else, from social situations to what type of jobs he'd like in the future. I told him something of myself, my habits as an older person, my experiences, and other things that friends would talk about. This allowed us to build up much more trust in each other than you can in three visitations. It allowed me to show our enthusiasm and our active interest in James.

When coaches had the chance to get to know the young people they were recruiting, it put them on a different level from those who were just talking about the size of their field house, the number of players graduating and leaving open spots on their team, and anything else that sounded good. Any time you see someone as often as I saw James Hardy, any questions that don't come out one time can be discussed on the next visit. The athlete gets to see the recruiter not just when everything is fine, but in many different situations—after a lost game, or when the recruiter is over-scheduled and irritable. Both the recruiter and the athlete can form opinions of each other as people.

One way around the three-visitation rule, by the way, is to "bump into" a prospect. The NCAA does not say you must ignore a prospect if you run into him by chance, and such things have come to be known as "bumps." With the new rule, we now have what we call professional bumpers. They time how long it takes an athlete to go to the bathroom and they happen to be in the corridor when he comes out. They learn his route to school and manage to be in the intersection at the same time. It becomes quite a game to see how many times one can "accidentally" run into a player and get across one or two more points without using up one of the three visits.

Recruiting and How to Handle It

THE CAMPUS VISIT

The real point of the home visit for many of the big-time universities is just to get the athlete to visit the campus. The house visits and initial personal contacts are often made by "recruiters" who have little involvement with the coaching staff. Many of them just promote the university and pressure the athlete into a campus visit. There is no meaningful, personal contact. You don't have to give in to this pressure. The important thing to keep in mind is that it is your future at stake and ultimately your decision to make. You will want to choose the schools that interest you most and visit only those. You want to use your time wisely.

An athlete is now only allowed to make visits to six campuses. This has cut down decidedly the number of trips the better athletes used to make. I think this change is probably for the good. I don't think that the athlete needs to make ten or fifteen visits. It just leads to confusion. (I should add that if you pay your own way to visit an institution, it does not count as one of your six visits; often a young man in a metropolitan area can visit two or three campuses on his own, and then take his six paid visits, possibly getting to as many as nine or ten schools.)

When an athlete visits a school, he's only allowed forty-eight hours on the campus, and of course he's going to see the best the campus has to offer. The trip may well have been planned months in advance, and the timing will have been selected to coincide with the athlete's particular interests. He will be invited at a time when the school can display its strongest athletic competition, its best postgame functions and parties, the best weather, and whatever else puts the campus in the best possible light, whether or not that's indicative of a nine month's stay.

If the athlete really likes the social life, his hosts will make sure that he visits on the greatest party weekend, in conjunction, perhaps, with the homecoming game. There will be attractive dates—in short, just about anything he enjoys in life will be available. No wonder he comes home thinking this particular school could be heaven.

THE ATHLETE'S PERSPECTIVE

ANALYZING YOUR ABILITY

One of the first jobs of the recruited athlete is to try to analyze his own abilities as well as possible. Too often local stand-outs have a false impression of their abilities, and this leads to numerous problems down the line.

The difficulty here is that everyone is usually biased. Parents generally think their offspring is better than he is. The coach is high on him because he's probably his best athlete. The athlete will have had some degree of success in the past, and it will seem very important from a local perspective.

Quite often coaches get involved in their own ego trips. Typically this is the high school coach who has been closely involved with a player throughout his high school career. He will often encourage the athlete to take trips to nationally prominent schools across the country knowing that they are not in the student's best interests. A coach may like to name-drop and play the role of being on a personal level with prestigious schools and big-name coaches. This is his way of trying to make his life more interesting and seemingly important.

Phil Smith's cousin, John Smith, was a fine player at Wilson High School in San Francisco. His coach, who was from the Midwest, went so far as to say that John could possibly go directly to the pros. He actually indicated that the Washington Bullets of the National Basketball Association would be looking forward to giving John a try-out, that they had expressed a genuine interest in him. Now John Smith was a fine high school basketball player, but this sort of influence could only confuse his perspective and add to the early hurdles all strong young athletes have to overcome.

John signed a Letter of Intent recently to attend the University of Arizona. Fortunately, he is a very level-headed young man. He is attending the University of Arizona not only to play basketball, but also to participate

Recruiting and How to Handle It

in the strong academic programs that school has to offer in his fields of interest. He was able to put academics right at the top of his priorities. Unfortunately, many young athletes are not so mature and their illusions of immediate stardom can prove disastrous.

A good example of someone who did not evaluate his ability honestly was a quarterback named Charles Dudish who signed a Letter of Intent with Georgia Tech seven or eight years ago. He was the subject of a national TV special on recruiting that showed him being hounded by some of the country's major football coaches. The film included scenes with Bear Bryant at the University of Alabama, and with recruiters from Notre Dame and four or five other major universities.

At that time you were allowed to announce your signings at press conferences (the NCAA no longer allows it), and when Charlie Dudish finally decided to go to Georgia Tech, it was like a scene straight out of Hollywood. They had the governor, the mayor of Atlanta, influential alums, the coaching staff, and several hundred people at a banquet room some place in Atlanta. They put the Letter of Intent in front of him and said, "Charlie, we don't want to put any undue pressure upon you, but if you are willing to announce your happiness with Georgia Tech, we certainly would love to have your signature at this time."

Charlie played it like a Hollywood actor. He squirmed in the chair, made several false starts of starting to reach for the paper, and must have spent four or five minutes enjoying all of the publicity, before he signed the Letter of Intent. Finally the flash bulbs went off, and he was acclaimed the next great player in the college ranks.

I am afraid that that was his high water mark. I followed his career, because for me this was such an interesting example of recruiting. Unfortunately, Charlie Dudish never got past third string.

HELPFUL CRITICISM

I would suggest that a young athlete who has had some initial recruiting contact, and is fairly certain that he is going to be talked to, try to find someone who will give him an objective appraisal. This can be a local junior college coach who knows that the athlete is going to go on to a four year institution and who has no interest in trying to recruit him himself. Such a coach can give an objective opinion as to the level at which the athlete could compete successfully. There are some very talented players at the small college level who would not even get playing time if moved up to a major university.

I suggest that each recruited athlete ask specifically, "If I could not make it at the university level, why would I not make it—what particular shortcomings would keep me from making it?" This should pinpoint weaknesses.

For example, if a player has many of the general skills, such as quickness and jumping ability, he may be able to disguise the fact that he is a poor offensive player from more than fifteen feet from the basket. In high school he probably does not have to shoot beyond that distance and he may be able to average twenty-five to thirty points a game. But he must learn that when he moves up to another level, the offensive area that he's been able to operate in may no longer be available to him. Despite his physical ability, if he is deficient as an outside shooter, this one flaw may prevent him from participating. And it will be too late to learn.

Once this is pointed out, he has to believe it. We find that regardless of how many people tell an athlete he is deficient in certain areas, until he is able to look in the mirror and tell the same thing to himself, he is not going to take the steps to solve his problems. Instead he is going to take the shortcuts to avoid dealing with them. Again, I suggest that people not involved with the athlete's decision be the ones to tell him about his weak points. Then he has to check back with his coach and/or his parents, and if he can honestly admit to problems and be able especially to confront his most important weakness, then he's made the first step toward effective self-evaluation.

What the athlete must do next is to picture himself in a year or two playing at the college level. What size are the people at the position he expects to play? If he's a very talented 6'1" guard who's a fine offensive player at the high school level, he should take a look around the country and ask how many 6'1" college guards are able to do the things at which he's strongest. Do they become the playmakers responsible for running the defense, whereas he's used to being the main threat offensively? Looking at the strong college teams, how big are their athletes?

Many 6'4" and 6'5" players are what we now call in-betweeners. They can perform very well at the forward positions at the high school level, but once they move on to college, if they are not exceptionally quick, or great jumpers, or extremely strong, they will almost always have to be played in the back court. And that requires a complete new set of offensive and defensive skills. They may not be willing to pay the price to learn these skills; and they will be on the road to defeat.

Young athletes must also analyze their environment. Many players are good in a weak league, and this can be misleading. A player might be able to score thirty points a game and be considered a tremendously fine shooter, but he may be getting all those shots because the level of competition is not good enough really to challenge his movements on the court. He has to be aware of this, and say to himself: "If I were playing in a stronger league, maybe I would still be able to shoot, but not as many times, and I might average seventeen, eighteen, nineteen points a game."

This is very difficult because it often means that people close to the situation must tell him that his high school teammates and competitors are not quite that good. This runs into pride and ego factors, things that are not easy to admit, and those involved will often end up distorting relative ability levels among players and leagues.

ESTABLISHING PRIORITIES

Once an athlete has determined that he is definitely going to be recruited, and has analyzed his abilities, he should make a conscious effort to establish priorities and set ground rules. This may well be critical to the success of his senior year. We strongly advocate that the athlete sit down with his parents, with his list of priorities, and take whatever time they need to analyze them carefully together. Hopefully, the parents will ask all the hard questions, and make sure that the athlete is aware of what his priorities really are. They may change somewhat, but not much. And once they are clear, the athlete is ready for the next step, the elimination of all but a few of the schools.

NARROWING THE LIST OF SCHOOLS

Eliminating schools can be very difficult; often an athlete has not visited the schools, has not even talked extensively with them. He's going to have to do his eliminating from his thorough list of priorities. Whatever his goal, to be an attorney, or a professional basketball player, or whatever, he must try to identify what is most important, and then try to match up with what the various schools have to offer.

Of course athletic participation in college will be important (though perhaps not most important), or he wouldn't be recruited. So there will be priorities to think about that concern only the athletic participation. What does he really want? Does he want to start as a freshman? Does he want just to get a uniform as a freshman? Does he feel he should play on the JV team as a freshman?

He has to try to be specific about these types of questions. And it's not easy. Down deep an athlete may really feel that he wants to play a lot as a freshman, but will say what he thinks he should say—that he will be content to be patient, that he realizes that he has a lot to learn. In fact, often he's telling the recruiter what he feels the recruiter wants to hear.

The non-athletic questions can be just as tough: What am I going to major in? What is the best type of school for me academically? What kind of social life do I want? Is that important to me? Am I the type that will be homesick? Do I care if it's a long way from home? Am I really looking forward to getting away from my Mom and Dad? Do I have a girlfriend close by that I don't really want to get too far away from? Or do I?

These must be put down in very concrete terms, and then matched against the various institutions.

A College Rating System

The important thing is to eliminate most of the institutions right away. It may help to develop a number system, grading each school on a point scale in each area. The following is a chart with the priorities which have proved important to the young athletes I have known:

Priorities	SCHOOLS						
	A	B	C	D	E	F	G
Athletics:							
Coach's and School's Credentials							
Playing Opportunities							
Style of Play							
Compatibility with Coaches & Team							
Academic:							
Career							
Immediate Interests							
Personal Help							
Physical Qualities of School:							
Equipment—Aesthetics							
Urban—Rural							
Size							
Climate							
Proximity to Home							
Fringe Benefits:							
Summer Job Help							
Alumni Career Help							

To use the chart, fill in ratings only for the priorities which are important to you, on a scale of 1 to 10, with "10" for best and a "0" for a school you feel rates really poorly. If one or two priorities are particularly important to you, count them twice: give a double rating (potentially a "20") for an outstanding school, and "10" for one in the middle, and so forth.

Some comments on the listed priorities might be helpful. The first item is "Coach's and School's Credentials." This refers to the record of the coach and school in helping advance the sports careers of their players. It would be of importance only to a player seriously interested in going on to professional sports; and for someone who really knows he will go to the pros, it could be of double importance. It is usually a matter of visibility, and "pro-type" play and coaching. The media exposure of UCLA in basketball helps build All-American reputations and professional interest; on the other hand, a football team which tends to use a lot of razzle-dazzle plays might scare off professional scouts looking for experience in "pro-type" play.

"Playing Opportunities" means just that, but it may not be as obvious as it seems at first. Say if you're a guard and all of a team's guards are seniors, the playing opportunity would look good unless this coach has a record of going after junior college transfers to step in when he's out of experienced players for a particular position. Maybe chances would be better if there were one or two open slots that matched your strengths.

"Style of Play" can be very important. It is perhaps the single greatest cause of later unhappiness. Whatever the sport, if the coach's style isn't the one you're used to and comfortable with, be careful! Perhaps you should adapt and learn a new style, but far too often it just doesn't work out.

The last priority under "Athletics" is "Compatibility with Coaches and Team." When you're being recruited, you see everybody's good side. So ask around and see if you can't find out what these people are really like. When you visit a school and meet the players, try to talk to the non-stars, the eleventh man on the basketball team, the third-string catcher in baseball. They'll be the ones who see the not-so-cheery side, and are probably less concerned about making a good impression on you.

The "Academic" concerns are divided into three categories, "Career," "Immediate Interests," and "Personal Help." The first two are probably self-evident: if you think you want to go into medicine, you'll want a school that can help you get there. If you aren't at all sure about a career but want a good liberal arts education, pick a school that prides itself on its liberal arts tradition.

"Personal Help" may not be so clear. Academic counseling can be extremely important for a heavily committed college athlete. Someone who can help with schedules and communication with teachers can be a godsend when travel schedules put pressure on the demands of the classroom. "Personal Help" may be available simply because of a low teacher-student ratio. It's much easier to develop relationships in classes of fifteen to twenty students than in mammoth lecture sections.

The "Physical Qualities" priorities should be fairly obvious. How well is a school equipped, athletically and in general? Is it a good place to be physically? Is it important to be in or near a major city, or do you want to be well away from big cities? Do you want a big school, or a small school? How about climate? And finally, do you want to be near home? Do you want your folks to be able to see you play? Or maybe it's important to get away.

The last category is "Fringe Benefits." About the only legitimate outside-financial-help during the school years is help in getting summer jobs. It can be very important to some. The other area is "Alumni Career Help," which can mean a lot but is difficult to gauge. It can only be a hope at best; but if you know that successful sports figures at a particular school have tended to get good opportunities through influential alumni, it would be a factor to consider.

Handbook for the Young Athlete

So let's say you fill out the chart and it looks like this:

Priorities		SCHOOLS						
		A	B	C	D	E	F	G
Athletics:	Coach's and School's Credentials	0	10	20	0	6	4	3
	Playing Opportunities							
	Style of Play	5	10	5	5	0	7	4
	Compatibility with Coaches & Team							
Academic:	Career							
	Immediate Interests	10	8	5	5	5	0	6
	Personal Help	0	0	10	5	5	8	0
Physical Qualities of School:	Equipment—Aesthetics	5	0	5	5	5	0	5
	Urban—Rural							
	Size							
	Climate							3
	Proximity to Home (Double rating used)	6	10	20	0	10	5	5
Fringe Benefits:	Summer Job Help	0	10	10	10	0	5	0
	Alumni Career Help							
	Total	26	48	75	30	31	29	26

Two of the priorities were especially important to you, "Coach's and School's Credentials," and "Proximity to Home." So you doubled up on your ratings for them. Several categories were definitely of less importance, so you skipped them altogether.

When you added up the score, you found that School C was well ahead. In this case it would clearly indicate that it looks the best in the things that count for you most, particularly since you gave it the only top rating in each of the two categories which are most important to you.

Sometimes the results won't be so clear. Two or more

schools may lead with almost the same total scores; or, the school with the highest total score may be deficient in an area that's important to you. Choosing isn't always clearcut and easy.

But the exercise of filling out the chart will help you organize your thinking and identify your priorities. And at the very least it should help you eliminate some of the schools that just don't measure up, where it counts with you.

As I said, I think any athlete should be able to cut down to not more than three or four schools just by carefully considering priorities and what the various schools have to offer. But whatever the system of selection, it is important to notify the people involved, both those still in the running and those that have been eliminated.

Often an athlete has difficulty telling schools that he is not interested in them. He may have developed a personal relationship with their recruiters and he feels some loyalty to them. He does not want to string them along, but at the same time he does not want to dash their hopes.

What he must realize is the importance of being honest with them, and with himself and his parents. He will be doing no harm to the recruiters or their colleges. They have other people they can recruit, and learning early of the cases where there is no real interest will allow them to spend their time in other areas. So they should get the word as soon as possible. If it is done by letter, that's fine: if it's done over the phone, that's fine; or in a personal confrontation, that's fine. The important thing is to do it.

So at this point, hopefully, the list will have been narrowed to just a few schools, and the task will be to do as good a job as possible of selecting among them. Whatever the system of selection, there must be a concentrated effort to know the people involved as well as possible. The athlete must try to distinguish sincerity from the good sales pitch, being aware of the fact that almost every school is going to say what the athlete wants to hear.

There was the example of a seven-foot center named Jawann Oldham, now playing for the University of Seattle.

He was an excellent player at Cleveland High School in Seattle, considered possibly the best high school team in the country, and he was actively recruited by most of the major universities around the country. It came down to Seattle and the University of Southern California. USC went so far as to involve in the case an alumnus of USC who was now a star professional football player. The star talked to Jawann on numerous occasions, and Jawann felt that he was keenly interested in him and in his career. For other reasons, Jawann eventually signed with the University of Seattle.

In his first year as a freshman he was a starter, and on one of his team's trips to Los Angeles he happened to run into the star. Of course, he thought he would go over and say "hi" to his good friend and when he did, the star didn't remember who he was, or what he ever had to do with the University of Southern California.

Parents can help separate the real from the phony. They've been around a while. They know that everybody has faults, and in dealing with people they can often see through someone who is really not interested in the athlete as a person. They may be able to help spot those who are interested only in his athletic talent, as a commodity—people who will forget the athlete once he's committed himself and will let him suffer along for three or four years at their school without any sense of responsibility.

Again, it must be remembered that the athlete is apt to be hearing exactly what a recruiter thinks he wants to hear. This can often relate to the academic opportunities that are important to a particular athlete. For example, Mark Wherle was an excellent basketball player at Jesuit High School in Sacramento, where I originally started my coaching career. He was also a very fine student, with an interest in math and a strong desire to be an engineer. Many of the schools that were actively recruiting him stressed the fact that their engineering schools were tremendous places, and that their athletes had never had any problem combining an engineering major with athletic competition. Nothing could have been further from the truth. There just isn't time to attend engineering school with the lengthy afternoon labs that are mandatory and be able to give a competitive sport the time it requires. You almost have to separate one from the other.

In Mark's case, he attended Rice, which has a fine engineering school, and after a brief semester of trying to combine engineering and basketball, ended up in economics. We had tried to get across to Mark the importance of taking a very realistic approach about whether or not he could do both things, and if not, to decide which was going to be more important to him. However, he had been strongly influenced by the universities that pushed their engineering programs, and made his decision on the assumption that they were telling him the truth. Whether he ended up picking the right school or not, his main reason for picking it was invalid.

Setting Recruiting Guidelines

The athlete will have his senior year of high school to go through, and it can be critical for him and his future. It should be a year for a lot of fun and a lot of work—getting good grades and improving athletic skills. If guidelines are not set up, the recruiters will completely dominate the senior year.

The athlete must realize that he has a loyalty and a responsibility to the team he's been playing for. He has to have the same loyalty and responsibility to his coach. The coach's efforts and those of the player's teammates in the past have helped put him in this position.

I advocate a policy of no recruiting contact during the season. Recruiters will have the time, if they are interested enough, to make sure they have appointments before the season, or immediately after the season. They will not neglect their opportunities to make contact if they really value the prospect as a person and as a player.

At any rate, guidelines should be worked out with the coach for times and places that will allow the recruiters to do their job without preventing the athlete from doing his. He, not the colleges, are setting the ground rules. He doesn't owe them anything. They are trying to recruit, and they should get an honest shot at it. But at the same time, the athlete wants to make sure he does exactly what is best for his interests.

So he sets the time periods. If he doesn't want to be bothered at night, which I think is a very good possibility, the recruiters should be told. Perhaps the home phone number shouldn't be given out. In many cases, it may be necessary to change the number to get one that's unlisted and give it only to the universities that he wants to visit.

The Campus Visit

When the decision has been made on which schools to visit, the athlete must remember that it is a time for him to learn all he can. He will have four years later for the good times if he does a good job now of picking the right place. So he must try to ask the important questions about the things which he has decided mean most to him. He must try to talk to people who have no reason to try to impress him. (As I said earlier, sometimes the marginal players on the team he hopes to make can be good people to talk to.)

In selecting a school, a very talented athlete must be aware that in many instances some of the team members are not going to be too elated about his coming. Quite often he has been a prolific scorer, and some of the veterans who have been effective point producers, and who have their own careers to be concerned about, may not be completely helpful to a young upstart who comes in, and who is supposed to average twenty-five to thirty points a game. There are ways in which they can make this young player's road very rough.

In practice sessions he will not get passes where he likes them, the defensive players will play him much more physically than they will other players, and he will be a target for everyone on the team. They will revel in trying to make him look bad, and if he's not aware of it, it's

Recruiting and How to Handle It

quickly going to get to his confidence and affect his thinking about whether or not he made the right decision. It can really snowball; and I've seen players go progressively downhill and never really bounce back once this type of thing hits them.

So when you evaluate the university, try to determine how much, if any, resentment there will be against you. Whose position will you be challenging; how is that player likely to react? How congenial is the rest of the team? If there will be hostility, can you take it? Do you want to take it?

THE LETTER OF INTENT

When the decision on a school has been made, the athlete may want to sign a Letter of Intent such as the one on page 200. The "Letter of Intent" is something relatively new and beneficial, both for recruited athletes and for the universities. Formally called the "Inter-Conference Letter of Intent," it is really a subscription membership. Athletic conferences and individual institutions voluntarily sign as members and agree to be bound by its rules. What it means is that if an athlete signs with any member university, and thereafter elects to disregard the Letter of Intent and attend any other university that's a member of the Letter of Intent Plan, he will have to sit out one year and at the same time lose one year of eligibility. So it is a potent mechanism for discouraging players from saying they're going to go to one place and ending up in another.

Up until the start of the Letter of Intent program, nine or ten years ago, we had a very difficult situation. Until the athlete actually sat down in class the first day of school, he was not considered an official member of your university.

There were many situations where players left for airports to attend one university and ended up across the country in some other place. Recruiters became adept at knowing the flight plans, and intercepting school bound athletes, buying them a Coke in the airport lobby until

Handbook for the Young Athlete

they missed their planes, and conveniently finding other planes to their own universities with coaches and university members waiting to greet them at the other end.

1978   NATIONAL LETTER OF INTENT   1978
(Administered by the Collegiate Commissioners Association)

☐ Football: Do not sign prior to 8:00 a.m. February 15, 1978 and no later than July 1, 1978
☐ Basketball: Do not sign prior to 8:00 a.m. April 12, 1978 and no later than July 1, 1978
☐ All other sports: Do not sign prior to 8:00 a.m. April 12, 1978 and no later than August 1, 1978

1. Place "X" in proper box above. Read reverse side before completing and signing this form in triplicate — one copy to be retained by student, two copies to be returned to the institution, one of which is to be sent to the appropriate commissioner.

2. THIS IS NOT AN AWARD OF FINANCIAL AID. If the enrollment decision in this letter is made with an understanding by the student that he is to receive financial assistance, he should have in his possession, before completing this Letter of Intent, a written statement from the institution involved which lists the terms and conditions, including the amount and duration of such financial assistance.

Name of student _____
(Type proper name, including middle name or initial)

This is to certify my decision to enroll at _____
Name of Institution

IMPORTANT - READ CAREFULLY

In making this certification, I have read all terms and conditions on page 1 and 2, fully understand them, accept and agree to be bound by them:

(1) All members of the cooperating Conferences and institutions (listed on the reverse side of this Letter) are obligated to respect my decision and to cease all recruiting activities with respect to me once a National Letter of Intent has been signed.

(2) I MAY SIGN ONLY ONE LETTER OF INTENT. If that Letter is rendered "null and void" I may not then sign a second Letter, but I remain free to enroll at any institution of my choice where I am admissible.

(3) If I elect not to enroll in the above named institution and enroll in another institution which is a participant in this agreement, my athletic eligibility at the institution in which I enroll will be limited in accordance with the regulations outlined on the reverse side of this Letter.

(4) If my parent or legal guardian fails to co-sign this Letter of Intent, it will be rendered invalid.

(5) This letter will also be rendered null and void if I have not, by the opening of its classes in the fall of 1978, met the requirements for admission to the institution named above, its academic requirements for financial aid to athletes, and the NCAA 2.000 GPA requirement.

(6) My signature on this form nullifies any agreements oral or otherwise that would release me or the institution from the conditions stated in this National Letter of Intent.

(7) This Letter of Intent will be invalid unless signed within fourteen (14) days after being issued. This Letter can be reissued.

(8) A prospective student signs a National Letter of Intent with an institution and not for a particular sport.

SIGNED _____   _____
                Student   Date and Time of Signature

SIGNED _____   _____
           Parent or Legal Guardian   Date and Time of Signature

ADDRESS _____   _____
                Street Number   City   State

Submission of this Letter of Intent has been authorized by

SIGNED _____   _____
            Athletic Director   Date

_____   _____
          Institution   Sport

- 1 -

Recruiting and How to Handle It

Individual universities got together and said this was not a very good working procedure, and they came up with the Letter of Intent Plan. It is not run by the NCAA.

Despite the fact that the Letter of Intent is supposed to eliminate post-signing competition, it is not quite foolproof. For instance, it contains a clause which stipulates that if financial aid is not available, then the Letter of Intent can be voided. If a young person has changed his mind, some schools will try to put pressure on the school he selected to withdraw financial aid, and allow him to get out of his commitment. One way to apply pressure is to threaten disclosure to the NCAA of recruiting violations; just the threat can be very scary for a school. There may be some question of exactly what the terms of financial aid were, permitting the argument that there was later a change in the terms which rendered the Letter of Intent void. If so, the athlete can go to another school. He could never sign another Letter of Intent, but would be considered a "free agent" to go elsewhere.

As a general proposition, once the student athlete is 100% committed to going to one place, and signs a Letter of Intent, he effectively tells the other schools that he has made a definite decision; and then he can get a little peace of mind, and go back to the normal land of the living that he has been missing for the past few months.

The Letter of Intent should help in putting the distractions of the recruiting experience out of the way. It will, if there has been a good job in investigating, and the athlete knew what he wanted when he signed. The abuses arise only when confused athletes encourage recruiters by vacillating—perhaps wanting to prolong the drama and attention-getting of the recruiting process.

There is a high price to pay. The college experience, and often life-long happiness are at stake. It is serious business and should be treated as such. And doing it right is, after all, just a matter of paying attention, and doing some careful investigating and honest thinking.

GV
704
.H36

Handbook for the
young athlete